AF647152

Yama

— The Glorious Lord of the Other World —

Reconstructing Indian History & Culture
(ISSN 0971-3824)

1. Society in Ancient India; by Sures Chandra Banerji (ISBN 81-246-0000-7)
2. Political Thought in Ancient India; by G.P. Singh (ISBN 81-246-0001-5)
3. Early Indian Historical Tradition and Archaeology; by G.P. Singh (ISBN 81-246-0005-8)
4. Vasantotsava: The Spring Festivals of India; by Leona M. Anderson (ISBN 81-246-0011-2)
5. Ecological Readings in the Veda; by M. Vannucci (ISBN 81-246-0009-0)
6. Vṛndāvana in Vaiṣṇava Literature; by Maura Corcoran (ISBN 81-246-0024-4)
7. Social History of the Tamils (1707-1947); by P. Subramanian (ISBN 81-246-0045-7)
8. Ancient Indian Coinage; by Rekha Jain (ISBN 81-246-0051-1)
9. Buddhism and Socio-Economic Life of Eastern India; by Bimal Chandra Mohapatra (ISBN 81-246-0055-4)
10. Chandragupta Maurya; by P.L. Bhargava (ISBN 81-246-0056-2)
11. Mṛtyu: Concept of Death in Indian Traditions; by Gian Giuseppe Filippi (ISBN 81-246-0072-4)
12. Yama: The Glorious Lord of the Other World; by Kusum P. Merh (ISBN 81-246-0066-X)
13. Sacred Complex of Ujjain; by D.K. Samanta (ISBN 81-246-0078-3)
14. Vedic View of the Earth; by S.R.N. Murthy (ISBN 81-246-0091-0)
15. Society in the Atharvaveda; by B.S. Kharade (ISBN 81-246-0093-7)
16. Orissan History, Culture and Archaeology; by S. Pradhan (ISBN 81-246-0117-8)
17. Education in Ancient India; by Mitali Chatterjee (ISBN 81-246-0113-5)
18. Surā: The Liquor and the Vedic Sacrifice; by M.B. Kolhatkar (ISBN 81-246-0114-3)
19. Human Ecology in the Vedas; by Marta Vannucci (ISBN 81-246-0115-1)
20. Governance in Ancient India; by Anupa Chandra Pandey (ISBN 81-246-0135-6)
21. The Cultural Glory of Ancient India: A Literary Overview; by Sures Chandra Banerji (ISBN 81-246-0137-2)
22. Kauṭilya's Arthaśāstra in the light of Modern Science & Technology; by Sunil Sen Sarma (ISBN 81-246-0187-9)
23. History of Jainism — With Special Reference to Mathurā; by V.K. Sharma (ISBN 81-246-0195-X)
24. Cultural Tourism in India: Museums, Monuments & Arts — Theory and Practice; by S.P. Gupta; Krishna Lal; Mahua Bhattacharya (ISBN 81-246-0215-8)
25. Ancient Indian Historiography — Sources and Interpretations; by G.P. Singh (ISBN 81-246-0228-X)
26. Republics, Kingdoms, Towns and Cities in Ancient India; by G.P. Singh (ISBN 81-246-0237-9)
27. Facets of Ancient Indian History and Culture — New Perception; by G.P. Singh (ISBN 81-246-0238-7)
28. Kamakhya — A Socio-cultural Study; by Nihar Ranjan Mishra (ISBN 81-246-0251-4)
29. History and Culture of Tamil Nadu as Gleaned from the Sanskrit Inscriptions Vol. 1 (up to c. AD 1310); by Chithra Madhavan (ISBN 81-246-0308-1).
30. Life Style of the Vedic People; by Pranati Ghosal (ISBN 81-246-0344-8)

Reconstructing Indian History & Culture, no. 12

Yama

— The Glorious Lord of the Other World —

Kusum P. Merh

D.K.Printworld (P) Ltd.
New Delhi

Cataloging in Publication Data — DK

[Courtesy: D.K. Agencies (P) Ltd. <docinfo@dkagencies.com>]

Merh, Kusum P., 1950-

Yama, the glorious Lord of the other world.
(Reconstructing Indian history & culture, no. 12).
Includes bibliographical references (p.).
Includes Index.
ISBN 812460066X

1. Yama (Hindu mythology). 2. Mythology, Hindu. 3. Vedic literature. 4. Gods, Hindu. I. Title. II. Series: Reconstructing Indian history & culture; no. 12.

ISBN 81-246-0066-X
First Published in India in 1996
Second impression in 2006
© Author

All rights reserved. No part of this publication may be reproduced or transmitted, except brief quotations, in any form or by any means, electronic or mechanical, including photocopying, recording, or any information storage or retrieval system, without prior written permission of the copyright holder, indicated above, and the publishers.

Published and printed by:
D.K. Printworld (P) Ltd.
Regd. office : *'Sri Kunj'*, F-52, Bali Nagar
New Delhi - 110 015
Phones : (011) 2545-3975; 2546-6019; *Fax* : (011) 2546-5926
E-mail: dkprintworld@vsnl.net
Web: www.dkprintworld.com

वैवस्वतं संगमनं, जनानां
यमं राजानं हविषा दुवस्य।

— ऋग्वेद, 10.14.1

vaivasvataṁ saṁgamanaṁ janānāṁ
yamaṁ rājānaṁ haviṣā duvasya।

— *Rgveda*, 10.14.1

तपसा धर्ममाराध्य,
पुष्करे भास्करः पुरा।
धर्मांशं यं सुतं प्राप,
धर्मराजं नमाम्यहम्॥

— *ब्रह्मवैवर्तपुराण, प्रकृतिखण्ड, 26*

tapasā dharmamārādhya,
puṣkare bhāskaraḥ purā।
dharmāṁśaṁ yaṁ sutaṁ prāpa,
dharmarājaṁ namāmyaham॥

— *Brahmavaivarta Purāṇa, Prakṛtikhaṇḍa, 26*

Dedicated to
my dear parents

Shri L.O. Joshi & Smt. Prabha Joshi

Preface

VEDIC mythology occupies a very important place among ancient mythologies. Antiquity of the language of the *Vedas*. Its various interpretations besides the numerous obscure and unintelligible lines have generated a notion that nothing in all mythologies is more difficult than an attempt to get the clear view of a Vedic god.

The post-*Saṁhitā* period has preserved the immediate reactions to the symbology of the *Vedas*. Most of the Vedic gods find a place in later Hindu pantheon also and a considerable change in the concept of these gods is noticed. In the course of time some deities gained tremendous importance, while some others were lost in the oblivion, some gained new attributes while some new gods also came up. As a result, the Ṛgvedic gods like Varuna. Agni, Viṣṇu, Indra and Yama are quite different from what they appear through the Purāṇic legends.

Among the Vedic gods, Yama has a unique place. The picture of Yama, as derived from the Vedic references is vague, inconsistant and even paradoxical. He is the son of Vivasvat, but he is called a king, and not a god. Though he was immortal like the other gods, he was the "first to die"; and though he died he is never called a mortal. He is a path-finder who discovered a new settlement for all the dead where they alive blissfully in his company. The worshipper desires to become immortal in the kingdom of Yama. In the *Purāṇas* Yama underwent an evolution. The king of the dead now became the god of death, or death personified.

I decided to take up his study in order to carry out a thorough and detailed investigation into the real character of this Vedic god, as derived from the Vedic texts and its development in the principal *Purāṇas.* This investigation required a journey through the *Saṁhitās* to the *Purāṇas*; which is not only very long, but also diverse in language, dicton and spirit. An analytical approach is used to examine the various interpretations of some obscure passages of the *Vedas*. It is hope that this exhaustive study would be valuable to scholars interested in this field.

I take this opportunity to express my profound gratitude to Prof. S.G. Kantawala, Former Head, Department of Sanskrit, Pali and Prakrit, Ex-Director, Oriental Institute, Baroda whose valuable guidance throughout the period of my this research can only be inadequately acknowledged.

I am also grateful to Prof. R.I. Nanavati, Head, Dept. of Sanskrit, Pali & Prakrit, M.S. University of Baroda. My sincere thanks are due to Dr. B.S. Mehta of Varanasi who not only took keen interest to my research, but also helped me in procuring some plates of Yama icons.

I am also obliged to my sister Dr. Sudha Pandya, Reader, Dept. of English, The M.S. University of Baroda, for helping me in several ways. I thank the M.S. University, Baroda to granting me permission to publish this book. I am thankful to the authorities of the American Institute of Indian Studies, Ramnagar, Varanasi, for providing me with the plates of Yama icons no. 1 to 8, and also to the National Museum, New Delhi for the photographs of Yama plate nos. 9 & 10, included in this book. I also wish to express my gratitude to the publishers, D.K. Printworld Private Lmited, New Delhi.

I retrospect, this work is an outcome of the constant encouragement I have received from my father Shri L.O. Joshi (Retired, I.A.S.). A great Scholar of literature, Sanskrit as well as English — he imbibed in me early in life, love for literature in general and Sanskrit in particular. I, therefore, dedicate this work to him and my mother who also has been a great source of inspiration to me.

I would like to express a deep sense of appreciation for my family — my husband Pradeep Merh and my children — Vani and Rohit — for their wholehearted support.

Kusum P. Merh

Contents

Abbreviations

ABrā	*Aitareya Brāhmaṇa*
ABORI	Annals of the Bhandarkar Oriental Research Institute, Poona
AgniP	*Agni Purāṇa*
AV	*Atharvaveda*
AGS	*Āsvalāyana Gṛhya Sutra*
ĀŚS	*Āśvalāyana Śrauta Sūtra*
ASP	Anandashram Press, Poona
AVSB	*Atharvaveda kā Subodh Bhāṣya*
BG	*Bhagavadgītā*
BhāgP	*Bhāgavata Purāṇa*
BrP	*Brahma-Purāṇa*
BṛUp	*Bṛhadāraṇyaka Upaniṣad*
BrvaiP	*Brahmvaivarta Purāṇa*
BVP	*Bhaviṣya-Purāṇa*
BVT	*Bhaviṣyottara Purāṇa*
Ch(s)	Chapter(s)
ChāUp	*Chāndogya-Upaniṣad*
Ed.	Edited by or Editor
Edn.	Edition

ERE	*Encyclopaedia of Religion and Ethics*
GP	*Garuḍa-Purāṇa*
GB	*Gopatha-Brāhmaṇa*
HDŚ	*History of Dharma-Śāstra*
HOS	Harvard Oriental Series
HVM	A. Hillebrandt's *Vedische Mythologie*, English Translation by Rajeswar Sarma
IHQ	*Indian Historical Quarterly*
JOIB	*Journal of Oriental Institute*, M.S. University Baroda, Baroda.
JaimUpBr	*Jaiminīya Upaniṣad Brāhmaṇa*
KP	*Kūrma-Purāṇa*
KāŚS	*Kātyāyana Śrauta Sūtra*
KaṭhaUp	*Kaṭhopaniṣad*
Mbh	*Mahābhārata*
MP	*Matsya Purāṇa*
ManuS	*Manu-Smṛti*
MāP or *Mark*	*Markaṇḍeya Purāṇa*
MS	*Maitrāyaṇī-Saṁhitā*
Ms	Manuscript
Nir	Yāska's *Nirukta*
NrP	*Narasiṁha Purāṇa*
Nigh	*Nighaṇṭu*
OST	Original Sanskrit Texts
PP	*Padma Purāṇa*
PaiP	*Paippalāda*
Rām	*Rāmāyaṇa* (cr. ed., Baroda)

PB	*Pañcaviṁśa Brāhmaṇa*
PGS	*Pāraskara Gṛhya-Sūtra*
RPVU	*Religion & Philosophy of Vedas and Upaniṣads*
ṚV	*Ṛgveda*
ŚB	*Śatapatha Brāhmaṇa*
ŚvetaUp	*Śvetāśvatara Upaniṣad*
SBE	*Sacred Books of the East*
Tai Ā or *TĀ*	*Taittirīya Āraṇyaka*
TB or *TBr*	*Taittirīya Brāhmaṇa*
TaiUp	*Taittirīya Upaniṣad*
TS	*Taittirīya Saṁhitā*
TMB	*Tāṇḍyumahabrahmaṇa*
VS	*Vājasaneyisaṁhitā*
ViP	*Viṣṇu Purāṇa*
VāyuP	*Vāyu Purāṇa*
ViDhP	*Viṣṇudharmottara Purāṇa*
YS	*Yājñavalkyasmṛti*
VM	*Vedic Mythology*
VMT	*Vedic Mythological Tracts*

List of Plates

PART I

Yama in the Vedas

1

Conspectus of the Vedic Literature

THE word *Veda* come from $\sqrt{vid}$ = to know. This word, primarily signifying knowledge, designated the 'Sacred Lore' "which was traditionally believed to enable the expert to know the superhuman powers and methods of influencing them."[1] The term *Veda*, therefore, means a whole great literature and not just one literary work. This great literature kept taking shape through many centuries and for many more centuries it was handed down to the next generation through verbal instructions. In this manner this sacred knowledge was passed on verbally for generations from the preceptors to the pupils, and survived in its purest form for an incredible length of time before it was written down.

In the Indian tradition the *Veda*s are termed as *Śruti* since they were, initially, only heard as spoken by the preceptor, and not read or written. The *Veda*s are also considered *apauruṣeya*, i.e., not composed by men. It is believed that this sacred literature was visioned by the ancient sages when they were 'issued like breath from the Self-Existent (*ŚB*, 11.5.8.1f; also *ṚV*, 10.90.9). The Vedic poets, therefore, are called seers (*ṛṣiḥ* = *ṛṣer darśanāt Nir.*, 2.11), because these compositions were not made but seen by them. Hence these Vedic *ṛṣis* are called the draṣṭāraḥ, not *kartāraḥ* of the

Vedas. With this concept of the nature of their origin, the authoritativeness of the *Vedas* cannot be questioned. The belief in the *Vedas* as 'seen' and not as 'composed' also shows the reverence with which they were learnt.

The *Vedas* consist of four classes of literary works. They are: (1) *Saṁhitā*, (2) *Brāhmaṇa*, (3) *Āraṇyaka* and (4) *Upaniṣad*.

The *Saṁhitās* are collection of prayers to different gods as well as chants and *mantras* for sacrificial purposes. This literature is constituted of four *Saṁhitās*: (1) The *Ṛgveda*, (2) The *Sāmaveda*, (3) The *Yajurveda*, (4) The *Atharvaveda*.

The *Brāhmaṇas* contain prose-texts and deal with sacrificial rites, religious duties and some legends. The *Āraṇyakas*, i.e., Forest-texts, contain the objects of meditation for the forest-hermits. The *Upaniṣads* contain higher philosophical reflections.

Date of the Vedas

There is no satisfactory evidence to prove the exact date of the compilation of the *Vedas* and, therefore, not a single work of Vedic literature can be accurately dated. On the basis of the language and contents the oldest of them is the *ṚV-Saṁhitā*.

On the linguistic grounds again, the *ṚV* may be said to be of about 1500-1200 BC but its contents are, in the oldest part, of a much more ancient date whereas some parts are of a later date. Many scholars have presented their views and findings in an effort to determine the age of *Vedas*, still the controversy persists. Some scholars assign the Vedic hymns to 3000 BC, others to 6000 BC. Tilak dates the hymns to about 4500 BC, *Brāhmaṇas* to 2500 BC and *Upaniṣads* to 1600 BC. Jacobi puts the hymns at 4500 BC. According to Winternitz the date of the *Vedas* is between 2500-2000 BC.[2] A generally accepted date of the *ṚV* is between 2000-2500 BC.

ṚV-Saṁhitā

It has been rightly observed that "the first place in the long row of books which contain the records of the Āryan branch of mankind belongs for ever to the ṚV."[3] This *Saṁhitā* has the distinction of being the oldest Indo-European literary monument. It also contains the earliest ideas about gods and religion as entertained by the ancient Āryans. Thus this *Veda* represents the earliest phase of evolution of the religious consciousness. This mammoth book was not written in its present form. Various hymns of the *ṚV* were composed at different times, with a number of seers contributing to the creation of this great work which was later compiled.

The *ṚV* is mainly a collection of *ṛcs* (stanzas) (*ṛc* < √*arc*, which are prayers to different gods like Agni, Varuṇa, Soma, Indra, etc. The only available recension of *ṚV* is the Sākala recension which including the 11 *Vālakhilya* hymns contains 1028 hymns.

On the ritualistic application of the hymns M. Winternitz observes that there is no doubt that a great number of the *ṚV* hymns arose independently of the sacrificial rituals. Although many of these hymns were used later on for sacrificial purposes, it does not prove that they were originally meant for this purpose.

Of the various recensions of the *ṚV* only one, namely the Śākala recension is available in an apparently complete form. Its 1028 hymns are divided in 10 *Maṇḍalas* (i.e., books). According to another division the *ṚV* has 8 *Aṣṭakas*. Each *Aṣṭaka* is further divided in 8 *Adhyāyas* (chapters). *Maṇḍalas* II-VII are called the 'Family-Books' (a term used by Geldner) because they contain family-hymns. Each of them is assigned by tradition to the eponym ancestor of a particular priestly family. The names of these *ṛṣis* are Gṛtsamada (II), Viśvāmitra (III), Vāmadeva (IV), Atri (V), Bhāradvāja (VI) and Vasiṣṭha (VII) respectively. The family-hymns are composed by the *ṛṣi* himself or by members of his family.

The family-books contain the knowledge of the sacrifices performed by the family and also some information or reminiscences of important events of that family or *gotra*. The eighth *Maṇḍala* of the *ṚV* is known as *Pragāthā Maṇḍala*, for it contains *Pragāthās* which were indispensable for *Udgātṛ* rituals. It is known as *Kāṇva Maṇḍala*, as many hymns are by Kāṇvas. The ninth *Maṇḍala* is also known as *Pāvamānīya Maṇḍala/Soma Maṇḍala*. It is a collection of hymns addressed to Pavamāna Soma. These hymns are believed to have been picked up from the other *Maṇḍalas*, compiled and placed in a separate *Maṇḍala*. About half a dozen hymns are, however, found scattered in other *Maṇḍalas*.[4]

The tenth *Maṇḍala* of the *ṚV* has some hymns containing philosophical thoughts as well as speculations on the problem of creation. These hymns, viz. *ṚV*, 10.90; 121; 129; are the earliest specimens of the Āryan philosophical thoughts. In X.121, i.e., the *Hiraṇyagarbha-Sūkta*, the Creator appears under the name of *Hiraṇya-garbha*, 'germ of gold'. The X.129 or the *Nāsadīya-Sūkta* is noteworthy for the daring speculations which finds utterance in so remote an age. It explains the origin of the world in a philosophical manner. The X.90 describes the creation of Universe from the different parts of the Cosmic Man (*Puruṣa*) who being thousand-headed and thousand-footed extended even beyond earth as he covered it.

The *Maṇḍala* X contains almost all what is said in *ṚV* about Yama and the Pitṛmedha (sacrifices for the dead). There are three hymns addressed to Yama. They are X.10; 14; 135. The X.15 is addressed to the Fathers. The X.16 and 18 are connected with the cremation of the dead and other funerary rites. This set of hymns connected with Yama and Fathers is termed as *Yama-Saṁhitā* on the analogy of *Soma-Saṁhitā* (the *Maṇḍala* IX) which contains all the Soma hymns. The fact that all hymns connected with Yama appear in the *Maṇḍala* X does not necessarily suggest that they were composed at a later date. It is quite possible that at the time of the compilation of the *ṚV* these hymns were brought together and placed in the *Maṇḍala* X, same as all the Soma hymns were collected in the *Maṇḍala* IX.

The Ṛgvedic seers attribute divinity to the striking phenomena of nature. The hymns are addressed to the deities like *Sūrya*, *Soma*, *Agni*, *Dyaus*, *Pṛthivī*, *Maruts*, *Vāyu*, *Āpaḥ* and *Uṣas*. Though several gods are praised in the Ṛgvedic hymns, it is not hard to discern an undercurrent of their oneness which is well-expressed in the *Ṛ**V*, I.164.46, according to which various gods are different manifestations of one Supreme Being (*ekam sad viprā bahudhā vadanti* — *ṚV*, I.164.46).

A study of the hymns of the *ṚV* is indispensable for getting an adequate account of the Indian thought. "They are a source of the later practices and the philosophy of the Indo-Āryans, and the study of these hymns is necessary for the proper understanding of subsequent thoughts."[5]

Sāmaveda

The word *Sāman* means melody and therefore the *Sāmaveda* is a collection of melodies. The texts used as musical notes in this *Saṁhitā* are almost wholly drawn from the *ṚV*. There are only seventy-five verses of the *Sāmaveda* which do not occur in the *ṚV*, so the *Sāmaveda* has little literary value and is of no importance in the study of the Vedic mythology.

Yajurveda

This *Saṁhitā* is essentially a guidebook for the *Adhvaryu* priest, who has to perform the sacrificial rites. There are several recensions of the *YV*, out of which six complete recensions are available. *Samhitās* of the Vājasaneyī school consist only the verses and formulae to be recited at the sacrifice. It does not contain the explanatory matter which is collected in the *Brāhmaṇas*. It is, therefore, called *Śukla Yajurveda*. In contrast to this the Black (*Kṛṣṇa*) *Yajurveda* contains both kinds of matter mixed up in the *Saṁhitā*. The six complete available recensions of the *YV* are: (1) *Mādhyandina* and (2) *Kāṇva*[6] of the *Śukla-Yajurveda* and (1) *Taittirīya*, (2) *Kāṭhaka*, (3) *Maitrāyaṇi* and (4) *Kāpiṣṭhala* of the *Kṛṣṇa-Yajurveda*. *Yajurveda* resembles the *Sāmaveda* in having been compiled for application to sacrificial rites only. But while the *SV* deals only with one part of the ritual, i.e., the Soma-sacrifice, the *YV* supplies the formulae for the whole sacrificial ceremonial. Like the *SV* it is also connected with the *ṚV* but while the former is extracted from the *ṚV*; the *YV*, though borrowing many of its verses from the same source, is largely an original production. Some important changes are noticed in connection with the gods. Prajāpati, who is introduced only in the latest hymns of the *Mandala* X of the *ṚV* is now the chief of the gods. Rudra of the *RV* is mentioned by the name Śiva as well as by Śaṅkara and Mahādeva. Visnu now occupies a more prominent place than in the *RV* and a new feature is his constant identification with the sacrifice. In the *YV* high importance is given to the sacrifice and the correct performance of its each and every detail.

Atharvaveda

The *Atharvaveda* means the *Veda* of the Atharvans, i.e., the knowledge of the magic formulae. It is also called a "prayer-book of the simple folk haunted by ghosts and exploited by brāhmins"[7]

The full title of the *AV*, i.e., *Atharvāṅgiras* (*AV*, 10.7.20) shows that is contained Atharvan as well as Aṅgiras. The former refers to the auspicious practices used for healing purposes (*Bheṣajyāni AV*, 11.6.14). The hostile practices and black magic belonged to Aṅgiras. The former is medicine and later is witch-craft. The *AV* is also called by a few other names. They are

(1) *Āṅgirasaveda* (*GB*, 1.8; *SB*, 13.4.3.8)

(2) *Brahmaveda* (*AV*, 5.5.6)

(3) *Bhṛgvāṅgiroveda* (*GB*, 3.1)

The *AV* is a collection of 730 hymns which contain about 6000 verses in its best preserved Śaunakīya recension. The other recension is Paippalāḍa, a part of which is available.

The *AV* is divided in 20 books (*kāṇḍas*). The 20th book almost entirely consists of the hymns which have been taken from the *RV*. Besides this about 1/7th part of the *AV* is taken from *ṚV*. The most interesting of all the *kāṇḍas* of *AV* is the fifteenth. It is composed in prose and is devoted to the mystic exaltation of Vrātya. The 15, 17, 18, 19, 20 *kāndas* are regarded as later additions, but there is no reason to doubt the antiquity of the major part of the *AV*. For the study of the history of Vedic people the *AV* is certainly the most important of all the four *Saṁhitās*. It contains popular beliefs and superstitions prevalent among people.

The *AV* contains songs and spells for the treatment of various ailments. Numerous charms are addressed to *takman* (fever) (*AV*, 5.2.2), who is imagined to be a demon. The subject-matter of the *AV* can be divided under the following heads:[8]

(1) *Bhaiṣajyāni Sūktāni* — prayers for the treatment of diseases.

(2) *Āyuṣyāṇi Sūktāni* — prayers for health and long life.

(3) *Pauṣṭikāni Sūktāni*—prayers for benedictions by which the farmers, shepherds, merchants and others hope to gain happiness in their undertaking.

(4) *Mṛgāra Sūktāni*—they contain general prayers for happiness and protection against danger and evil.

(5) *Prāyaścitta Sūktāni* — these are expiatory formulae and spells for cleansing oneself of guilts and sins.

(6) *Strīkarmāṇi* (women's rites) — magic songs referring to marriage and love, e.g. 3.25.

(7) *Abhicārakāṇi* — they deal with exorcism against demons, wizards and enemies.

(8) *Rajakarmāṇi* (king's rites)—these are a rather large class of magic-songs which are intended for the needs of the kings. They contain exorcism and formulae against enemies as well as songs and charms belonging to the magic-rites which refer to the life of a king.

(9) Philosophical and cosmogonical verses.

Brāhmaṇas

The *Brāhmaṇas* form the second part of the *Veda*. They are ritual text-books intended to guide the priest through long and complicated sacrificial rites. Elaborating the sacrificial ceremonies with the combination of the verses and rites, a new class of literature took shape in these theological treatises entitled *Brāhmaṇas*. In contrast with the *Vedas*, which are poetical in matter and form, the *Brāhmaṇas* are prosaic and written in prose. The *Brāhmaṇa*-texts together with the prose part of the *YV* and *AV* are the early prose-text which Sanskrit as a popular language has produced.[9] They represent the oldest prose writing of the Indo-European family.

The period of *Brāhmaṇas* was also that of important changes in the religious thoughts. A great stress was laid on sacrifice, the observance of caste-system and *āśramas* and the superiority of the priest.

The *AB* and *KB* are the *Brāhmaṇas* of the *ṚV*. Of them the former is older in date and bigger in bulk, but the later is rich in contents. Two *Brāhmaṇas* of the *SV* are preserved; they are (1) *Jaiminīya-Brāhmaṇa*, (2) *Tāṇḍya-Mahābrāhmaṇa*, (also called *Pañcaviṁśa Brāhmaṇa* on the basis of its twenty-five chapters).

Of the *Kṛṣṇa-Yajurveda*, in the *Taittirīya* school, there is the oldest and the most important *Brāhmaṇa*, viz. *Taittirīya Brāhmaṇa*. The ritual explanation of the *Śukla Yajurveda* is to be found in extraordinary details in the *Śatapatha-Brāhmaṇa*. This *Brāhmaṇa* is available in two recensions, viz. *Mādhyandina* and *Kāṇva*.

The *Gopatha-Brāhmaṇa* is attached to the *AV*. This *Brāhmaṇa* consists of two books. The matter of the former half is, to a considerable extent, original, the rest being borrowed from books XI and XII of the *ŚB* besides a few passages from the *AB*. The main motive of this portion is glorification of the *AV* and that of the fourth priest, i.e., the Brahman priest.

Āraṇyaka

They are the concluding portions or appendices to the *Brāhmanas*. *Brāhmaṇas* discuss the rituals to be observed by the householder but when in his old age the house-holder enters the *vānaprastha āśrama* and lives in the forest, some substitute for the rituals is supplied to him in the *Āranyakas*. At this stage the symbolic and spiritual aspect of the sacrifices is meditated upon. Thus here the meditation replaces the actual performance of the sacrifices. The *Āryanakas* form a transition-link between ritualism of the *Brāhmanas* and the philosophy of the *Upaniṣads*. The *Āranyakas* and *Upaniṣads* were originally called *Vedānta*; literally, the concluding part of the *Veda*. The *ṚV* has *Aitareya Āraṇyaka* which is attached to the *Aitareya Brāhmaṇa* and *Śāṅkhāyana* (*Kauṣītakī*) *Āraṇyaka* which also forms the concluding part of *Śāṅkhāyana* (*Kauṣītakī*) *Brāhmaṇa*. The *Kṛṣṇa Yajurveda* has *Taittirīya Āraṇyaka*. The *Śukla Yajurveda* has *Bṛhadāraṇyaka*, the last six chapters of which constitute the *Bṛhadāraṇyakopaniṣad*.

Upaniṣads

Upaniṣads form the concluding part of the *Veda*. They are also called *Vedānta*, literally the end of the *Veda*, "not only because they came at the end of the Vedic period or they were taught at the end, i.e., completion of the Vedic instruction but also because the later philosophies found in them are the final aim of the *Veda*."[10] Thus this name (i.e., *Vedānta*) suggests that the *Upaniṣads* contained the essence of the Vedic teachings. The term *Upsniṣad* is derived from *upa* + *ni* + √*sad* which means 'to sit down near someone'. This refers to pupils sitting down near the preceptor at the time of instruction. Later this term was applied to a secret communication or doctrines which the pupil learnt from the preceptor towards the completion of his studies. The texts which contained these doctrines came to be called *Upaniṣads* and they are the foundation of many later philosophies.

This term, i.e., *Vedānta*, used to denote the *Upaniṣads* is applicable to them because (1) they, on the basis of relative literary chronology, stand at the end of the *Vedas*, (2) they were taught to the pupil towards the completion of his studies, and (3) they formed the last portion of the daily Vedic recital.

The number of the treatises called *Upaniṣads* is quite large, but some of them are not as old as others. The oldest *Upaniṣads* are partly included in the *Āraṇyakas* or the 'Forest-texts' and partly appended to them.

It is difficult to determine the chronology of the *Upaniṣads* due to different strata of composition in the various *Upaniṣads*. R.D. Ranade[11] observes that the various 'tests' used for determining the chronological order of the *Upaniṣads*, i.e., (1) the test of the language, the style, the vocabulary, grammatical peculiarities, (2) prose or verse style of the *Upaniṣads*, (3) the regular ideological development of the ideas like that of the 'Two Souls' or of the Transmigration, etc. are not sufficient criterion to serve the purpose.

The 13 major *Upaniṣads* are divided in these groups.[12]

I. *Bṛhadāraṇyaka* and *Chāndogya*

II. *Īśa* and *Kena*

III. *Aitareya, Taittirīya* and *Kauśītaki*

IV. *Kaṭha, Muṇḍaka* and *Śvetāśvatara*

V. *Praśna, Maitrī* and *Māṇḍūkya*

BṚHADĀRAṆYAKA UPANIṢAD

This *Upaniṣad* contains six chapters.

In the first chapter there is a good description of the Cosmic Person considered as a sacrificial horse and a parable to establish the Supermacy of *prāṇa* which is followed by a number of creation myths put together. The second chapter contains the famous conversation between Gārgya, the proud brāhmin and Ajātaśatru, the quiescent kṣatriya king. The great sage Yājñavalkya is introduced making the division of his estate between his wives. The sage Yājñavalkya becomes the prominent figure in the chapters three and four, and as in chapter two he is seen discoursing with his wife Maitreyī, similarly he is seen in the chapter three discoursing with a number of philosophers in the court of the king Janaka and in chapter four with Janaka himself. These passages contain philosophical teachings of Yājñavalkya. The next two chapters contain a number of miscellaneous reflections on ethical, cosmological and eschatological matters, and the celebrated parable of the senses.

The doctrine of *karman* is seen developed in the *BṛUp* and is explained like this:

> Just as an embroiderer undoes a small portion of a piece of embroidery, and out of it creates a different, quite new and more beautiful form, so man, when he has stripped off his body and has rid himself of non-knowledge, creates for himself a different, quite new and more beautiful form.[13]

The *ChāUp* contains eight chapters. It declares the great fundamental dogma of the identity of *Brahman* with the *Ātman* (chapter III) and the earliest statement of the doctrine that this manifold world is unreal (chapter V). The chapter V is noteworthy for its theory of transmigration. It also declare the one-ness of the individual soul and the Supreme Self by saying *tat tvam asi* (thou art that). The ethical basis the Upaniṣadic doctrine is expressed by a simile:

> As water does not stick to the leaves of the lotus flower, so evil actions do not stick to him who knows this that the Self is Brahman. (*ChāUp*, IV.14.3).

This is not to be construed to mean that a knower is given all laxity to do evil actions. The simile rather shows that the knower was regarded as inherently incapable of doing evil action. The sixth chapter contains the philosophy of Āruṇi who establishes an absolute equation between individual and Universal Spirit.

Īśa and *Kena* both are named after the initial words of

these treatises. *Īśa Upaniṣad* (40th chapter of the *VS*) contains only 18 verses and gives a valuable mystical description of *Ātman*, a description of the ideal sage who remains unruffled in the midst of temptations and sorrows, an adumbration of the doctrine of *karmayoga* and finally a reconciliation of the claims of knowledge (*jñāna*) and work (*karma*). *Kena Upaniṣad* consists of four sections, of which the first two are composed in verse and the last two in prose. The verse part of the *Upaniṣad* gives an argument for the existence of *Ātman* as the inspirer of the various sense functions, it also favours the worship of the Ultimate Reality conceived as *Ātman* and finally makes an essay in spiritual agnoiology telling in a paradoxical fashion that those who know really do not know and those who do not know may alone be said to know the Ultimate Reality.

AITAREYA UPANIṢAD

There are three chapters of this *Upaniṣad*. The first is given to a description of the creation of the world by the Primeval *Ātman* through *Virāj*. The next chapter contains the famous philosophy of 'Three births', probably belonging to the sage Vāmadeva, Vedic sage mentioned in the *ṚV*, 4.27.1. The idea of the life after death is introduced in this chapter.

TAITTIRĪYA UPANIṢAD

This last four of the ten sections of the *TA* constitute the two *Upaniṣads* of the *Taittirīya* school, viz. chapter VII to IX forming the *Taittirīya Upaniṣad* and the chapter X forming the *Mahānārāyaṇa Upaniṣad*.

KAUṢĪTAKI UPANIṢAD

Kauṣītaki Upaniṣad is divided in four chapters of which the first is merely an enlarged variant of the description of the path of the gods and the path of the Fathers as occurring in the *Chāndogya Upaniṣad* and *Bṛhadāraṇyaka Upaniṣad*. According to the philosophy of the *Kauṣītaki Upaniṣad prāṇa* is the first principle of life, then the principle of consciousness, and then is equated with Ultimate Reality, namely the *Ātman*. This *Upaniṣad* also contains a number of social customs of that time.

The *Kaṭha*, *Muṇḍaka* and *Śvetāśvatara Upaniṣads* are related to each other as all of them aim at visaging the highest philosophical truths in a poetic manner and thus became the chief sources from which the *Bhagavadgītā* and later philosophical poems freely borrow. The only difference between them being that the *Kaṭha Upaniṣad* is more or less a metaphysical work, the *Muṇḍaka* is an emotional work and the *Śvetāśvatara* is a commixture of philosophy and mysticism. "All the three *Upaniṣads* seem ..... to have been written at the time when the *Sāṁkhya* and *Vedānta* had not yet parted ways".[14]

The whole of the *Kaṭha Upaniṣad* which deals with the legend of Naciketas contains ideas about immortality of the soul as well as suggestion for the attainment of *Ātman*. Two of the most important features of *Kaṭha* are the description of the "chariot of the body" and the death and dream approaches to the problem of Reality.

MUṆḌAKA UPANIṢAD

Muṇḍaka Upaniṣad derives its name from being the *Upaniṣad* of the tonsured (*muṇḍa*), an association of the ascetics who shaved their heads. Its cosmology is suffused both by *Sāṁkhya* and Vedāntic ideas. Its metaphysics is based on Vedic ideas and has a ritualistic tinge. While as a work which can incite to mystic thought, it has no parallel in the whole literature of the *Upaniṣads*.

ŚVETĀŚVATARA UPANIṢAD

Śvetāśvatara Upaniṣad derives its name from an individual author. In this *Upaniṣad* lie embedded side by side the *Sāṁkhya* and Vedāntic doctrines of cosmology, psychology and metaphysics and it is a very valuable *Upaniṣad* for the genetic study of the parting of the two great systems, i.e., the *Sāṁkhya* and *Vedānta*.[15] It exhibits various *Vedānta*-

doctrines which do not figure in the earlier *Upaniṣads*. Among these may be mentioned the destruction of the world by *Brahman* at the end of the Cosmic Age (*kalpa*) as well as its periodic renewal out of *Brahman* and especially the explanation of the world as an illusion (*māyā*) produced by *Brahman*.

PRAŚNOPANIṢAD

It is written in the prose. The nature, the style and the manner of presentation of the argument in it are comparatively modern. The six sages are mentioned as going to the sage Pippalāḍa to learn wisdom and each of them asks him a question. The order of these questions is thus that they adduce an evolving philosophy from Pippalāḍa. These question concern the origin of matter and life (*prāṇa*) from Prajāpati, the superiority of life (*prāṇa*) over the other vital powers, dreaming and dreamless-sleep, meditation on the syllable *Om*, and the sixteen parts of man.

MAITRĪ UPANIṢAD

This *Upaniṣad* consists of seven chapters written in prose. Its many quotations from other *Upaniṣads*, the occurrence of several late words, developed *Sāṁkhya* doctrine presupposed by it — all combine to render it a stamp of lateness. The text can be divided in two strata and the first stratum consisting of the first four chapters is comparatively earlier.

The main body of the treatise expounds the nature of *Ātman*. The king Bṛhadratha goes to Śākāyana and begs of him what he himself has learnt from the sage Maitrī who may thus be regarded as the promulgator of the doctrine of this *Upaniṣad*. The first point in his philosophy is a description of the pure noumenal self who "arising from the body shines in his own greatness", and second is the description of the phenomenal self called *bhūtātman* who is subject to the influence of his good and bad actions and who, therefore, undergoes transmigration.

MĀṆḌŪKYA UPANIṢAD

It is a very short prose *Upaniṣad* and its importance lies in the fact that it lays the foundation of the later Vedāntic philosophy. It is used more than any other *Upaniṣad* by the author of the well-known later epitome of the *Vedānta* doctrine, the *Vedāntasāra*. The great originality of the *Māṇḍūkya Upaniṣad* consists in positing the four states of consciousness, namely, wakefulness, dream, sleep and a fourth unnameable state of consciousness.

Vedāṅga

Contrary to the 'revealed literature', i.e., the *Vedas*, there is another class of works which is regarded as a human work. This class of literature is closely associated with the Vedic literature and it is called *Vedāṅga* (literally — limbs of the *Veda*), the auxiliary sciences of the *Veda*. The *Vedāṅga* are six in number and they contribute towards the proper understanding of the *Vedas*. They cover six subjects which help in the proper understanding, recitation and sacrificial use of the Vedic *mantras*. These six subjects are: (1) *Śikṣā* (phonetics), (2) *Kalpa* (rituals), (3) *Vyākaraṇa* (grammar), (4) *Nirukta* (etymology), (5) *Chandas* (metre), and (6) *Jyotiṣ* (astronomy).

The *Vedāṇga* literature is written in *Sūtra*-style.

The earliest references to the *Vedāṅgas* is found in the *Muṇḍakopaniṣad* (1.1.5) where they are mentioned as *aparā vidyā*. In this passage the term *parā vidyā* refers to *Brahma-vidyā*, i.e., the knowledge of *Brahman*, while *aparā vidyā* refers to all the four *Vedas* along with the six *Vedāṅgas*.[16]

ŚIKṢĀ

These works termed as *Prātiśākhyas* instruct the student in the correct pronunciation, accent, euphonic changes which the sounds undergo in the composition of the words, and other such topics which come under Vedic phonetics. Thus the *Prātiśākhyas* are the oldest books on this subject. They are the earliest specimen, if occasional excursions in the

Brāhmaṇas are excluded, of the Indian endeavour in the field of the science of linguistics.

As the name suggests the *Prātiśākhyas* belong to every recension of a Vedic *Saṁhitā*. The following *Prātiśākhyas* are available to us

(1) *Ṛgveda Prātiśākhya* (ascribed to Śaunaka),

(2) *Taittirīya Pratiśākhya*,

(3) *Vājasaneyi Prātiśākhya* (both ascribed to Kātyāyana),

(4) *Atharva Prātiśākhya* (supposed to belong to Śaunakas),

(5) *Pañca-vidha Sūtra* (It belongs to the *Sāmaveda* and shows the manner in which the *Sāman* are to be sung at the sacrifice.

KALPA

The period of *Kalpa-Sūtras* is roughly estimated to be from 400 BC-200 BC.[17] The practical side of the Vedic religion can be seen in the *Śrauta* and *Gṛhya Sūtras* which deal with different, but complementary topics relating to the rituals. They are manuals for providing guidance for performing the complicated and long sacrificial rites. They provide valuable explanations of the *Brāhmaṇas*. In this way they are directly connected with the *Brāhmaṇas*. No *Kalpa-Sūtra* represents rigidly any one *Saṁhitā*. Even though a *Sūtra* generally follows some *Saṁhitā*, materials from other *Saṁhitās* are also included in it.[18]

According to their subject-matter, the *Sūtras* are divided in two categories:

(1) *Śrauta-Sūtras*

(2) *Gṛhya-Sūtras*

Śrauta-Sūtras

They provide guidance about the several rites performed at the sacrifices. They deal with elaborate forms of rituals in which the presence of a priest and usually of many priests in necessary. They teach the laying of the three sacrificial fires and performing big sacrifices.

Gṛhya Sūtras

They deal with the rituals and other duties of the housholders. They also contain instructions on various customs, ceremonies and functions performed at the different stages of life of a man. They describe five great sacrifices, i.e., the daily-sacrifices to the Brahman, gods, Fathers, men and creatures.

Two complete collections of the *Sūtras* of the *ṚV* are available. They are *Āśvalāyana* and *Śāṅkhāyana Śrauta* and *Gṛhya Sūtras*. The *Sāmaveda* has *Śrauta-Sūtra* of Maśaka, Lātyāyana, Drāhyāyaṇa; and *Gṛhya-Sūtras* by Jaimini, Gobhila and Khadira. The *Kṛṣṇa Yajurveda* has both the *Śrauta* and *Gṛhya Sūtras* by Mānava, Baudhāyana, Bhāradwāja, Āpastamba and Hiraṇyakeśin. The *Śukla Yajurveda* is represented by Kātyāyana *Śrauta-Sūtra* and Pāraskara *Gṛhya-Sūtra*. The *AV* has *Kauśika-Sūtra* which contains an accurate account of the magic rites which are accompanied by the formulae of the text.

Dharma Sūtra

This is another class of the *Sūtras* which especially deals with customary laws and practises. The difference between the *Gṛhya* and *Dharma Sūtras* is that "the weight in the *Dharma-Sūtra* is laid on the wider relation of a man with the state, so that those sections, which deal the family became condensed and subordinate."[19] They enumerate the duties of people according to their *varṇa* and *āśrama*. The beginning of civil and criminal law can be seen there. The important subjects covering the civil law are taxes, inheritance and position of women. In the criminal laws the assault, adultary and theft are the main topics. The *Dharma-Sūtras* of Gautama, Baudhāyana, Āpastamba and Vasiṣṭha are considered to be the oldest and the most important of the *Dharma-Sūtras*. Their importance lies in the fact that they contain references to religion and that the gradual change from the Vedic religion to Purānic religion is noticed in them. The *Gṛhya Sūtras* and the *Dharma-Sūtras* are of a special value since they preserved for the posterity the domestic side of the religion practised by the ordinary householders, as opposed to the great sacrifices which were solely in the hands of the priests.

Śūlva-Sūtras

This is another class of the *Sūtras*, directly connected with the *Śrauta-Sūtra*. They provide minute details regarding the measurement of the place of sacrifice and the fire-altars. They may, therefore, be regarded as the oldest books in geometry.

VYĀKARAṆA

The only representative of this *Vedāṅga* is the *Aṣṭādhyāyī* of Pāṇinī. The principal subject of Pāṇinī was *bhāṣā*, the language of the common people and not the sacred language of the seers. The Vedic grammar, therefore, receives only sectional treatment from Pāṇinī.

NIRUKTA

This class of works also have only one representative viz. Yāska's *Nirukta*, since the works of Yāska's predecessors (mentioned by Yāska in his *Nirukta*) are not available to us.Yāska's treatise is a commentary on the *Nighaṇṭu*, which is comprised of a list of the obscure words of the *Vedas*. This list (i.e., the *Nighaṇṭu*) was prepared in an attempt to protect those words from being unintelligible to the future generations.

CHANDAS (METRE)

Very little literature is now available on this *Vedāṅga*. The *Nidāna-Sūtra* (which has ten *prapāṭhakas*) belonging to the *SV* deals with metre.

JYOTIṢ

There is no work available at present dealing with ancient astronomy in *Sūtra* style. The *Jyotiṣ-Vedāṅga* is a later work of practical utility. It gives some rules for calculating and fixing the days and hours for performing the different sacrifices. Earlier works are lost to us.

Vedic Gods

The compilation of the *ṚV* extends over a long period of time and hence it also contains the religious and philosophical thoughts prevailing in that period. Thus, the *ṚV*, being the oldest Indo-Āryan literary document, represents the earliest phase in the evolution of the religious consciousness.

The religion in its widest sense means men's conception of divine and supernatural powers and also a belief that their welfare depended upon those powers. This belief finds expression in various forms of worship. Myths are woven around a god describing his origin, his actions, his companions and enemies, etc.

The Ṛgvedic hymns are addressed to various gods, like Agni, Indra, Varuṇa, Soma, etc. and goddesses like Uṣas, Rātri, etc. Through his prayers to the various gods, the worshipper wants to get wealth, good health, victory, progeny and in short all the worldly happiness. The epithet *deva* (brilliant) (from √*div*), which was originally applicable to sky, sun, moon, dawn, fire and lightening, etc., was afterwards extended to earth, storm, rain, and even night. Yāska calls every object of worship a *devatā*.

The Vedic poetry and the Vedic mythology are, to a considerable extent dominated by priestly conventions. These details often obscure the mythology and sometimes present it in a different shape making an attempt to get a clear view of Vedic god very difficult. Moreover, the language of the *Vedas*, which is far removed even from the earliest commentators and exegetes like Yāska, Sāyaṇa and others, is difficult and obscure at many places. The obscurity as well as deviation in the meaning, due to various possible interpretations of the *mantras*, have also contributed to some extent to the vagueness in the true picture of a Vedic divinity. Sāyana's commentary, though very helpful, deals mainly with the ritualistic application of the hymns and the mythology contained in them is mentioned only secondarily. Nevertheless, Sāyaṇa quotes Yāska and Śaunaka to elucidate the mythology connected with the text. The personality of many a Vedic divinities is complex and heterogeneous, since their characteristic features are not only inconsistent and incomplete but sometimes, even mutually contradictory. This can be attributed to the fact that the Vedic mythology is essentially an evolutionary mythology which has been reacting and responding to the various vicissitudes in the cultural history of the Vedic age.[20] It can be assumed that in the different stage of evolution, the Vedic mythology was dominated by different gods, which has resulted in the complexity to their personality. To get a clear view of the personality of a god, therefore, it is necessary to study it as a growing personality and the whole mythology as an evolutionary mythology.[21]

Some Vedic myths seem to have started with an attempt to explain some natural phenomenon which puzzled the Vedic seers' minds. In the process the natural phenomenon got deified and myths grew around it. The Vedic poets were the children of nature. Many natural events or phenomenon filled them with awe, admiration and reverence, which got expression in worshipping them as gods and seeking their blessings. Thus a great majority of the Vedic gods, excluding Prajāpati and other later conceptions, can be connected with some element or event of nature. The dawn filling the sky with its golden light was personified as Uṣas. The thunder preceding a downpour was imagined to be Indra's fight with Vṛtra in order to get the rains released from his hold-up (*ṚV*, 2.11.5, 2.14.2, *AV*, 18.89.7). The natural phenomena like the sun's definite course, its daily appearance, the thunder, the storm, etc. also posed intellectual difficulty for the Vedic seer to which he attempts to find an answer by personifying the natural phenomenon and weaving a myth around it. These myths are, therefore, essentially early explanation of the mystery of natural phenomena observed by man. To Vedic poets a natural event was the work of a divine being resembling a human agent. Thus many powers of nature were deified. As these powers are closely associated with each other, the deities who represent them are also similar in character. Thus most of the Vedic gods like Dyaus, Sūrya, Agni, Savitṛ Uṣas, Maruts, Parjanya, Pṛthivī are symbolic representation of various elements and powers of nature. It is also seen that certain aspects of one deity have got separated in the form of another deity; for example, Vivasvat, Savitṛ, Mitra, Pūṣan are four gods representing different aspects of the sun's glory. Savitṛ, i.e., the inspirer, Pūṣan, the life-giver and Vivasvat, the luminous were at first epithets of the sun, then names of the sun and finally they became independent solar gods beside Sūrya. The general line of mythological evolution of the deified phenomenon of nature is like this.

First, the phenomenon of nature, then its personification, then (in some cases) separation of some abstract conception of some prominent quality of the deity, and possibly again the personification of that quality of deity.

In some cases, like Uṣas where the name of the deity is the same as its natural phenomenon the personification is not complete. Such gods represent the natural phenomenon as well as its presiding deity. Both of them exist in the poet's mind and find expression in turns. Dyaus, Pṛthivī, Sūrya, etc. fall in this category. Of many hymns whose deity is said to be Uṣas, Sūrya or Pṛthivī, etc. the subject-matter is primarily or even exclusively not that deity but a superhuman and, in most cases, a kind power behind a physical phenomenon. Therefore, the personification of these deities is not complete. The personification of Agni and Soma is also checked due to their visible forms, i.e., the element of fire and the sacrificial drink respectively, which are called by the same name. But in other cases the name of the deity is not same as that of the connected natural phenomenon. The origin of Indra and Varuṇa cannot be easily traced back to some natural phenomenon as the personification in such cases is complete,

Prayers to the Gods

The prayers to the Vedic gods extol their attributes, their

form, their deeds, and also their companion gods.[22] Through these prayers the worshipper wishes for the favour of the gods bestowed upon him in the form of prosperity, good health, long life and progeny of strong sons.

Gods at Sacrifice

The Vedic gods are invoked by worshippers and urged to accept the offerings made to them. On being invoked the gods come to the sacrifice in their luminous chariots drawn by steeds, etc. Various offerings are made to them at the sacrifices. The gods get these offerings through Agni. Soma is the favourite drink of the gods which the sacrificer makes sure to offer. Gods are also offered milk and honey.

The Vedic gods are sometimes invoked in pairs, e.g. Mitrā-Varuṇau, Agnī-Ṣomau, and sometimes also in groups. Rudra, however, is an exception who dislikes being invoked along with other gods. The worshipper wishes not to make Rudra angry by inviting him to the sacrifice along with other gods by reciting a common invocation *Mā tvā Rudra cukrudhāmā namobhiḥ/mā duṣṭutī vṛṣabha mā sahūtī//* (*ṚV*, 2.33.4).

Abstract Deities

There are some deities who are deified forms of abstract ideas. *Śraddhā* (faith), *Manyu* (anger), Viśvakarman (the world's master-builder) and Prajāpati (lord of creatures) are abstract deities. Nearly all these deities appear in the tenth *Maṇḍala* of the *ṚV*.

Minor Deities

Minor deities like Ṛbhus, Apsaras, Gandharvas also appear in the *ṚV*. Several demons and evil-spirits are mentioned as enemies of the gods whom they subdued. However, in the *ṚV* *asura* does not mean an enemy of the gods as in the epics and later literature. In the *ṚV* it means "one possessing wonderful powers"[23] or 'god'[24]. For evil demons the word *dāsa* or *dasyu* is used.[25] Non-Āryan aboriginal habitants are also called *dāsa* and *dasyu*.

Fathers

Apart from the gods the dead also received worship from the living members of their families. For the Vedic people death was not the end of one's existence. The ancestors, called *pitṛ* (Fathers), continue to be respected as elders in the family. They are worshipped like gods and offered food and water. Thus, the worship of the ancestors is connected with the sense of solidarity of the family.[26]

Characteristics of the Vedic Gods

Most of the Vedic gods are personification of some element or event of the nature. They possess certain distinguishing characteristics, while many attributes and powers are common to all the deities. All of them are described as brilliant, powerful and benevolent.

INDEFINITE CHARACTER

Unlike the Greek gods, the Vedic gods have no clear outlines to distinguish them fully from each other. There is a lack of distinctive attributes. Moreover, the epithets of one god are often shared by many other gods. Thus a Vedic god possesses many attributes which are common to several gods and the few distinctive attributes which he has are also sometimes transferred to other gods. This has often resulted in the indefiniteness of the character of the god. Several gods are said to have produced the sun, placed it in the sky and prepared a path for it. This practice has resulted in the gods having very few individual characteristic qualities. Too many figures are overlapping and too many offices are commonly held by two or more deities. Agni is also given a thunderbolt, he wins cows and waters (*ṚV*, 1.59.6) — all attributes belonging to Indra. Viṣṇu and Indra are both mentioned as possessing powers belonging to the other. Agni is said to be knowing all the created beings (*ṚV*, 3.55.10) whom he watches (*ṚV*, 10.187.4). At another place (i.e., *ṚV*, 3.62.9) similar words are said for Pūṣan. About Agni,[27] a terrestrial god it is said that he stretched the heaven and earth (*ṚV*, 3.6.5) and that his greatness exceeds that of the heaven.[28] (*ṚV*, 1,59.5)

TRANSFERENCE OF EPITHETS

One Vedic god receiving the epithets of another god is not rare. Often the epithets of one god are shared by many gods. Agni (*ṚV*, 1.59.6; 3.20.4) as well as Soma (*ṚV*, 9.26.3; 28.3; 9.37.5; 9.98.5) is called a "Vṛtra-slayer" (*vṛtrahan*).[29]

This is an epithet of Indra since the killing of Vṛtra is considered to be the most heroic deed of Indra.[30] Bṛhaspati too receives many epithets like *vajrin*, 'killer ofVala', 'releaser of cows', etc. which are mainly ascribed to Indra.

IDENTIFICATION

Due to the lack of definite characteristics and the transference of distinctive epithets one god is sometimes identified with other gods. The opening verses of the *ṚV*, 2 is marked by the identification of Agni with all gods, i.e., Dyaus, Indra, Viṣṇu, Rudra, Bhaga, etc. Aditi is identified not only with all gods, but with all that has been and shall be born; air and heaven. The tendency of identifying one god with another has led to a monotheist doctrine — "All gods are same, only sages describe them differently." (*ṚV*, 1.164.46)

DEPENDENTNESS

The Vedic deities are also represented as dependent on other gods. Varuṇa and Sūrya are subordinate to Indra; Varuṇa and Aśvins submit to the power of Viṣṇu. Indra, Mitra, Varuṇa, Aryaman, Rudra cannot violate the ordinances of Savitṛ.

MORAL TONE

The character of the Vedic deities is moral. All the gods are truthful and wise. They are friends and guardians of honesty and righteousness. Varuṇa is considered to be the chief upholder of the moral law, i.e., *ṛta*.

BENEVOLENCE

The Vedic gods are benevolent and kind-hearted. They bestow prosperity upon the worshippers and their attitude towards them is very friendly. Prayers to these gods express profound love, respect and admiration. As friends of the sacrificer they destroy his enemies.[31]

HOSTILITY OF THE GODS

Some gods are described displaying hostility. Agni, Sūrya and Indra (*ṚV*, 3.48.4; 6.18.2; 4.10.12; 10.79.4) are the killers of their parents. Indra is said to be breaking the harmony of heaven. He appears to have fought against the gods (*ṚV*, 4.30.3), broken the chariot of Uṣas (*ṚV*, 2.15.6) and threatened to slay Maruts (*ṚV*, 1.170.2).

ORIGIN OF THE GODS

The Vedic gods are in general described as the children of Heaven and Earth and sometimes of other gods. In the *ṚV*, 10.63.2 a triple origin is ascribed to the gods and here they are said to have been born from Aditi, from waters and from the earth (*ṚV*, 1.139.11). In one entire hymn (*ṚV*, 4.18) the birth and infancy of Indra are mentioned. The birth of Agni is referred to in many stanzas of the *ṚV*. The birth of Aśvins, Maruts, Uṣas and others are mentioned. The generations of deities is also referred to in many stanzas, while some earlier (*pūrve*) gods are also referred to (*ṚV*, 7.21.7 etc.).

MORTALITY OF THE GODS

In the *AV*, 11.5.19; 4.11.6 it is said that all gods were originally mortals. In the *ṚV* too it is suggested that the gods were mortals first and were granted immortality by Savitṛ (*ṚV*, 4.54.2 = *VS*, 33.34); by Agni (*ṚV*, 6.7.4; *AV*,4.23.6). They obtained immortality by drinking Soma (*ṚV*, 9.106.8, cf. 9.109.2-3). In the *ṚV*, 10.53.10 also they are said to have acquired immortality, but by what means is not clear.

The *Brāhmaṇas* state about the mortality of all gods *ŚB*, 10.4.3.3) and of the individual gods, e.g. Indra (*AB*, 8.14.4), Agni (*AB*, 3.4) and Prajāpati (*ŚB*, 10.1.3.1). The gods are said to have overcome death by austerity (*AV*, 11.5.19) also *TB*, 3.12.3.1). In the *TS*, 7.4.2.1 the gods are stated to have overcome death by performing certain ceremonies (i.e., sacrifices).

ANTHROPOMORPHISM

A few anthropomorphic features of the gods are described. These features represent the main activity of that god. Head, face, mouth, cheeks, eyes, hair, shoulders, belly, jaws, arms, hands, fingers, feet of the gods are mentioned. Head, arms, hands and chests are described as powerful assets of the warrior Indra. The arms of Sun are his rays. The tongue and limbs of Agni are but his flames. The belly of Indra is described to show his ability to drink an enormous amount of Soma.

HENOTHEISM

The prayers to Vedic gods describe their attributes and powers. The Vedic poets engrossed in praising a particular deity exaggerates his attributes and enthusiastically eulogises him as the highest god, therefore, many gods seem to have exalted to the position of the supreme god. This tendency has added to the indefiniteness to the personality of these gods. In the *Ṛ̣V*, 2.1.3-4 where Agni is identified with six deities, two of them are Indra and Varuṇa who hold a very high position in the Vedic mythology. Varuṇa is considered to be the highest god, while Indra is an extremely popular warrior god with almost one-fourth of the *Ṛ̣V* hymns addressed to him.[32]

This undeniable communalism among the Vedic gods has led Max Müller to propound his theory of Henotheism or Kathenthiesm, i.e., the individual gods alternately regarded as the highest. This theory has some element of truth but cannot be accepted in its full bearing. The feature of many Vedic gods alternately attaining the position of the highest god can be ascribed to the extraordinary zeal of the Vedic seer in eulogizing the particular god who is the subject of his composition. This has resulted in the epithets and remarkable feats of one god being transferred to another which forms the basis for the idea of Henotheism.

The hymns of the *ṚV* were composed during a long literary period and so it is not far-fetched to believe that different gods were given importance at different spells during this long period. It is not, therefore, necessary to believe that many gods were given the highest importance simultaneously. As Zimmermann has rightly observed "the indefinite shape and office of many gods as well as the absence of one recognised head in the Vedic pantheon is responsible for the possible though not real usurpation of Supremacy."[33] The tendency of the Vedic religious thought is far from henotheistic. Many of the gods are frequently brought together in a *dvandva* compound or mentioned in groups. None of them is raised above the rest. Moreover, in the hymns addressed to All Gods (v*iśve-devāḥ*) even the minor gods are also praised along with the bigger deities. In this light it is difficult to accept the suggested henotheism in the Vedic mythology.

Among the Vedic gods no one is recognised as the master of other celestials like Zeus or Jupiter is in the Greek mythology. Zimmermann observes that "the Henotheism is out of question for a simple reason that ancient India did not possess a pantheon in the strict sense of the word, with a head acknowledged by all the gods."[34]

Henotheism in the Vedic gods can be attributed to an under-current of the thought that all the gods are different manifestation of one Supreme Principle. This has led the Vedic seers to arrive at the great monotheistic doctrine that "all the gods are same, only sages describe them differently", (*ṚV*, 1.164.46). In the *ṚV*, 1.16.50 it is stated that Agni takes the form of any god who is being invoked.

The Vedic gods are not always described as independent of the rest. Even the great Varuṇa is subordinate to Indra. Sometimes their interdependence is also seen, for example, Savitr is said to 'rule over Indra' (*ṚV*, 2.28.9), who lords over Sūrya (*ṚV*, 1.101.3) the concrete basis of Savitṛ.

Number of Gods

In the *Nir*, 7.5 Yāska says that according to his predecessors there were only three deities. They are

(1) Agni — whose sphere is the earth

(2) Vāyu — whose sphere is the atmosphere

(3) Sun — whose sphere is the heaven.

Each of these gods receives many appellations on account of his supereminence or the diversity of his functions, just as a priest according to his function is called Hotṛ (the sacrificer), Adhvaryu (the director of the sacrifice), Udgātṛ (the chanter) and *Brahman* (the possessor of the sacred lore). This view may be based on such passages as the *ṚV*, 10.158.1.[35] Śaunaka too upholds the idea of three deities, other deities being different manifestations of these three (*Bṛhaddevatā*, 1.69).

In the *ṚV*, 1.139.11 the number of gods is stated to be thirty-three,[36] who, in the groups of eleven each belong to the three regions of the universe, i.e., the earth, the mid-region and the heaven. The 5th chapter of the *Nighaṇṭu*, on which Yāska (*Nir*, 7.5-12.46) comments enumerates a number of minor deities and deified objects. The number of gods, therefore, far exceeds in each division.

Some drastic deviation in respect of the number of gods is also found. In the *ṚV*, 10.52.6 the number of gods is given as 3329 and in the *AV*, 11.5.2 it is 6333.

Classification of the Gods

The Vedic gods are classified in different ways. Though in the *ṚV*, 8.30.1 it is stated that — "None of you gods is small, all of you are verily the great", they are distinguished in the *ṚV*, 1.27.13 as great gods and small gods, old gods and young gods. But this distinction is nowhere explained.

Yāska (*Nir*, 7.5) adheres to the triple classification of gods as given in the *ṚV*, 1.139.11 which divides the gods on the basis of their place of habitat in nature or in cosmos. They are:

(1) Terrestrial gods (*pṛthivī-sthānāḥ* — *Nir*, 7.14-9.43)

(2) Intermediate gods (*antarikṣa-sthānāḥ* or *madhyama-sthānāḥ* — *Nir*, 10.1-11.50).

(3) Celestial gods (*dyu-sthānāḥ* — *Nir*, 12.1-46).

It is significant to note that the list of gods contained in the *Nighaṇṭu* (chapter 5) on which Yāska (*Nir*, 7.5-12.46) comments, the names of Tvaṣṭṛ and Pṛthivī appear in all the three spheres, those of Agni and Uṣas in both the terrestrial and the aerial and those of Varuṇa, Yama and Savitṛ in the aerial as well as the celestial.

On the basis of the number of hymns addressed to a god as well as the frequency with which their names are mentioned in the *ṚV*, the Vedic gods can be divided into the five categories:[37]

(1) Indra, Agni, Soma;

(2) Aśvinā, Maruts, Varuṇa;

(3) Uṣas, Savitṛ, Bṛhaspati, Sūrya, Pūṣan;

(4) Vāyu, Dyāvāpṛthivī, Viṣṇu, Rudra;

(5) Yama, Parjanya.

This statistical standard, however, cannot determine the place of a god in the panthcon. For instance, Varuṇa is celebrated (mostly along with Mitra) in only about thirty hymns and his name is mentioned about 250 times. In comparision to this Aśvina claim over fifty hymns and their names mentioned over 400 times. Yet in the Vedic mythology Varuṇa holds a far more important place, even higher than that of Agni and Indra. Thus, such a classification which is based on statistics does not tell about the position held by a particular god in the Vedic pantheon.[38]

Another classification is based on the relative age of that mythological conception, i.e., (i) Indo-European, (ii) Indo-Iranian and (iii) Indian. But this is also not free from objections. Though Rudra, Bṛhaspati, Viṣṇu, Pūṣan may be considered purely Indian, there is nothing to ascertain the age of other mythological conceptions. No god except Dyavs can be definitely traced back to Indo-European age. Thus this classification is open to a serious objection that there are no means to determine the order of origin of the gods.

M. Bloomfield[39] has classified the gods the following categories:

(1) Pre-historic — imported by Āryans into India, i.e., Varuṇa;

(2) Transparent ot half-personified — the divine personifications whose naturalistic basis and whose starting point in human consciousness is absolutely clear.

(3) Translucent gods whose origin has been obscured by the later developments of their personalities, i.e., Viṣṇu, Indra, Pūṣan, Aśvins.

(4) Opaque gods, who refuse to reveal their origin.

(5) Abstract or symbolic gods: They embody an action, a wish, a fear in shape of a good or evil divinity.

Varṇa-based Classification

Just like men who are divided in four categories based on the four *varṇas*, i.e., brāhmin, kṣatriya, vaiśya and śūdra, the gods are also stated to be divided in these four social orders. Sāyaṇa in his commentary on the *AB*, 1.9[40] mention this with reference to the creation theory of the *VS*. According to this *Varṇa*-based division the gods are classified in the following manner:

(1) Brāhmin gods — Agni and Bṛhaspati

(2) Kṣatriya gods — Indra, Varuṇa, Soma, Rudra, Parjanya, Yama, Mitra,[41] Īśāna

(3) Vaiśya gods — Vasus, Ādityas, Rudras, Viśvedevāḥ, Maruts

(4) Sūdra gods — Pūṣan.[42]

Dumezil[43] has divided the Āryan gods in three main classes. They are (1) moral, (2) military, and (3) economic. According to him Mitra and Varuṇa, represent the first class of the gods.

Indra and Vāyu are presentative of the second class and the Aśvins of the third.[44]

Zimmermann has pointed out that none of these classifications is free from defects.[45] The traditional classification of Yāska is based on the classification on the origin, nature and activity of the gods which is not fully ascertained. It is very difficult to get a clear view of the Vedic gods to be able to classify them in these categories as (1) terrestrial, (2) atmospheric and (3) celestial gods.

A historical division into Indo-European, Indo-Iranian and Indian deities would require complete informaion about the date of every god in all these periods. But the available data leaves doubt about the dates of many gods.

The division proposed by M. Bloomfield[46] into pre-historic, transparent, translucent, opaque and abstract or symbolic gods is based on the historical and exegetical principles "and is likely to suffer from the faults of both these principles".[47] It is not ascertained which god belongs to pre-historic period and a god can be considered transparent or translucent on the basis of varying interpretations, hence according to Zimmermann, it is best to revert to Yāska's classification.

To serve a practical measure Vedic gods are also divided in two broad groups — major gods and minor gods. But the major or minor character of a god cannot be determined solely on the basis of statistical consideration. J.R. Joshi suggests the rationale for such classification, according to which the gods who play in a direct manner — a significant role in the evolution of the basic mythology of the *ṚV*, are considered major divinities.[48] According to him the basic mythology of the *Veda* may be said to be constituted of such concepts as cosmic, ethics, hero-worship, fire-worship, Soma-ritual, fertility-rites and the pre-Vedic non-Āryan religious element and related to these concept are the gods Varuṇa, Indra, Agni, Soma, Viṣṇu and Rudra respectively. The major character of a few other divinities like Pūṣan can be attributed to the cultural-historical consideration. The distinct and prominent individuality of Yama may be regarded as suggesting his character as a major divinity in the *Veda*.[49]

Notes

1. J. Gonda, *A History of Indian Literature*, Vol. 1, Fasc. 1, p. 7.
2. M. Winternitz, *History of Indian Literature*, Vol.1, p. 310.
3. M. Max Müller, *History of Ancient Sanskrit Literature*, p. 63.
4. *Vide* A.A. Macdonell, *A Vedic Reader*, p. 152.
5. S. Radhakrishnan, *Indian Philosophy*, Vol. I, p. 66.
6. "Kāṇva and Vājasaneyi *Saṁhitā* are practically identical" B.K. Ghosh, *Vedic Age*, p. 243, fn. 43.
7. M. Bloomfield, A Monograph on *AV* published in Grundriss referred to by B.K. Ghosh, *op. cit.*, p. 243, fn. 45.
8. *Vide* M. Winternitz, *op. cit.*, p. 132.
9. J. Eggeling, Trans. *ŚB*, *SBE*, Vol. XII, p. xxv.
10. M. Winternitz, *History of Indian Literature*, Vol. I, p. 234; *vide* Asoke Chatterjee Sastri, *Upaniṣadyoga and Pātañjalayoga — A Comparative Approach*, pp. 2 ff.
11. R.D. Ranade, *A Constructive Survey of the Upaniṣadic Philosophy*, pp. 18 ff.
12. R.D. Ranade, *op. cit.*, p. 16.
13. *BṛUp*, IV.4, Translated by M. Winternitz, *op. cit.*, p. 259.
14. R.D. Ranade *op. cit.*, p. 28.
15. *Ibid.*, p. 30.
16. *dve vidye veditavye iti ha sma yad brahmavido vadanti parā ca eva aparā ca tatrā parā Ṛgvedo Yajurveda Sāmavedo, Atharvavedaḥ Śikṣā-Kalpa-Vyākaraṇa-Nirukta-Chanda-Jyotiṣam iti atha parā yayā tadakṣaram adhi gamyate — Muṇḍakopaniṣad*, 1.1.5.
17. A.B. Keith, *RPVU*, Part I, p. 28.
18. *Ibid.*, p. 27.
19. E.W. Hopkins, *CHI*, p. 229.
20. *Vide* R.N. Dandekar, "Some aspects of Vedic Mythology", *University of Ceylone Review*, January, 1954, p. 3.
21. Zimmermann observes that "though other mythologies may show changes and evolution, these development, after all, do not affect the whole pantheon and it is just the rise and fall of the individual gods, but it is the evolution of the whole Vedic pantheon that makes this mythology so important".

    Vide S.J. Zimmermann, *Hymns of the Ṛgveda*, Appendix II, p. xx
22. *stutis tu nāmnā rupeṇa karmaṇā bāndhavena ca — Bṛhaddevatā*, 1.17.
23. R.N. Dandekar, *VMT*, p. 54.
24. M. Winternitz, *A History of Indian Literature*, p. 28.
25. For a brief account of evil-spirits *vide* H.D. Velankar *Ṛgveda, Maṇḍala*, VII, Introduction, pp. xiv ff.
26. M. Winternitz, *op. cit.*, p. 28.
27. Also Varuṇa, *ṚV*, 7.86.1.

28. J. Muir comments that these epithets might have been originally used for some other god for whom they were more appropriate. They were later transferred to other gods including Agni. (*O.S.T.*, Vol. V, p. 279).
29. It is obvious that Vṛtra here is not the demon Vṛtra whom Indra killed, but an enemy in general. It shows that the word has undergone a semantic change.
30. R.N. Dandekar observes "the various antagonist tribes whom the Vedic Indians, under the heroic leadership of Indra vanquished in the course of their onward march came to be collectively referred to as "Vṛtra or Vṛtrāṇi" and Indra came to be regarded as "Vṛtrahā" — R.N. Dandekar, *op. cit.*, p. 15.
31. For prayers see J. Gonda, *History of Indian Literature*, Vol. 1, fasc. 1, p. 108.
32. Out of 1028 hymns (including the *Vālakhilya* hymns) of the *ṚV* nearly 250 are addressed to Indra.
33. S.J. Zimmermann (ed.), *Peterson's second edition of Hymns of the Ṛgveda*, Appendix II, p. xxiii.
34. *Ibid.*
35. *sūryo no divah pātu vato antarikṣāt/*
    agnir naḥ parthivebhyaḥ // — *ṚV*, 10.158.1.
36. Cf. *ṚV*, 8.30.1; *AB*, 1.10.
37. A.A. Macdonell, *VM*, p. 15.
38. A.A. Macdonell, *op. cit.*, p. 20; A.B. Keith, *RPVP*, pp. 93-94.
39. M. Bloomfield, *Religion of the Veda*, p. 96.
40. *Vide* A.B. Keith, Transl. *AB*, 1.9, *HOS*.
41. *mṛtyu* according to the *ŚB*, 14.4.2.22.
42. Similar division of gods is found in *ŚB*, 14.4.2.24 "Brahman was alone. He created Kṣatriya gods — Indra, Varuṇa . . . Vaiśya gods — Vasu and Śūdra gods — Pūṣaṇ", *ŚB*, 14.4.2.23-25.
43. Referred by J.R. Joshi *Some Minor Divinities in the Vedic Mythology and Rituals*, Introduction, p. 2.
44. Dumezil's threefold classification of the Indo-Iranian gods is rejected by Theime (P), *Mitra and Aryaman*, New Heaven, 1957; J.R. Joshi *op. cit.*, Introduction, p. 2, fn. 10.
45. S.J. Zimmermann, *op. cit.*, Appendix II, p. xxiii.
46. M. Bloomfield, *The Religion of the Veda*, p. 96.
47. S.J. Zimmermann, *op. cit.*, Appendix II, p. xxiii.
48. J.R. Joshi, *op. cit.*, pp. 4 ff.
49. *Vide* chapter 10, "Epilogue".

2

Yama's Family and Associates

Etymology

The vocable *yama* occurs in the *Ṛ̣V* with a difference in accent and yields two different meanings which generally correspond with the accent. The oxytone *yamá*, i.e., having acute accent on the last syllable means 'a twin'. In this sense it occurs several times in the *Ṛ̣V* generally in the dual masculine or feminine. Yama was a twin, born with Yamī (*Ṛ̣V*, 10.10.4), and so he acquired this appellative name. In a few places Agni too, who was a twin born along with Indra, (*Ṛ̣V*, 6.59.2) is called 'Yama' for the same reason.[1] According to Güntert[2] the word *yama* can be linguistically connected with two series of words: on one hand with Avestan *yema*, Lettic, *jumis*, Mir. *emuin*—all meaning twins; on the other hand with Latin *geminus*, *gemellus* and Greek *didumos* which means both a twin and a hermophrodite.[3] On the basis of the linguistic consideration and on the analogy of other primitive mythologies it can be deduced that the term *yama* which connotes 'a twin' is an expressive appellation of a god (i.e., Yama) and it highlights his original character.

An etymology of the word *yama* is suggested in the *Ṛ̣V*, 10.14.14 where this god is prayed to grant (*ā yamat*) a long life. Here the vocable *yama* is derived from √*yam* to grant, to give. In the *Nirukta*, 10.19 also *yama* is derived from √*yam* ~ √*yacch* and it denotes 'one who grants (fulfils) the wishes of the worshippers. Sāyaṇa gives this derivation of *yama* in his commentary on the *ṚV*, 1.66.8.

Hopkins remarks that the pun of *yamat ā*, in *ṚV*, 10.14.14 in the sense of 'stretch out' shows that the sense of twin is lost from the name and as yet no thought of a restrainer (from √*yam*, to control) was there in the poet's mind. The *Śabda-kalpa-druma* also derives it from √*yam*~ √*yacchh*, to give, and further gives some more meanings of this root.[4]

The *TS*, 2.1.4 deals with the etymology of this word in a more specific manner. It says that Yama separated (*ayuvat*) the strenth from the gods, hence his name is Yama. Here the term *yama* is derived from √*yu*, to separate; to take hold of; or to get possession. In this context Sāyaṇa remarks that since Yama deprived the gods of their power, he got the name *yava*, derived from √*yu* to separate. This *Yava* became *Yama* due to the change of letters (*varṇa-vyatyaya*).[5] Thus from √*yu* the vocable derived is *yava*, and *va* of *yava* is replaced by *ma* making the formation as *Yama*. This can be taken as a case of dissimilation because here the phoneme *v* is lost and the phoneme *m* is substituted in its place.[6]

Referring to the etymology of *Yama* in the *TS*, 2.1.4 and Sāyaṇa's remark thereon Fatah Singh explains the similarity of the two words *yava* (i.e., barley) and *yama*. The *Yava* has two parts distinctly marked, yet not separated.[7] Yama too has in his original character of a primeval bisexual being, two personalities inseparably united in one form. The derivation of *Yama* from √*yam*, to restrain, though normally possible, is not acceptable in this case, i.e., *yama* on account of the difficulties of the Vedic accentuation it would create.[8] It does not also agree with the personality of the Vedic Yama. It was only at a later stage in the evolution of Yama-mythology that Yama came to be regarded as a controller on account of his self-control or because of his control over humanity.[9]

The vocable *yama* also stands for some other gods, i.e., for Vāyu in the *ŚB*, 14.2.2.11, and Āditya in *ŚB*, 14.1.3.4.[10]

Yama's Abode

Yāska classifies the Vedic gods in three divisions on the basis of their dwelling region:

(1) Terrestrial gods (*Nir*, 7.14-9.43)

(2) Aerial gods (*Nir*, 10.1-11.50)

(3) Celestial gods (*Nir*, 12.1-46)

According to this classification Yama can be called a celestial god, as his abode is said to be in *dyu* (*ṚV*, 10.64.3). It is to be noted that in the *Nighaṇṭu*, on which Yāska comments enlists the gods of allied spheres and functions in its fifth chapter, Yama appears in more than one category of the gods. He is enumerated among the aerial (*Nigh*, 5.4) as well as the celestial gods (*Nigh*, 5.6), and Yāska also discusses this word at both the places. In the *Nir*, 10.20 Yama finds a place among the aerial gods. Here Yāska comments that Agni is also called Yama.[11] It is obvious that Agni gets this name, which basically means 'a twin', on account of his being Indra's twin[12] and it can be assumed that this Agni (i.e., belonging to the mid-region) is the 'lightning', which can be safely called Yama (a twin) because he is born with Indra (i.e., thunder),[13] another dominant deity of the mid-region[14] (*Nigh*, 5.4).

At another place (*Nir*, 12.29) Yama appears among the celestial gods and referring to the *ṚV*, 10.135.1 it is stated that Āditya is here called Yama. Sāyaṇa has given two parallel interpretation of the 10.135.1, one of them being in connection with Yama and the other being in connection with Āditya. He interprets the second hemistich as: Yama 'drinks' in the company of gods and 2. Āditya 'goes' along with the rays (by interpreting 'Yama' as 'Āditya'. *deva* as 'rays' and *saṁpibate* as *saṁgacchate*.[15]

As discussed earlier the vocable *yama* is at some places used as an adjective, or an epithet of a deity, or even as a substitute noun of some deity (as in the *ṚV*, 1.66.8; 6.59.2 discussed above). Obviously when the vocable *yama* is under such usage it does not stand for the god Yama.

As a son of Vivasvat, Yama is a solar god and occupies a

place in *dyu* (heaven). At more than one place Yama's abode is conceived to be situated in a very high region of *dyu*. Out of the three spheres of *dyu* which are brightened by Savitṛ, two are near Savitṛ, while third-one is a passage for the dead souls to enter the realm of Yama (*ṚV*, 1.35.6). Sāyaṇa considers *tisro dyāvaḥ* occurring in this stanza as denoting the three worlds, i.e., *dyu* (heaven), *antarikṣa* (mid-region) and *pṛthivī* (earth). Out of these, *dyu* and *pṛthivī* belong to Savitṛ, because they are brightened by the sun, while the middle region is for the dead for going to Yama's world.[16]

The difficulty with this interpretation is that it mentions two regions, *dyu* and *pṛthivī* (i.e., heaven and earth) being brightened by the sun excluding the third-one (i.e., the mid-region), which is situated in the middle of those two regions. The difficulty can be removed, if the *ṛc* is interpreted as follows:

There are three spheres of heaven which are illumined by Savitṛ. Out of them two are near Savitṛ, while the remaining one which is brightened variously is near Yama.[17] This third sphere of heaven, which belongs to Yama, can be inferred as the highest. There are some very clear references to this in the *ṚV* as well as in other *Saṁhitās*.

In the *ṚV*, 10.14.8 Yama's abode is menticned to be in *parame vyoman*, i.e., in the uppermost heaven. It is significant because the third step of Viṣṇu is mentioned to be in the highest heaven (*ṚV*, 1.154.5, 6).[18] Macdonell observes that the third step of Viṣṇu is indentical with the highest step.[19] The highest step of Viṣṇu is represented as his abode and is also connected with the ideas concerning the life after death. The pious men, after their death live happily in the abode of Viṣṇu (*ṚV*, 1.154.5). The *ṚV*, 10.14.8 suggests that *parame vyoman* is Yama's abode. The *VS*, 12.63; *AV*, 6.84.4; *ŚB*, 7.2.1 *TĀ*, 6.42 also state that Yama's abode is in the *uttame nāke*, i.e., the highest heaven. The *AV*, 18.2.48 says that the Fathers live in the third heaven, which is called *pradyauḥ*. According to this stanza the lowest *dyu* contains waters (i.e., the clouds), the middle one contains stars and the third-one (which can be inferred as the highest) is the place of the Fathers (and hence that of Yama too). According to the *ṚV*,

9.113.8, Yama's dwelling place is stated to be in *avarodhanam divaḥ*, i.e., the innermost part of the heaven.[20]

It is situated at a far off place in the remote recess of the sky and a long distance has to be covered to reach there. This is also expressed by the *ṚV*, 10.14.1 that Yama himself had travelled to lofty heights to reach this region, where he secured a place for the departed souls.

In *ṚV*, 10.58.1 about a man, who is apparently dead or unconscious, it is said that his mind has gone to Yama, to a very far off place.[21] The *VS*, 12.63 speaks of Yama along with Yamī as being in the highest heaven. In the region of Yama the Fathers live blissfully. The Vaśā cow fulfils all the desires (*AV*, 12.4.36). It is conspicuous that although the *Yamaloka* is connected with death and the life thereafter, the fear of the *Yamaloka* or the dreadful ideas of the life therein are not present here. On the contrary, the worshipper prays for being granted a permanent stay in the world of Yama (*ṚV*, 9.113.8).[22]

Here the dead souls, who are exalted to the position of the Fathers live blissfully with their benevolent kind Yama. Yama's place (*sādanam*, 10.135.7) was built by the gods. The music is played here and Yama is propitiated with eulogies (*ṚV*, 10.135.7).

When a dead soul reaches the kingdom of Yama, he is received with warmth by Yama. Yama grants him a place there and also a right to share the oblations offered to himself. Yama also declares that by reaching there, the dead soul has become his own (*AV*, 18.2.37).[23]

Yama is invariably connected with the south quarter (*AV*, 9.7.20).[24] The *ṚV*, 3.27.2 is a rare instance where Indra, who is generally called the 'lord of the east' is called the 'lord of the south direction' (*AV*, 3.27.2).

Yama's house, it is stated, was built by the gods (*ṚV*, 10.135.7). The *AV*, 18.4.55 says that *pañca-janāḥ* made the *harmya* for Yama. Sāyaṇa quotes *Nir*, 3.8 which states the *pañca-janāḥ* as 'Gandharvas, the Fathers, the gods, the demons and goblins'. Here an alternative group of five men *pañca-janāḥ* according to another view, is the four *varṇas* and *niṣāda.*[25]

Yama's *harmya* is taken to be a tomb or mound of dead by Ehni.[26]

Parentage

In the *ṚV* there is a brief but clear account of Yama's divine parentage. The *ṚV*, 10.17.1 states that Yama's mother was Vivasvat's wife. In the *ṚV*, 10.15.1 Vivasvat is mentioned as Yama's father. Yama's patronymic 'Vaivasvata' also refers to his father's name (*RV*, 10.164.2; *AV*, 6.112.2).

This patronymic 'Vaivasvata' refers also to Manu, who is also a son of Vivasvat, but in such cases it is followed by his own name viz. 'Vaivasvata Manu'. When not followed by any name the term 'Vaivasvata' connotes Yama[27] and when it is followed by a proper noun 'Manu' it refers to Manu.

Yama's Father

As noted earlier, 'Vivasvat' is Yama's father. The vocable *vivasvat* also occurs with a variation in the accent which yields another meaning of the word. 'Vívasvat' denotes the sun-god, the father of Yama (*ṚV*, 1.44.1; 10.17.1), while 'Vivásvat' means a sacrificer[28] and it is frequently mentioned in connection with the sacrifices and sacrificial activities. Agni is called a messenger of Vivásvat (*ṚV*, 1.58.1; 4.7.4; 8.39.3; 10.21.5).

Indra rejoices in the prayer of Vivásvat (*ṚV*, 8.6.29) and places his treasure beside him. Soma is cleansed by the daughters (i.e., fingers) of Vivásvat (*ṚV*, 9.14.5). Thus it is clear that the vocable *vivasvat* when accentuated differently connotes two meanings — (1) Vívasvat — a god who is the father of Yama, (2) Visvásvat — a sacrificer. The meaning can be determined on the basis of the accent. Barring a few cases (*ṚV*, 1.46.13; 1.31.3) this difference in meaning generally corresponds with the variation of the accent. It is apparent that Vivásvat, the sacrificer,[29] has an identity different from that of the god Vívasvat, who is the father of Yama. The exactness of the accent leaves little room for confusion.[30] The indifference to the usual accent at some places can be attributed to the possibility of the Vedic accent losing their importance towards the end of the Ṛgvedic period, and these two words getting mixed up.[31]

The vocable Vívasvat is formed as a present participle from the intensive from *vivas* of √*vas*, to shine.[32] This derivation is given in the *ŚB*, where it is said that Āditya Vivasvat illumines (*vi - vaste*) night and day (*ŚB*, 10.5.2.4).

In the context of a sacrificer the word *Vivásvat* is formed by shortening the second syllable of the perfect participle Vivāsvat from *vivās* to worship.[33] Sāyaṇa derives it from √*vas*, *nivāse*

(1) *vivasanam vivaḥ tad yuktam viśiṣṭa nivāsopetam*[34]

(2) abiding in the chamber of sacrifices.[35]

Vivasvat is prayed to grant a long life to the worshipper. In the *ṚV*, 8.67.20 it is prayed "May the shafts of Vivasvat not strike them before the old age".[36] In the *AV*, 18.3.63 Vivasvat is prayed to make the worshipper immortal. The *ŚB*, 10.5.24 explains the god Vivasvat's name by saying that he brightens night and day. It calls him Āditya, and this name is found elsewhere also (*MS*, 1.6.12). Thus Vivasvat is conceived as a god of light. Considering the etymology it can be said that originally he represented the morning Sun.[37] In the *YV* (*VS*, 8.5, *MS*, 1.6.12) and the *Brāhmaṇas* Vivasvat is called Āditya, while in the post-Vedic literature it is a common name of the sun.

Vivasvat is also considered as the morning sky, which is gradually becoming bright, or as the god of bright sky in general, be it the diurnal sky shining with the radiance of the sun or the nocturnal sky lit by the moon-light.[38]

Oldenberg[39] comparing Vivasvat with the Avestan Vivañhvant, the first mortal who prepared Haoma, believes that the reasons for considering Vivasvat a god of light are insufficient and that he represents simply the first sacrificer and ancestor of human race.[40] But this theory of parallelism between the Avestan Vivañhvant and Vedic Vivasvat is, on the whole inadeqaute to account for all that is said of Vivasvat. The etymology of Vivasvat establishes his connection with light and brightness. His connection with Aśvinā, with Agni and with Soma, as well as the importance laid upon his seat, can be explained by the theory that he is the sun, especially the rising Sun.[41]

According to Bergaigne the character of sacrificer is prominent in Vivasvat, hence he is Agni, of whom sun is a form.[42] Here it is clear that he confuses Vivásvat, the sacrificer with Vívasvat the sun-god. It appears that he overlooked the accent in the word which has resulted in the difference.

Yama's Mother

According to the *ṚV*, 10.17.1 Tvaṣṭṛ's daughter Saraṇyū was Yama's mother and the wife of Vivasvat. This *ṛc* records her disappearance. The next *ṛc* (i.e., 10.17.2) informs that she was concealed (by the gods, *vide* Sāyaṇa on the *ṚV*, 10.17.2) for the sake of the mortals, and another woman resembling Saraṇyū (Savarṇā)[43] was given to Vivasvat by them (i.e., by the gods). Saraṇyū bore Aśvinā and when this happened she abandoned (*ajahāt*) two pairs of twins (*ṚV*, 10.17.2). It may be noted here that the verb *ajahāt* in the *ṚV*, 10.17.2 is interpreted differently by scholars. Sāyaṇa interprets *ajahāt* as *tyaktavatī janitvatī iti arthaḥ*, i.e., as, "gave birth to". According to Muir *ajahāt* means 'abandoned'.[44] Griffith also translates it as 'deserted'.[45] Suryakanta gives the meaning of √*hā* as (1) to leave; (2) to produce, to give birth to[46] and thus he covers both the meanings of *ajahāt*.

Another important word of this stanza is *martyebhyaḥ* which is also interpreted in two ways —

(1) *As Ablative Plural* — as the ablative plural it denotes that she was hidden "from the mortals". J. Muir's and R.T.A. Griffith's interpretation of *martyebhyaḥ* as ablative plural creates a difficulty viz. who were these *martyāḥ* from whom Saraṇyū was hidden.

(2) *As Dative Plural* — in the second way the word *martyebhyaḥ*, is taken as dative plural and it denotes

> then that "she was hidden for (the sake of) the mortals". Sāyaṇa follows this meaning and interprets that Saraṇyū was hidden for the sake of a mortal progeny (*martyebhyaḥ manuṣyebhyaḥ tad utpattyartham apagūhitavantaḥ* — Sāyaṇa on *ṚV*, 10.17.2) K.F. Geldner also interprets *martyebhyaḥ* as dative plural.[47]

The text (*ṚV*, 10.17.1-2) does not provide anything to suggest as to who concealed Saraṇyū, and why was she concealed. Furthermore, there is also a question, viz. in what way the motive behind the replacement of Vivasvat's wife was particularly beneficial to the mortals, and another question is here: if she was hidden from the mortals who were they. All these questions remain unanswered.

The data provided by the *ṚV* is inadequate for knowing the complete story of Saraṇyū and her offsprings who are mentioned as 'two pairs of twins'. Yāska (*Nir*, 12.10) gives the following story in this connection —

> Saraṇyū the wife of Vivasvat gave birth to a twin. One of the children was male and the other female.[48] After placing another woman resembling herself (for their care) Saraṇyū ran away in the form of a mare. Vivasvat took the form of a divine horse and followed her. After that Aśvinā were born. Manu was born to Savarṇā, i.e., Saraṇyū's look-alike.
>
> Here Savarṇā is clearly an appellative and not the proper name of that woman. She might have got this appellative due to her similarity (in looks) with Saraṇyū, the wife of Vivasvat.

Bṛhaddevatā

The *Bṛhaddevatā* (6.162-7.6) provides some more details of this story but there is no fundamental difference from Yāska's version, Tvaṣṭṛ gave his daughter Saraṇyū to Vivasvat in marriage and a twin was born. These children were Yama and Yamī. Saraṇyū placed her children in the care of a woman, who was similar to her in looks. She then transformed herself into a mare and went away. She had taken care of keeping Vivasvat ignorant of all this. Vivasvat could not discern this change and took that woman as his wife Saraṇyū. Manu was born to her. Thereafter, on knowing that she was not Saraṇyū and that Saraṇyū had gone away in the form of a mare, Vivasvat too transformed himself into a horse and went to Saraṇyū. Saraṇyū recognised him. Another twin was born to them — and these two children are Aśvinā, also named Nāsatya and Dasra.

Sāyaṇa's account of the story is based on *Bṛhaddevatā*, 6.162-7.6 and he also quotes it in his commentary on the *ṚV*, 7.72.2. To this account Sāyaṇa adds that when Saraṇyū left her home she went to the lands of Uttara Kuru.

On the basis of the *ṚV* account, the details provided by Śaunaka and Yāska and with the help of Sāyaṇa's and Geldner's interpretations, the story may be worked out as follows:

> Saraṇyū was the wife of Vivasvat and Yama's mother. The gods desired the creation of a mortal progeny. With this intention they hid the immortal Saraṇyū from Vivasvat as she, being immortal could not have produced a mortal progeny. Therefore, after the birth of her first twin, i.e., Yama and Yamī — the immortal children of Saraṇyū, they (the gods) concealed her. Making an exactly similar woman, who is aptly called Savarṇā, i.e., having the same appearance (literally the same colour), they gave to Vivasvat as his wife. From this woman, i.e., Savarṇā, Vivasvat got a son called Manu. Thus Manu was the mortal son of Vivasvat by Savarṇā, who was not an immortal being. The gods had a definite purpose in this whole affair which was their desire to create a mortal progeny. Later Vivasvat and Saraṇyū also become parents of another twin, i.e., Aśvinā. It may be noted that

> here *martyebhyaḥ* interpreted as dative plural supports the idea of creation of the human race through Manu.

On the basis of this story it can be concluded that from Vivasvat two types of progenies sprang up, viz. (1) the mortal, (2) the immortal.[49] It is significant to note that the female parent is different in these cases. Thus human progeny started from the first mortal, i.e., Manu, the son of Vivasvat. He is called the progenitor of the human race (*manuṣ pita* — *ṚV*, 1.8.16; 2.33.13). All mortals are called *mānavas*, i.e., the sons of Manu (*mānavyo hi prajāḥ* — *TS*, II.5.6).

It must be noted that the *ṚV*, 10.17 does not allude to Manu as the son of Savarṇā or Saraṇyū, Max Müller observes that the fable of Manu might have came in at a later date.[50]

The *Nirukta*, 12.19 considers Saraṇyū as the night who is the wife of sun and who disappears as the sun rises.

Max Müller has discussed in detail the problem of Saraṇyū.[51] According to him Saraṇyū is dawn and Savarṇā is the gloaming or the evening. He observes that Savarṇā is not a proper name and means no more than the word implies, i.e. 'a wife similar to the first'. The evening is similar to the dawn in appearance, i.e., colour, so the name Savarṇā is appropriate. Day and night are the two children of dawn. In the mythological dialect the day is the twin brother Yama and night is his twin sister Yamī.[52] The disappearance of Saraṇyū after the birth of the twin refers to the disappearance of dawn, when it is day. Thus Max Müller visualises the whole episode depicted in the *ṚV*, 10.17.1-2 as a natural phenomenon. He works out the equation in this manner — "Saraṇyū is wedded to Vivasvat, i.e., dawn embraces the sky; Saraṇyū has left her twins (Yama and Yami, i.e., day and night) i.e., the dawn has disappeared, it is day; Vivasvat takes a second wife, i.e., the Sun sets in the evening twilight."

In the *ṚV*, 10.10.4 Yama and his twin sister Yamī are said to be the children of Gandharva and *apyā yoṣā* (the water-nymph). Udgītha[53] and Veṅkaṭa[54] take Gandharva as 'Āditya' and *āpyā yoṣā* as his wife Saraṇyū. Sāyaṇa also considers *apyā yoṣā* to be Saraṇyū, the wife of Āditya.

The *ṚV*, 10.10 consists of a dialogue between Yama and Yamī. This dialogue-hymn has led to an assumption that Yama and Yamī were the parent of humanity.[55]

Yamī is the seer of the *ṚV*, 10.154. This hymn is addressed to the dying sacrificers and it tells about the different drinks offered to them in the next world — *soma* to some, *ghṛta* to others and *madhu* (honey) to yet others. According to *TĀ*, 2.20 *soma* is offered to the Sāman-singers, *ghṛta* (i.e., clarified butter) to those who performed sacrifices with *Yajus* and honey to those who recite *Atharvans*.

The *MS*, 1.5.12[56] contains an episode connected with Yama and Yamī and it tells why the gods created night. According to the story Yamī mourned the death of her brother. She could not be consoled because she thought, 'he died but today'.

The gods, in their bid to comfort her, decided to create night. They created night and it became yesterday. Then she could endure her bereavement.[57]

In some passages e.g., *TS*, 3.3.8 where Agni is called Yama, Yamī is identified with the fire-altar.

Yamī's original personality as Yama's sister is retained in the *Brāhmanas*. According to the *TMB*, 10.10.21.2 Yamī helped Yama to ascend to heaven with the help of a hymn. In the human sacrifice a barren woman is to be offered to Yama and to Yamī is offered a woman who has delivered twins.[58]

Yama's Messengers

Yama's messengers are mentioned in dual (*ṚV*, 10.14.12; *AV*, 5.30.6) as well as in plural *AV*, 8.2.11; 8.11. Two Dogs, the owl (*ulūka*), the pigeon (*kapota*) as well as bad dreams and *mṛtyu* are called Yama's messengers.

TWO DOGS

Amongst his messengers a comparatively fuller account of the two dogs is available (*ṚV*, 10.14.10-12). The epithets which describe the two dogs are:

(1) Sārameyau (*Ṛ*V, 10.14.10)

(2) Udumbalau (*ṚV*, 10.14.12)

(3) Uruṇasau (*ṚV*, 10.14.12)

(4) Caturakṣau (*ṚV*, 10.14.11)

(5) Asutṛpau (*ṚV*, 10.14.12)

Sārmeyau

These dogs are sons of Saramā and hence they got this metronymic (*ṚV*, 10.14.10). Saramā was a messenger of Indra (*ṚV*, 10.108.2) who had been sent to the Paṇis with his message. Paṇis are a group of 'demons of the upper air'[59] and primarily the enemy of Indra. They captured Indra's cows and hid them in the mountain (*ṚV*, 10.108.11) Bṛhaspati found out their whereabouts and Saramā was assigned the job of carrying Indra's message. The *ṚV*, 10.108 contains a dialogue between the Paṇis and Saramā. At first she was mocked at and then persuaded by the Paṇis to become their sister and stay with them sharing their kine.

This proposal was immediately turned down by Saramā who warns the Paṇis of Indra's deadly weapons.

There is nothing in the *ṚV* showing directly that Saramā was a bitch. The *Nir*, 11.25 calls it the 'bitch of gods' Sāyaṇa also describes Saramā as *deva-śunī* (Sāyaṇa on the *ṚV*, 10.14.10).

In the *AV*, 4.20.7 a four-eyed bitch is mentioned and according to M. Bloomfield this four-eyed bitch is Saramā, the mother of the two four-eyed dogs of Yama.[60]

The *JBr*, 2.438, 440 also contains the Saramā-Paṇi story. Here too her connection with the gods as Indra's messenger is clear but it is not expressed that Saramā is a bitch.

In the *ṚV*, 7.55.2-3 this vocable occurs in its singular form as *Sārameya*, but in this context it does not stand for Yama's messenger-dog. Sāyaṇa explains the word as 'born in the race of Saramā'. It shows that gradually *Sārameya* became a synonym of dog in general.[61]

Yama's dogs possess a ferocious appearance. Both of them have four-eyes and a broad nose (*ṚV*, 10.14.12). They are Śabala, i.e., brindled in colour. In the *AV*, 8.1.9 one of them is spoken of as Śyāma, while the other one as Śabala. M. Bloomfield considers *Śyāma* and *Śabala* to be the proper names of these dogs.[62] In that case here a word which is an adjective in dual (*ṚV*, 10.14.11) becomes, in singular, the proper name of one of the dogs (*AV*, 8.1.9).

Udumbalau

Another epithet used for Yama's dogs is *udumbalau* (*ṚV*, 10.14.12; *AV*, 18.2.3) Sāyaṇa explains it as *Vistīrṇabalau* Monier Williams and Suryakanta[63] translate it as 'copper-coloured', Macdonell,[64] Hillebrandt[65] and Oldenberg[66] do not translate it and Macdonell comments that there is no means of throwing light on its sense.

Usually the word *udumbalau* is translated as 'brown' or 'copper-coloured' on account of its supposed identity with *Uḍumbara*—i.e., the fig-tree, the fruit of which is light brown in colour.[67]

F.B.J. Kuiper observes that taking *udumbala* for *uḍumbara* is purely conjectural; Sāyaṇa's explanation is also not satisfactory, and since dogs are called *śabalau* in the *Ṛ*V, 10.14.10 there is no reason to suppose that *udumbalau* at this place denotes a colour at all. He further says that this word can be connected with the *Muṇḍa* word *uḍumbara* meaning 'fat, obese', on the basis of *ḍum-ḍum*, meaning having protruded 'stomach'.[68]

The *Kāṭhaka Saṁhitā* (8.2) identifies *udumbara* with *ūrjas*, i.e., vigour, and according to this text, wherever the gods distributed *ūrjas* (i.e., the vital power) there arose *udumbara*. Thus according to the Vedic tradition *udumbara* signifies vigour, and so Sāyaṇa's translation as *vistīrṇabalau* cannot be dismissed altogether.

Caturakṣau

On *Caturakṣaḥ* which is another epithet of the Yama's dogs, Bhaṭṭa Bhāskara comments — "having two marks above the two normal eyes".[69] This ingenious explanation of the epithet 'four-eyed' accounts for the number 'four' by the two marks and two normal eyes which together give an impression of four eyes. (Thus according to him the epithet *caturakṣāḥ* appears to be fictitious). Sāyaṇa explains this epithet as having another pair of eyes above his (normal) eyes'.[70] According to M. Bloomfield the term *Caturakṣaḥ* indicates here the capacity (of the dogs) to see both in day and night.[71]

This epithet seems to be a figurative expression suggesting the sharp sightedness and alertness of the dogs. Agni is also called *caturakṣaḥ* (*ṚV*, 1.31.13), which can be satisfactorily interpreted only as 'sharp-sighted', and is a suitable poetic epithet for Agni.[72]

Asutṛpau

These dogs are also called *asutṛpau* (*ṚV*, 10.14.12), Venkaṭamādhava and Sāyaṇa explain it as 'pleased in taking away the lives'. This explanation is acceptable to Keith[73] who translates is as 'delighting in lives'. Velankar translates it thus — "those who feel happy in seizing the asus (spirits) of men."[74] Macdonell also comments that the literal meaning of the term *asutṛpau*, delighting in lives implies delighting in taking them while they wander among men as Yama's messengers.[75]

FUNCTIONS OF THE DOGS

Guards

These two dogs are the guards of Yama's house and also of the path (*ṚV*, 10.14.11), which leads to his realm. They sit on this path (*AV*, 18.2.12) as watchful guards, and a deceased is advised to hasten past them and join, without hindrance, the Fathers who rejoice in the company of Yama (*ṚV*, 10.14.10).

In connection with their role as guards, Macdonell remarks, that though there is a possibility, there is not sufficient evidence for supposing that they keep out the soul of the evil-doers.[76]

Guide of the Souls

It can be deduced from the *Ṛ̣V*, 10.14.11 that they are guides to a soul who is proceeding on Yama's path. Their help is sought for reaching the blessed dead who are enjoying the company of their lord Yama. Here a contradiction with the *RV*, 10.14.10 is seen where they appear to be stopping the souls from entering the realm of Yama, but this lack of harmony in their functions is not actual. In this connection Velankar[77] rightly remarks that here the deceased is not advised to run past these dogs in order to avoid an encounter with them, on the contrary, he is advised to run to them[78] and seek their help on his way to Yama's kingdom. The next *ṛc* also renders support to this interpretation of *atidrava sārameyau* (*Ṛ̣V*, 10.14.10), where Yama is requested to entrust the dead man to these dogs, till he reaches his destination mentioned in the *Ṛ̣V*, 10.14.10cd.

Thus the main function of these dogs is to see that the souls of the dead reach Yama's kingdom without any obstruction or difficulty. This is similar to the duty of their Avestan counterpart who frightens the fiends trying to snatch away the souls of the dead.[79] That the fiends can harm the dead is also suggested in the *Ṛ̣V*. It is stated that *apeta vīta* (*Ṛ̣V*, 10.14.9) should be recited at the time of cleaning a place for cremation (*ĀŚS*, 4.2.10). The object is to drive the fiends away from the cremation place. According to Sāyaṇa this *ṛc* is addressed to the fiends who might be present there at the time of cremation.

There is no clear evidence of any such function of the Yama's dogs as the divider of souls as good and bad.[80]

The task of these dogs as messengers is also not very clear. The *Ṛ̣V*,10.14.12 states that they move among people. The object of the *AV*, 8.1 is to enhance the life of a dying person and it is wished: "May these two dogs of Yama, one

Śyāma and the other Śabala not come near you." (*AV*, 8.1.9).

This suggests that, at the bidding of their lord Yama, these dogs move among the people and approach a person whose death is near. In the *PGS*, 1.10.24 there is a dog-spell, requesting the dogs (evidently of Yama) to leave the child alone "verily, your mother is Saramā, your father is Sīsara and Śyāma and Śabala are your brothers". In the *HGS* we have mention of a dog-demon Sīsaramā (clearly a compound of Sīsara and Saramā). The fact that he is a demon whose sons, according to the *PGS*-passage are Yama's messengers connects the dogs with sinister association. Even today the typical mournful baying of a dog is considered omnious. It is believed to be a portent of the impending death of someone living nearby. Thus the arrival of death is connected with the wail of a dog and hence a wailing dog is driven away to avert the arrival of death.

The function of these dogs, therefore, seems to consist of tracking out among men those who are about to die, and in keeping guard on the path of Yama. They also guide a soul on his way to Yama's world.

IDENTITY OF THE DOGS

The *Kāṭhaka Saṁhitā*, 33.14 takes these two dogs of Yama as day and night.[81] Dayānanda Sarasvatī also holds the same view.[82] S.D. Satvalekar[83] takes them as denoting day and night, as they also move and have access in all the four directions. The four sections of day and night are their eyes. The day is brown (*śabala*) and the night is black (*śyāma*). It is important to note that the words *śyāma* and *śabala* are used for the night and the day respectively in the *JaimUpBr*, 2.6, as well as the *Kauṣītaki Brāhmaṇa* (2.9).

Western scholars hold a variety of opinions. According to Bergaigne[84] they are the forms of Yama (as Agni) and Yamī. Ehni takes them as south-wind and the north-wind.[85] Bloomfield identifies them with the sun and the moon.[86] This idea seems to be based on the few references, e.g., *AV*, 6.80, *TBr*, 11.2, where the sun and the moon are called heavenly dogs. In *MādhŚB*, 11.1.5.1 also moon is called a heavenly dog.

The *AV* (*Paip*, 3.22.5) makes a notable statement that the four-eyed dog overlooks, by night, the sphere of night. Here also moon is called a heavenly dog. It is observed that the sun and moon course across the sky. The abode of light and the blessed is situated beyond that. As they constantly watch the race of men dying day-by-day they are regarded as daily choosing people for the final journey. In connection with the sun and the moon the term *mithu-dṛśā* (i.e., seen alternately — *RV*, 1.29.3) can be easily understood as sun and moon alternate their presence.

The *TBr*, 1.1.2 states that two *asuras* flew up in the sky and became two heavenly dogs of Yama. It explicitly tells that there are two dogs in the heaven, and they are Yama's dogs. It also tells that they were originally the *asuras* named Kālakāñjas. In order to reach heaven they piled up a fire-altar. With the intention of foiling their attempt, Indra disguised himself as a priest and placed a brick in the fire-altar. But when the *asuras* climbed up to heaven, Indra pulled out this brick which resulted in the fall of the *asuras*. The *asuras* who fell down became spiders, but two of them flew up and became the two heavenly dogs of Yama. The Kālakāñjas also appear in the *AV*, 6.80.2 where they are mentioned as having attained godship. There they are mentioned as three in number.

Max Müller considers these dogs as representing the mythological conception of Time in its two aspects as morning and evening.[87] Bruce Lincoln observes that hell-hounds in both Greek and Vedic mythology hold an important intermediary position at the border of this world and the next, between life and death, hope and fear, good and evil. Thus, according to him, the hell-hound is the moment of death, the great crossing over, the ultimate turning point.[88]

Yama's dogs appear to be of Indo-European origin, because in other ancient mythologies too dogs are connected with the 'lord of the other World'. In the Greek mythology, Hades, who is the god of the underworld and a brother of Zeus, has a three-headed hound named Kerberos, whom Zeus appointed as the messenger of the gods to the dark kingdom of Hades.[89] Kerberos is a three-headed dog while Śyāma and Śabala (the dogs of Yama) are two, but they are mentioned as having four eyes. 'Kerberos' is allied to the word Karbura meaning spotted and variegated. It is significant that 'Śabala' the name which describes one of Yama's dogs also means the same. Kerberos is described as having serpents entwined around his body, which would naturally make him look variegated.[90] Kerberos was the watch dog of Hades. Stationed at the gates, Kerberos allowed people to enter but devoured them, if they tried to leave.

'Sārameyaḥ' is an epithet of Yama's dogs which has some similarity with Hermes who in the Greek mythology is the messenger of the gods and is called Mercury by the Romans. He was the son of Zeus and Maia, and patron of travellers and shepherds. He wore a winged cap and had wings attached to his ankles, enabling him to travel from place to place with the speed of the wind.[91]

Max Müller observes that the word *sārameya* approaches very near, linguistically as well as philologically, to Hermeres or Hermes, who is the guide of the travellers and particularly of the souls who travel on their last journey, he is the psychopompos.[92] In this functional aspect also Hermes can be compared with the dogs of Yama who have a similar responsibility.

In the Avesta also a dog guards the path to the next world. The Kinvat bridge, which leads to the next world is said to be guarded by a four-eyed and yellow-eyed dog. He scares away the fiends and saves the souls of the holy ones to be dragged to the hell. According to the Vendidad VIII. 14-22, when a man dies and his soul parts from the body, the evil corpse-demon (Druz-Nasu) falls upon the dead.[93] This demon is driven away by the means of 'the look of the dog'. In practise a yellow dog with a spot over his each eye, or a white dog with yellow ears (because the dog who guards the path to the next world is described as 'four-eyed and yellow-eared'), is brought near the dead body. It is made to look at the dead whereupon the demon flees back to hell.[94] An allowance of bread is also made for the dogs three times in summer and two times in winter. On this account it is wished that they should come to assist the soul at the Kinvat bridge.[95] Vendidad XIII.9 states if two dogs, i.e., the shepherd-dog and the house-dog passes by the house, they should not be driven away from there.

In the Egyptian mythology also 'Anubis', a jackal-faced dog is the conductor of the dead.

BIRDS

The *ṚV*, 10.165 contains several verses about the pigeon and the owl. Here the pigeon is clearly mentioned as the messenger of Yama, who is identified with *mṛtyu* (death) itself. The pigeon is called *Nirṛti's* messenger too (*ṚV*, 10.165.4). Hooting of an owl as well as a pigeon placing its foot near fire (settling near Agni, i.e., reaching well inside the house[96]) are considered bad portents (*ṚV*, 10.165.4). According to the *AGS*, 3.7.7 this hymn (*ṚV*, 10.165) is recited if a pigeon enters the house. In this hymn the pigeon is called *pakṣiṇī hetiḥi*, i.e., a winged missile (*ṚV*, 10.165.2,3).[97]

In *AV*, 6.29.2 both the pigeon and the owl are called the messengers of *Nirṛti*. They are sent by their master, but sometimes they come on their own. Gods are prayed earnestly that the *kapota* be expelled from the house and the ill-omen be rendered inefficacious. According to the *Kauśika Sūtra*, 46.7, the *AV*, 6.27 and the following two stanzas are recited while the great consecration (*mahā śānti*) is being poured. These stanzas are used for averting the ill-omen when a pigeon or an owl enters the house. In *AV*, 6.28.3 Yama is identified with *mṛtyu* and hence the presence of a pigeon who is Yama's messenger, is feared. In the *Brāhmaṇas* and *Gṛhyasūtras* also a pigeon's entry in the house is considered ominous (*PB*, 5.8; *AGS*, 4.15; *KS*, 5.5).

According to the *AV*, 10.3.6 the ominous shreak of a bird is rendered futile by wearing a particular amulet. If a person sees some evil dream, if a wild beast runs an evil course (*pāpam sṛtim*), if there is too much sneezing, if the evil utterance of bird is heard, the *varaṇa*-amulet is said to protect him from all these ill-omens.

Commenting on these stanzas S.D. Satvalekar observes that they are obscure and it is difficult to say what forthcoming misfortune these birds indicate. He further suggests that since pigeons are used for sending messages, it may be that, it is prayed here that the pigeons who carry messages should bring good news, and not a death or defeat of their warriors.[98] In the *Mbh* the pigeons along with vultures, fire-flies and bees are considered to bring ill-luck (*Mbh*, 13.104.14 f.) Red-footed birds and pigeons are particularly inauspicious (*Mbh*, 5.143.18 f; 7.6.56). It is a horrible portent for a person if a pigeon alights on him.[99] It is also said that a red-brown owl with green eyes attacking a crow foretells misfortune (*Mbh*, 5.143.18 f; *Rām*, 7.6.56). In the *Matsya-Purāṇa* also *kapota* and *ulūka* are stated to be precursors of ill-fate. A pigeon entering the house forebodes death of the house-holder (*MP*, 237.6), while the hooting of an owl forebodes the loss of property as well as death of the family head (*MP*, 237.13). To nullify this portant it is advised to recite stanza *devāḥ kapotaḥ* (*ṚV*, 10.165).

DREAM

In the *AV*, 16.5.1 dream is identified with death itself. It is also called 'Son of Yama' (*AV*, 6.46.1). This stanza is addressed to *svapna* (dream). It is important to note that it is not *duḥṣvapna* or the evil dream who is addressed here. The text states that the name of *svapna* is *araru*[100] and his mother is Varuṇānī. According to Sāyaṇa on the *ṚV*, 7.87.1 Varuṇa is connected with darkness.[101] The *TS*, 2.1.7.4 also says that the day is said to belong to Mitra and night to Varuṇa.

In the present stanza (*AV*, 6.46.1) Varuṇānī, i.e., wife of darkness is said to be the mother of dream. In the next stanza (*AV*, 6.46.2) the dream is prayed to save the worshipper from evil dreams.

Dream is also called *karaṇa*, (instrument) of Yama. He comes from the region of Yama and enters the mortals and causes (brings) evil dreams (*AV*, 19.56.1).

Dream is also called the son of Grāhi (disease),[102] Nirṛti (destruction), Nirbhūti (poverty) Parābhūti (defeat) etc. (*AV*, 16.5).

The dream mentioned as son of Yama (*AV*, 6.46.1) and of

Grāhi, and others (*AV*, 16.5) only reflects the belief that a bad dream forebodes these undesirable situations. It is considered to be a portent of ill-luck, disease, poverty, destruction and also of death. Similarly a bad dream is not a son of Yama in the literal sense of the word. Yama presides over the evil dreams (*duḥsvapnādhidevo Vaivasvato* — Sāyaṇa on *ṚV*, 10.164.2), and therefore Yama's auspicious sight is sought by the worshipper for the dissipiation of the evil dreams. The god who is addressed in the hymns about dream or evil dream is, therefore, Yama. The *AV*, 16.5,6,7,8 are connected with the evil dreams. The *ṛṣi* of these verses is Yama and they are addressed to *svapna* (i.e., the dream). The refrain of the poem is the prayer to *svapna* urging him to save the worshipper from the evil dreams— *sa naḥ svapna duḥsvapnāt pāhi.*

MṚTYU

Mṛtyu is called a messenger of Yama (*AV*, 18.2.27). He takes the life of the dead to the Fathers (*TS*, 18.27; *AV*, 18.2.27). Like Yama, he is also mentioned as holding a *padbīśa* (foot-fetter) (*AV*, 16.8.32). Though Yama is not considered to be a god of death in the *ṚV*, there are a few references in the later Vedic literature which almost identify Yama and Mṛtyu. In the *KaṭhaUp* Yama is repeatedly called Mṛtyu establishing their complete identification.

Mṛtyu is conceived to be death, i.e., the phenomenon of cessation of life, or Death as personified. As a divinity representing death he is different from Yama, who is the regent of the departed. Yama is offered oblations of *ghī* (*ghṛta*) with a prayer that he should grant a long life to the worshippers (*ṚV*, 10.14.14). Death is sought to be warded off through Yama's help and the worshipper desires assurance (*AV*, 3.14.4).[103] The *TB*, 1.8.6 has a prayer for deliverance from death and it is addressed to Yama. This suggests that Yama is not considered a killer but a savior.

In the *ṚV mṛtyu* is primarily the phenomenon of death. Gradually he came to be apotheosised as a divinity presiding over death. There are four *ṛcs*, *ṚV*, 10.18.1-4, addressed to

Mṛtyu and Sāyaṇa observes that Mṛtyu is the name of a god who kills everybody.[104] In the *ṚV*, 10.18.1 Mṛtyu is prayed to go away by a different path, i.e., a path which is his own and is distinct from the path of the gods. He is also prayed not to harm the progeny.[105]

In the next stanza the relatives of the dead are addressed. It says that after effacing Mṛtyu's foot-step and thereby avoiding the path of death they would now have a longer and better life: "May you O sacrificers! enriched with progeny and affluence be cleansed (*śuddha*) and pure (*pūta*)."[106] It is wished that those who are living should remain separate from the dead: "may our invocation to gods today be successful; let us go forward to merriment and laughter, assuming a longer and better life. I erect this circle of stones for the protection of the living, so that none other of them may approach this limit. May they live a hundred years, occupied in many holy works, and keep death hidden by this mound."[107]

In the *ṚV*, 10.18.1 *Mṛtyu* is prayed to go away on his own path which is distinct from that of the gods (*itaro devayānāt*) and to spare the progeny of the sacrificer (*ṚV*, 10.18.1; *VS*, 35.7; *AV*, 2.2.21). This suggests that the path of *Mṛtyu* is the *pitṛyāṇa*. It is significant to note that he is called *cakṣuṣmat* (one who has eyes, i.e., one who sees properly) and *śṛṇvan* (one who hears properly)[108] with a wish that he would see his own path and go away by it and also listen to the prayers of the worshippers. In the *AV*, 18.2.27, Mṛtyu is called *pracetas*, i.e., wise, and there he is mentioned as a wise messenger of Yama.[109]

Though Yama is not considered to be a god of death in the *ṚV*, he is regarded with a certain amount of fear due to his indirect connection with death, so much so that it is tempting to identify him with Mṛtyu in the *ṚV*, 10.165.4d (also *AV*, 6.28.3; 63.3).

As a pigeon, who is Nirṛti's messenger, comes near the place of the sacrifice, the sacrificer wants to make atonement for this and prays to gods for the well-being of his "bipeds and quadrupeds" (i.e., his people and his cattle). As seen earlier the hooting of an owl as well as pigeon's entry in the house is considered to be very inauspicious because it forebodes ill-fate for the house-head. It is earnestly prayed that the bird who has entered the house be auspicious: "may Agni accept our oblations and may this pigeon depart from here". It is also wished that this bird, who is as dreadful as a winged weapon (*pakṣiṇī hetiḥ*), should not harm anybody. It is prayed that "may the shriek of the owl be in vain, may the pigeon's entry in the house be in vain". Salutations are offered to Yama who is called the god of death and who has sent his messengers, i.e., the pigeon and the owl. (*ṚV*, 10.165.1-4)

In the *ṚV*, 10.165.4d Yama comes to be identified with Mṛtyu, who is at an other place called his messenger. Yama has no direct connection with death, while Mṛtyu is the divinity presiding over death, but here these distinct personalities are getting mixed up.

Sāyaṇa renders *mṛtyave* as *māryitre* (i.e., a killer) and takes it as an adjective of Yama. S.D. Satvalekar follows Sāyaṇa and renders this pada as *tasmai mṛtyave mārakāya Yamāya namaḥ astu.*[110]

Griffith translates it (i.e., the *ṚV*, 10.165.4 cd) thus — "To him who sent it as an envoy, to him be reverence paid, to Death, to Yama."[111] This rendering of *tasmai Yamāya namo astu mṛtyave* (*ṚV*, 10.165.4cd) creates an impression that here reverence is being paid to two deities, i.e., Death (*mṛtyu*) and Yama, but the context does not permit this because a dove is mentioned to be a messenger of Yama and Nirṛti and not of Mṛtyu. Griffith does not take *mṛtyu* in this *ṛc* to be an adjective of Yama as Sāyaṇa does. Possibly he is addressing a single deity, i.e., Yama by two names, i.e., Yama and Death. This is not a sole instance where Griffith is taking Yama as Death. He calls a dove "an ill-omened bird, the messenger of Mṛtyu"[112] instead of that of Yama. Here in 10.165.4 too Griffith seems to be addressing Yama by two names by translating "to Death, to Yama".

Antaka is said to be the son of Mṛtyu in the *AV*, 8.10.(4) 7.[113] In the *VS*, 39.13 Yama is mentioned by the side of Mṛtyu and Antaka.

Mṛtyu is mentioned as having a number of weapons. He holds a noose (*pāśa*) which is a special weapon of Varuṇa.

Through sacrifice men seek to free themselves from the thousands of nooses of Mṛtyu.[114] Like Yama, Mṛtyu also holds the foot-fetters (*padbīśa*).[115] He is said to be making people motionless by using the thunderbolt (*vajra*).[116] Thus Mṛtyu is credited with holding the noose, the foot-fetters and the thunderbolt which are the special weapons held by Varuṇa, Yama and Indra respectively. Apart from these weapons, Mṛtyu is also mentioned as holding wooden maces (*sthāṇu*) (*AB*, 12.3).[117]

Mṛtyu is, as noted above, a wise messenger of Yama and he takes the deceased to the Fathers (*TS*, 18.27; *AV*, 18.2.27). In the *AV* he is mentioned as the lord of the creatures (*prajānām*) while Yama is mentioned as the lord of the Fathers (*pitṛṇām*) (*AV*, 5.24.13; 14).[118]

Thus, Mṛtyu rules over all living beings. The causes of death such as diseases prevail all over the world and so there are no restrictions over his activities (*ŚB*, 13.3.5.1).[119] He himself is immortal (*ŚB*, 10.5.2.4). In fact he was created by Prajāpati above all mortal beings as their consumer (*ŚB*, 10.1.3.1). Hunger is also called death. The *ŚB*, 10.6.5.1 reads as follows:

> Verily there was nothing here in the beginning, by Death (this) (Universe) was covered, by hunger because Death is hunger.[120]

From the ritualistic point of view of the *Brāhmaṇas*, the holy works, i.e., sacrifices, are necessary for a man to escape recurrent deaths. If one does not offer oblations Death would get hold of him in every world and if he offers oblations to Death, he wards off in every world Death, even hunger (*ŚB*, 13.5.1.2).

Even gods were freed from the fear of death after performing sacrifices. Afraid of death they had rushed to Prajāpati who instituted the Dāśarātra and Viśvajit sacrifice for them. By these sacrifices the gods defeated death and thus they became immortal (*JB*, II.329-31).

Death separates the world of living beings from that of

the dead. In the event of a death it is even more strongly wished that death should not come again and kill others. The Adhvaryu who is performing the *śāntikarman* after the cremation of the deceased is done, puts an obstruction (*paridhi* *ṚV*, 10.18.4), a rampart — a line of demarcation between the living and the dead, which no one should cross. This *ṛc* is employed by *AGS*, 4.6.9 in the *śānti-karman* which is performed after the collection of the bones. The Adhvaryu places the obstruction saying: "I place (here) this barrier (stone) for the (protection of) other living beings (relatives, sons and the like) so that none of them may go this goal (that the departed went). May they live for a hundred prosperous autumns! May they keep off death by means of mountain (the stone).[121]

According to Sāyaṇa, with the uttering of this verse a stone is placed as an obstruction for the safety of others' lives *anayā jīvarakṣārtham pāṣāṇaṁ paridhi-rūpeṇa sthāpayanti* (Sāyaṇa on *ṚV*, 10.18.4) Wilson translates *paridhi* as 'a circle of stones'.[122]

P.V. Kane comments that *paridhis* here are the encircling sticks of the sacrificial wood such as *palāśa, khadira* placed round the fire. With *imaṁ jīvebhyaḥ* (*ṚV*, 10.18.4) the fire is surrounded on three sides by wooden sticks and a stone is placed on the north with the reciting of the last quarter of the *ṛc* as stated in the *AGS*, 4.6.10.[123]

The mountain (*parvata*) mentioned in the *ṚV*, 10.18.4d is, according to Sāyaṇa 'a heap of stones' symbolising a mountain placed in order to obstruct death, the killer, from coming again.[124]

Mahīdhara refers to *KāŚS*, 21.4.24 and explains that the Adhvaryu deposits a huge lump of soil (*mṛt-khaṇḍam*) between the village and the cremation ground.

Thus *parvata* which is explained as a heap of stones by Sāyaṇa and as a huge lump of soil by Mahīdhara[125] symbolises a mountain which is difficult for Mṛtyu to cross and strike the people again.

Though Yama's jurisdiction, in the *ṚV*, is beyond death, he gradually came to be identified with *mṛtyu* (death). In the

KaṭhaUp Yama appears as a preacher of the secret of the life after death. Here a complete identification of Yama and Mṛtyu is seen because Yama is repeatedly addressed as Mṛtyu.[126] At some places *mṛtyu* is used as just another name of Yama.[127] Vājaśravas angrily says — "To Death I give thee" and Naciketas proceeds towards the abode of Yama pondering "Is there any work of Yama which he will perform today through me" (*KaṭhaUp*, 1.1.5). Thus it is seen here that on being given to *mṛtyu* Naciketas understands that he is given to Yama. Śaṅkarācārya, identifying Mṛtyu with Vaivasvata Yama, comments *mṛtyave Vaivasvatāya tvāṁ dadāmi iti.*[128] Thus it is clear that Mṛtyu is considered to be Yama. This is further established by Yama being addressed as Mṛtyu at several places.

FATHERS

Fathers are called Yama's companions (*ṚV*, 10.15.8; *AV*, 19.9.51). He is also their king, with whom they live in the third heaven (*AV*, 5.24.14). They enjoy in the company of Yama (*Yamena ye sadhamādam madanti* — *ṚV*, 10.14.10) and Yama is also mentioned as enjoying the company of the Fathers (*ṚV*, 10.15.8), Yama is their lord (*Yamaḥ pitṛṇām adhipatiḥ*— *AV*, 5.24.14), and he is frequently called *pitṛmat*. The *ŚB*, 7.1.14 also states that Yama is the king and the Fathers are his people.

The term *pitaraḥ* is generally used for the ancestors. Originally *pitṛ* means a protector or a guardian[129] and hence it denotes 'father'. It can be assumed that gradually the plural form, i.e., *pitaraḥ* came to be used for the dead forefathers, and later still for all the dead. Though the term *pitaraḥ* is extensively used for the ancestors, it is also sometimes used for denoting a different sense e.g., (1) wisemen (*ṚV*, 10.88.18), (2) men sitting in assembly (*sabhāsadaḥ*, *AV*, 7.12.1), (3) warriors (*ṚV*, 6.75.9; *VS*, 29.46), (4) *prāṇa* (or the life-breath) (*ṚV*, 10.130.1), (5) seasons (*VS*, 2.32). In the *Brāhmaṇas* the term *pitaraḥ* used for denoting seasons (*ŚB*, 2.6.1.4; 32, *TB*, 1.4.10.8; 1.3.10.5, etc.).[130]

All the dead souls who have gathered in the world of Yama form a special community and this is called *pitaraḥ*. In this connection the rites from cremation to *śrāddha* are important because they enable the deceased to join the rank of the *pitaraḥ* (Fathers). It is said that through the *saṁskāras* after birth one conquers earth and through the *saṁskāras* after death, heaven (Baudhāyana, *Pitṛmedha*, 3.1.4). Great importance is given to the rites to the Manes. *ManuS* (3.203) says that the rite in honour of the manes is more important than the rite in honour of the gods.

The term *preta* refers to the dead for whom obsequial rites have not been performed.[131] According to P.V. Kane the word *pitaraḥ* is used in two senses, viz. (1) a man's three deceased ancestors, (2) the early or ancient ancestors of the human race that were supposed to inhabit a separate world (*loka*) by themselves.[132]

Creation of Fathers

The *ṚV*, 10.130.6 indicates that the Fathers along with *ṛṣis* and *manuṣyas* were made at the time of the primeval sacrifice. In the VS, 14.29 also the creation of the Fathers is mentioned (*navabhir astuvata pitaro as ṛjyanta*— *VS*, 14.29).

Mahīdhara explains that Prajāpati prayed with the nine *prāṇas* (vital breaths) and then the Fathers like Agniṣvātta etc. were created. He explains the nine *prāṇas* mentioned here by quoting *ŚB*, 8.4.3.7 which states that there are nine *prāṇas*—seven belonging to the head region and two to the lower region.[133] The creation of the Fathers is found in *ŚB*, 8.4.3.7 with more details.

In *AV*, 10.10.26 and also in *AV*, 11.7.27 it is indicated that the Fathers were considered to be a separate class of people like gods, *gandharvas*, *asuras* and men.

According to the *TB*, 2.3.8.2 Prajāpati first made the *asuras* and afterwards he made the Fathers. Thus here also they are spoken of as a separate class because they were created separately. Obviously here *pitaraḥ* is not a collective name for all the dead.

According to *TB*, 1.3.10.4 there are two kinds of Fathers: (1) divine and (2) human. Sāyana explains that divine Fathers are those who are the lords of the *pitṛloka*. Human *pitṛs* are those who being dead attain that world through repast.[134] Thus it can be said that those who passed of old and those who follow the countless ancient Fathers constitute a group of *pitṛs* who are the invisible, powerful, immortal, divine beings. According to the *ŚB*, 13.8.4.12 the Father and men never mix together. They lead separate lives and they are not seen together here. The Fathers are said to be rejoicing in the company of Yama (*ṚV*, 10.14.10). Yama is called *pitṛmat*, i.e., a companion of the Fathers (*ṚV*, 10.14.4). At the *mahāpitṛyajña* Yama and the Fathers are invited conjointly to accept the oblations (*ṚV*, 10.15.8). It was Yama who after himself dying first found out a new path for the dead souls to follow (*ṚV*, 10.14.2). Yama is the lord of the Fathers (*AV*, 18.2.25; 5.24.14). The *ŚB*, 13.4.3.6 states that Yama is the king and the Fathers are his people. At the sacrifices the Fathers are also invited and honoured. Like Yama they too are offered oblations with the call of *svadhā* (*ṚV*, 10.15.14, *AV*, 18.2.49; *TB*, 3.3.6.4).

Abode of the Fathers

The Fathers reside in the midst of heaven (*ṚV*, 10.15.14) and their place is in the highest heaven (*ṚV*, 10.14.8) which is also the abode of their lord Yama (*VS*, 19.45, *TB*, 2.6.3.4, *ŚB*, 18.1.18-19, *JaiUp*, 1.12.2). Their region is situated in the third heaven which is nearer to the sun. According to the *AV*, 18.2.48 the Fathers live in the third heaven.[135]

According to *PB*, 9.8.5, *TB*, 1.3.10.5 (*tṛtīye vā itaḥ loke pitaraḥ*) also the Fathers live in the third world from here. The author of the *GB*, 1.2.4 has them placed in the *svarga-loka* (heaven). As noted earlier it is not a matter of fact that the deceased went to the abode of the Fathers, because the *AV*, 12.2.45 implores Agni to let those who are dead reach to the region of the manes. The funeral rites are performed in order to enable the deceased to reach this region.[136] Being the subject of Yama, the Fathers are also connected with Yama's direction, i.e., the south direction (*MS*, 4.9.5). The

ŚB, 3.1.1.7 states that south direction is the direction of the Fathers (*yā dakṣiṇā dik sā pitṛṇām*, *ŚB*, 3.1.1.7).

The *ŚB*, 13.8.1.5 tells that the door of the *pitṛ-loka* is in the south-east, while that of heaven is said to be in the north-east (*ŚB*, 6.6.2.4). Death is the dividing line between the Fathers and men and so they do not mix together. They lead separate lives. Fathers are invited to the sacrifices, where they receive great honour. Like Indra and other goods they came to the sacrifice in chariots (*ṚV*, 10.15.10). They are often spoken of as *somyāsaḥ*, i.e., Soma-loving (*ṚV*, 10.15.1;5; 8) and are fondly invited at the time of drinking Soma, and to witness how immortal (Soma) has entered the mortals (men). At the sacrifice the Fathers sit to the right side of the altar. A.A. Macdonell, observes that the Fathers sits to the right of the altar, i.e., in the south direction because the south is the region of Yama and the Fathers.[137] They sit in a peculiar way with their knees on the earth.[138] They are told by Prajāpati to keep their sacred thread on the right shoulder and bend the left knee while sitting. When they asked Prajāpati the manner in which they were expected to live, he told them they would eat the food offered every month with the accomplishment of *svadhā*. He also told the Fathers that the moon shall be their light.[139]

Food is offered to the Fathers at least once a month. It is believed that in the *śrāddha-pakṣa*, i.e., the dark half of the month Āśvina they come to the houses of their kin to seek food.

Attitude Towards the Living

The attitude of the Fathers towards the living beings is that of friendship. They do not possess a hostile nature and so prayers to them are not due to any fear.

People look upon their ancestors with affection and esteein. Even after death they are considered a part of the family. They are supposed to come to a wedding in the family to see and bless the bride (*AV*, 14.2.73), like the living elders do. It emphasises the interest the dead are supposed to take in the affairs of the living and the sense of continuity that was felt to bind the living with the dead.[141] The Fathers are said to possess power to influence the life of their descendents on earth for good or evil. Hence there are passionate appeals to the Fathers to help their sons and grandsons, etc. on earth and not to injure them in any way. In the *AV*, 18.4.82, 83 salutations are offered to the wrath of the Fathers (*namaḥ vaḥ pitaro manyave*) as well as to their dreadful and cruel deeds. It is intended here that the anger of Fathers would not be directed to the worshipper.

Prayers to the Fathers

The Fathers who are kind, gentle and righteous, beneficient and harmless are prayed for success, for victory over enemies, for the gift of rains and abundance of food. They are prayed to show their goodwill, to be gracious towards men, to bless them with health and strength and protect them against dangers (*ṚV*, 1.106.3, 6.52.4, 75.9, 7.35.17; *AV*, 2.12.4, 18.1.51; 2.11, 30; 3.14, 15, 48, 58). They are prayed for the gift of rains and abundance of food. They are requested to protect the sacrificers (*ṚV*, 10.15.1; 5). They are propitiated to avert their anger for any sin the descendents might commit through human weakenesses (*ṚV*, 10.15.6) and not to injure (punish) them for the faults which they, being (erring) humans, have done.[142]

The Fathers wish to continue their line of progeny and they endow the human beings with the power of procreation (*ṚV*, 10.56.60). In this they have a special interest, as the continuation of the rites to the Fathers can only be kept up by continuing the family line. In the *ŚB*, 13.8.1.6, the Fathers are said to keep their contact alive with this world through the offsprings.

The Fathers are also connected with light. They are said to pervade the whole world and illumine it (*ṚV*, 10.56.5). They adorned the heaven with the constellations (*ṚV*, 10.68.11).[143] The *ṚV*, 3.38.3 states that the Fathers measured the two world with measuring rods and made them broad. They found out the hidden Agni and brought forth the dawn (*ṚV*, 7.76.4). In battles they are invoked as warriors (*ṚV*, 6.75.9).

In the *VS*, 2.33 the Fathers are worshipped to secure the prosperity and children. They are requested to grant (handsome) sons like Aśvins 'who put on lotus garlands'. In the *VS*, 19.58 the Fathers are requested to come to the sacrifice and enjoy the offerings. They are also requested to pronounce blessings (*adhi bruvantu*) and extend their protection on their descendents. They are prayed to make the sacrificers lords of wealth (*vayaṁ syāma patayo rayīṇām*).

In the *AV* the Fathers are prayed to save sacrificers from sins (*AV*, 11.6.11). They are propitiated to bestow riches, sons and longevity to their progeny (*AV*, 18.3.14; 4.62). Yama along with the Fathers protects the vessel of the food cooked for sacrificial purpose (*AV*, 12.3.8). They bestow a happy and long life to people (*AV*, 12.3.8).

Different Classes of the Fathers

Three grades of the Fathers are mentioned in the *Ṛ**V*, 10.15.1 as lower (*avara*), medium (*madhyamāḥ*) and high (*parāsaḥ*). Sāyana explains that those who have performed sacrifices according to *Śruti* are *uttama*, those who have performed according to *Smṛti* are *madhyama* and those devoid of any *saṁskāras* are *adhama*. In the *AV*, 18.4.80, 81, 82 *svadhā* oblations are offered to the Fathers who are sitting (1) On the earth (*pṛthivī-sadbhyaḥ*). (2) On the mid-region (*antarikṣa-sadbhyaḥ*) and in the heaven (*diviṣadbhyaḥ*). This suggests that the Fathers had access to all the three worlds. They are classified as ancient (*pūrvaiḥ*) and recent (*paraiḥ*) (*AV*, 18.3.48, also 72).

The *ṚV*, 10.15.4 mentions two classes of Fathers. They are: (1) those who are cremated, and (2) those who are not cremated. In the *VS*, 19.60 this stanza appears with only a little difference. Here the term *agnidagdhāḥ* and *anagnidagdāḥ* replaced by *agniṣvāttāḥ* and *anagniṣvāttāḥ*. This shows that the meaning of *agniṣvātta* in the following way — *yān agnir eva dahan svādayati te pitaro agniṣvāttāḥ*. It tells that the Fathers who are tasted by Agni at the time of cremation are *agniṣvāttas*. Others being those who are not cremated. These modes of disposal of the dead are referred to in the *Ṛ V* as well as the *AV*. In the *Ṛ V*, 10.18.11, 12 the dead is told to go to the mother earth which is to enclose him, as a mother covers her child with a garment. Thus it is a clear reference to the burial of the dead. These words are also applied to another rite by which the bones of the cremated, collected in an urn, are deposited in earth, and hence Oldenberg holds the view that these verses are in connected with the burial of such as urn.[144]

According to A.B. Keith who disagrees with Oldenberg, both these modes of the disposal of the dead, i.e., cremation and burial were practised in the Ṛgvedic age as two alternative methods. Later when burial was given up for cremation these verses were used for the burial of the bones, "but the fact remains that the verses are burial verses, that the *RV* treats burial and burning on the same footing."[145]

Besides cremation the other modes for the disposal of the dead are mentioned in the *AV*, 18.2.34. The dead might be buried (*nikhātāḥ*), they might be cast away (*paroptāḥ*) or they might be exposed (*uddhitāḥ*). Those cast away may refer to a practise, as in Iran, of throwing the dead body to the beasts to devour[146] *uddhitāh* seems to mean exposed on trees, which is referred to in *ŚB*, 4.5.2.13 for the expiation of a particular sin.[147]

Since modes of the disposal of the dead other than cremation were also practised, *anagniṣvātta* is used to denote such Fathers who were not cremated. It may also include those whose cremation could not be done due to certain reason like loss of their dead bodies as in some cases of drowning.

In the *VS*, 19.58 *agniṣvātta* Fathers are invited to come to the sacrifice by *devayāna*, enjoy the oblations offered to them with the utterance of *svadhā*.

Fathers come to sacrifice and sit on the strewn grass (*barhis*) spread out for them, so they are called *barhiṣadaḥ*. They are prayed to come and accept the *svadhā* oblations offered to them (*Ṛ V*, 10.15.3; *VS*, 19.56, *AV*, 18.1.45).

Aṅgiras is a class of the Fathers which is frequently

mentioned in the hymns connected with Yama. They are mentioned as special companions of Yama. Yama is said to prosper with the Angiras (*ṚV*, 10.14.3; *AV*, 18.1.4, with some variation). Yama is invited to come with Aṅgiras and sit on the *āsanas* spread out for them.

Two Paths

The concept of the two paths, i.e., the *devayāna* and the *pitṛyāṇa*, mentioned in the later Vedic literature is not very clear in the family-books of the *ṚV*. The *ṚV*, 1.109.7 however records that, "by the sun's rays, the Father attained a heavenly region". It is sufficient to suggest that this path is the *devayāna* which passes through the sun and leads to the total emancipation. The *ṚV*, 10.18.1 is a prayer to Mṛtyu. This stanza mentions *devayāna* and indirectly tells about another path which is different from the *devayāna* (*itaro devayānāt*) and which is here said to be the path of Mṛtyu (i.e., that of repeated births and deaths!).

The *ṚV*, 10.88.15 (also *VS*, 19.47; *ŚB*, 12.8.1.21) tells about the two paths for the mortals — one is that of the gods and the other one is that of the Fathers. The path by which the Fathers come to sacrifices is called the *pitṛyāṇa*, whereas the other path by which the gods come to sacrifices is called the *devayāna*. Sāyaṇa while commenting on this *ṛc* quotes the *Bhagavadgītā*, 8.24-26 to explain the two paths; one leading to the liberation and the other to the recurrent births.

After his death everybody passes through either of these paths. The *ŚB*, 12.8.1.21 states that by means of these two paths the Fathers go to the world of heaven.

In the *MS*, 1.3.37 it is said that the deceased has gone by the path of *Rta* through the moon to the gods. It also states that moon is the eye of the Fathers, which lights up their path. Thus it is clear that the path which takes the mortals to the gods through moon is *devayāna*.

The *ṚV* does not mention the recurrent births. Though the germs of the doctrine of transmigration can be seen even in *ṚV*, the doctrine of rebirth was not yet formulated.[148]

Gradually the *pitṛyāṇa* began to be considered the path of rebirth while *devayāna* that of the total liberation. (*ŚB*, 10.4.3.1-10).

The *Upaniṣads* mention two paths open to the mortals after their death:

One of them is the bright path, i.e., *devayāna* and the other is the dark path, i.e., *pitṛyāṇa*. They are also conceived as *arci-mārga*, and *dhūma-mārga*. Those who perform charitable deeds in their lives follow the *pitṛyāṇa* after their death, while those who lead a life of piety and austerity enter the path of the gods (*ChāUp*, V.10.1-2). The souls taking up the *devayāna* are said to reach the region of *Brahman*, (*ChāUp*, V.10.1; *BṛUp*, 6.2.15) while the *pitṛyāna* leads to rebirth (*ChāUp*, 5.10.3-6).

The *ChāUp*, (V.10.1-6) provides in full details the intermittent stages of both the paths. According to it he who follows the *pitṛyāṇa* enters first into smoke, then into night, the dark half of the month, six months of the year when the sun is in the southern course, the sky and finally it reaches the moon. He remains there till the remnant of his good deeds remain. After that he descends through ether, wind, smoke, mist, cloud, rain, herbs, grains and seeds. Those who eat the food and procreate, become manifold. Through the assimilation of the food by men he enters a womb and is born again.

Those souls, who go by *devayāna* enter successively into flame, day, bright half of month, six months of the year when the sun in its northern course, sun, moon, lightening, and finally into *Brahman* never to return (*ChāUp*, 4.15.5-6).

It is clear here that though all the dead go to moon, those coming by *pitṛyāṇa* stay there and after receiving the fruit of their good deeds return to earth to be born again. But it is different for those coming by *devayāna*. For them the moon is a transit station.

According to *KauBr* all those who depart from this world go, without exception, to the moon. For reaching up to moon no separate paths like *devayāna* or *pitṛyāna* are mentioned. From moon they (according to their knowledge and action) go either by *devayāna* which leads to *Brahman*, or (the name *pitṛyāṇa* is not used) they enter upon a new birth; whether as worm or a fly, or a fish, or a bird, or a lion, or a boar, or serpent, or a tiger, or a man, or something else.

Thus it is clear that according to the *KauUp* the dead do not take the *devayāna* or *pitṛyāṇa* right from the earth. All the dead go to the moon first and from there take up *devayāna* to reach *Brahman*. Others come down to earth in a renewed birth.

KauUp, 1.4 presents a development in the concept of *devayāna*.[149] It does away with the relays of the *devayāna* which are recognised in the *ChāUp*, and substitutes new ones. It tells that when the soul comes to the path of the gods he first goes to the world of Fire, then successively to that of wind, Varuṇa, Sun, Indra and Prajāpati and then finally to the world of *Brahman*.

From the above discussion it is evident that while the word *devayāna* is categorically mentioned in the *ṚV*, the other path which is the path of the Fathers is hinted by *itaro devayānāt*. It is in the later Vedic literature that the idea of these two paths was crystellized.

Notes

1. *Indrāgnyoḥ yugpat utpannatvāt agner yamatvam* — Sāyaṇa on the *ṚV*, 1.66.8.
2. *Der arische Wellkönig and Heiland*, p. 334 — referred to by R.N. Dandekar, *VMT*, p. 132.
3. R.N. Dandekar observes that on the strength of evidence of the analogies of other primitive mythologies and linguistic evidence it can be assumed that the original character of Yama was that of a bisexual being who immolated himself for the cause of progeny. His character further evolves into that of a 'twin' and later into the 'first to die' and then into the ruler of the dead — R.N. Dandekar, *op. cit.*, p. 132.
4. *Śabda-Kalpa-druma*, Vol. IV, p.19.
   (i) $\sqrt{yam}$ *niyamane-yamayati niyamayati jīvānāṁ phalāphalam iti.*
   (ii) $\sqrt{yam}$ *viratau-yacchati pāpat sādhuḥ iti.*
   (iii) $\sqrt{yam}$ *pariveṣaṇe-yāmayati annam dwijāya gṛhī.*
5. *Vyatyaya* is occurrence of one for another — K.V. Abhyankar, *A Dictionary of Sanskrit Grammar*, p. 374.

6. In dissimilation, one of the two successive phonemes is replaced by another, often with the same general type of articulation, the liquids and nasals *l, r, m, n, ṇ, ŋ* are specially subject to dissimilation'. (R.V. Hall, *Introduction to, Linguistics*, p. 137). In this phonetic change "a succession of identical articulations or phonemes or group of phonemes is altered by a total or partial loss of one of them" (Edger H. Sturtevant , *An Introduction to Linguistic Science*, p. 95).
7. Fatah Singh, *Vedic Etymology*, p. 188.
8. *Vide* R.N. Dandekar, *op. cit.*, p. 140.
9. *saṁyamī vijitendriya, BVP*, 26.6.
10. *Vide Śabdakalpadruma*, Vol. IV, p.19.
11. *Nir*, 10.20, *Agnirapi Yama ucyate.*
12. *Indrāgnyor yugapat utpannatvāt Agner yamatvam*—Sāyaṇa on the *ṚV*, 6.59.2.
13. Indra is 'primarily' a thunder god — A.A. Macdonell, *V.M.*, p. 54.
14. In the *Puruṣa-sūkta* Indra and Agni are said to have sprung from the mouth of the Cosmic Man (*ṚV*, 10.90.13).
15. *dīvyanti iti deva raśmayaḥ* — Sāyaṇa on *ṚV*, 10.135.1.
16. Sāyaṇa on the *ṚV*, 1.35.6.
17. *Vide* Skandasvāmin on the *ṚV*, 1.35.6.
18. There are two views regarding the three steps of Viṣṇu. According to one view the three steps are three stations, i.e., sunrise, zenith and sunset. This view is favoured by Yāska's predecessor Aurṇavābha (*Nir*, 12.19) and also by most European scholars (Whitney, Max-Müller, Haug, Kaegi, Deussen, etc. referred to by Macdonell, *VM* p. 38). According to the other view they are three levels: sunrise, mid-air and zenith, Macdonell (*VM*, p.38) remarks that the third step of Viṣṇu shows no trace of being connected with the sunset. Yāska takes zenith as the Viṣṇupada. Griswold too conceives *paramapada* as zenith (*The Religion of the Vedas*, p. 284.)
19. A.A. Macdonell, *VM*, p. 38; *AV*, 18.2.48.
20. *yatra rājā Vaivasato, yatra avarodhanam divaḥ*/—*ṚV*, 9,113.8.
21. *yat té Yamam vaivasvatam mano jagāma dūrakam*/—*ṚV*, 10.58.1.
22. *yatra rājā Vaivasvato yatra avarodhanam divaḥ. . . tatra mām amṛtam kṛdhi*/—*ṚV*, 9.113.8.
23. *dadāmyasmā avasānam etad, ya eṣa āgan mama ched abhūt iha* ।
Yamascikitvān pratyetad āha mamaiṣa rāyā upa tiṣṭhatām iha ॥
—*AV*, 18.2.37.
24. *Indraḥ prāṅg tiṣṭhan dakṣinā tiṣṭhan Yamaḥ*/—*AV*, 9.7.20.
25. Sāyaṇa on the *AV*, 18.4.55.
26. Referred to by A.A. Macdonell, *VM*, p. 173.
27. *ṚV*, 10.14.1.
28. *Vide* S.S. Bhawe, *Soma Hymns of the Ṛgveda*, Vol. I, p. 52.
29. Vivasvat is an honorific name for the sacrificer — A. Hillebrandt, *HVM*, Vol. II, p. 216.
30 "In the view of this, Wacknernagel's opinion (*Alt. Gram.* II, p. 19, Sec.

6B) that Vivasvat is one of the words which show change in the accent without corresponding change in the meaning cannot be fully accepted." — S.S. Bhawe, *op. cit.*, Vol. I, p. 52.

31. *Vide* S.S. Bhawe, *ibid.* p. 51.
32. The correct form ought to be 'Vivasat'. The actual form Vivasvat appears to be the contamination between the present participle 'Vivasat' and the perfect participle "Vivasvās" (the absolutely regular form "Usivas" being out of consideration here). Consequently Sāyaṇa has a lot of difficulty in explaining this form. (*Vide* S.S. Bhawe, *op. cit.*, p. 51).
33. *Vide* S.S. Bhawe, *ibid*, p. 51.
34. Sāyaṇa on the *ṚV*, 1.44.1.
35. Sāyaṇa on the *ṚV*, 5.11.3.
36. Here Sāyaṇa takes "Vivasvat" meaning 'Vaivasvata', i.e., Yama and accordingly his explanation may be translated as: "May Yama not kill us before old age". (Sāyaṇa on *ṚV*, 8.67.20).
37. A.A. Macdonell (*VM*, p. 43) and Ehni (referred to by R.N. Dandekar, *VMT*, p. 121) take him to be the morning Sun.
38. Ehni, *Der Vedische Mythus des Yama*, pp. 19, 24.
39. H. Oldenberg, *Die Religion des Veda*, p. 122.
40. Men are stated, to be progeny of Vivasvān Ādityaḥ. (*TS*, 6.5.6.2; *ŚB*, 3.1.3.4).
41. *Vide* A.B. Keith, *RPVU* pt. I, p. 113.
42. A. Bergaigne, *La Religion Vedique*, Part I, p. 81.
43. It does not suggest that Savarṇā is the name of that woman. This may be a case of an appellative used as proper noun.
44. J. Muir, *OST*, Vol. V, p. 228.
45. R.T.H. Griffith, *The Hymns of the Ṛgveda*, Part II, p. 404.
46. Suryakanta, *Vedic Dictionary*, p. 743.
47. Geldner, *Der Ṛgveda*, Comm. on *ṚV*, 10.17.2 — *Sie Verbargen die Unsterbliche Vor den Sterblichen.*
48. *yamau mithunau janayāñcakāra/*—*Nir*, 12.10.
49. But Yama, though immortal by birth had died by sacrificing himself in the primeval sacrifice — See chapter 4, "Yama and Creation".
50. F. Max Müller, *Lectures on the Science of Languages*, II, p. 620.
51. *Ibid.*, p. 620 ff.
52. *Ibid.*, p. 629.
53. Udgītha on the *ṚV*, 10.10.4 — *Gandharvaḥ gavām raśmīnām udakānām vā dhārayitā Ādityah; appūrvaṁ dattā ityarthaḥ yoṣā ca strī Saraṇyūśca Tvaṣṭruḥ duhitā ityarthaḥ.*
54. *Gandharvaḥ Ādityaḥ; apyā-yoṣā antarikṣa-sthitā tasya Ādityasya bhāryā/* — Venkaṭa on the *ṚV*, 10.10.4.
55. For details see Chapter 4.
56. Also *Kāṭhaka Saṁhitā*, 7.10.
57. Parallel episodes are seen in other mythologies also viz. Isis

mourning her brother-husband Osiris in the Egyptian mythology: Yimak mourning Yima in the Iranian mythology and Nanna mourning Bladr. Bladr has an identity very much similar to that of Yama. — *Vide* S. Bhattacharji, *Indian Theogony*, p. 96.

A fundamental difference is that Yama is never mentioned as a brother-husband of Yamī, but as a brother only (*RV*, 10.10; *MS*, 1.5.12)

58. *ŚB*, 3.8.14.
59. A.A. Macdonell, *VM*, p. 157; "Paṇis are often mentioned with Dāsas and Dasyus as enemies of the Aryans" (*Vide* for details. *The Vedic Age*, by R.C. Majumdar and A.D. Pusalkar, pp. 252-53).
60. M. Bloomfield, *The Hymns of Atharvaveda*, *SBE*, Vol. 42, p. 404.
61. *Amarakośa*, 2.10.21.
62. M. Bloomfield *op. cit.*, p. 404.
63. Suryakanta, *Vedic Dictionary*, p. 180.
64. A.A. Macdonell, *A Vedic Reader*, p. 172.
65. A. Hillebrandt, *Leider de Ṛgveda*, p. 119.
66. Oldenberg, *Die Religion des Veda*, p. 575.
67. Grassmann, *Wortebuch Zum Rigveda*, p. 253.
68. F.B.J. Kuiper, *Proto-muṇḍa words in Sanskrit*, p. 25.
69. Bhatta Bhāskara on *TS*, 5.5.29.2 — *caturakṣaḥ caksnoh upari bindu-dvaya vān*.
70. *Uparibhāge punar api akśidvayam* — Sāyaṇa on *ṚV*, 10.14.10.
71. M. Bloomfield identifies these dogs with the sun and the moon. (*JAOS*, 1893, Vol. XV, p. 162; also *Religion of Vedas*, p. 105).
72. Sāyaṇa interprets the four eyes of Agni as its flames — Sāyaṇa on the *ṚV*, 1.31.13. Agni's farsightedness is also expressed in his another epithet, i.e., *dūredṛśa* — *ṚV*, 6.10.4, 7.1.1, etc. — one who can see from a distance or one who can be seen from a distance — Sāyaṇa.
73. A.B. Keith, *RPVU*, Vol. II, p. 406.
74. H.D. Velankar, *Ṛksūktaśati*, p. 254 fn. 12.
75. A.A. Macdonell, *A Vedic Reader*, p. 172.
76. A.A. Macdonell, *VM*, p. 173.
77. H.D. Velankar, *op. cit.*, p. 254.
78. This meaning can be derived by taking *śvānau* as accusative dual.
79. *The Zend-Avesta*, tr. by J. Darmesteter & L.H. Mills, *SBE*, Vol. IV, p. 219 n. 219.
80. Cf. A.B. Keith, *RPVU*, p. 406.
81. *etau vai yamaśvā ahaśca rātriśca*/—*Kāṭhaka Saṁhitā*, 33.14.
82. *Ṛgveda Bhāṣā-Bhāṣya* on the *ṚV*, 10.14.10.
83. S.D. Satvalekar, *AVSB*, 18th *Kāṇḍa*, p. 151.
84. A. Bergaigne, *La Religion Vedique*, I.89.
85. Quoted by M. Bloomfield, "Śyāma and Śabala", *JAOS*, Vol. XV, p. 169; also referred to by R.N. Dandekar, "Yama in the Veda", *VMT*, p. 120.

86. M. Bloomfield, *op. cit.*, pp. 163-72.
87. F. Max-Müller, *Lectures on the Science of Language*, Vol. II, p. 593.
88. Bruce Lincoln, "The Hell-hound", *Journal of Indo-European Studies*, 7 (3-4), 1979, pp. 273-85.
89. Richard Cavendish, *An Illustrated Encyclopaedia of Mythology*, p. 134.
90. S. Bhattacharji, *Indian Theogony*, p. 71.
91. *The Lexicon Webster Dictionary*, Vol. II, p. BT. 155.
92. F. Max Müller, *op. cit.*, p. 593.
93. *The Zend-Avesta*, *SBE*, 4.219, 219 n; *Pahlavi text*, tr. by E.W. West, *SBE*, 24.293.
94. Vendidad VIII, 14-22.
95. *Pahlavi texts*, tr. by E.W. West, *SBE*, Vol. 24, p. 293.
96. Sāyaṇa on *ṚV*, 10.165.4, *Agnim atigṛha madhye padaṁ karoti.*
97. *pakṣopeta . . . . . hanana hetuḥ*, Sāyaṇa on *ṚV*, 10.165.2.
98. S.D. Satvalekar, *AVSB*, Transl. *AV*, 6.27-29.
99. *ghoraṁ kapotasya nipātam āhuḥ* — *ṚV*, 2.12.43; 3.197.5.
100. *Araru* = Killer √ṛ to kill — *vide* S.D. Satvalekar *AVSB*, p. 137.
101. Varuṇa is darkness — *vide* S.D. Satvalekar, *AVSB*, p. 137.
102. Grāhi is similar to Nirṛti, because both of them have destructive nature, but they cannot be considered identical (cf — Grāhi is almost a synonym of Nirṛti — S. Bhattacharji, *op. cit.*, p. 101) because in the next stanza Dream is called Nirṛti's son.
103. *Vide* S. Bhattacharji, *Indian Theogony*, p. 49.
104. *mṛtyo sarveṣām māraka etat nāmaka deva* — Sāyaṇa on *ṚV*, 10.18.1.
105. *mā naḥ prajām ririṣo mā uta vīrān/*—*ṚV*, 10.18.1. Sāyaṇa takes *prajā* as daughters and there offsprings. Mahīdhara renders it as *santatim*, i.e., descendents.
106. *śuddha* means pure from the decay caused by the sins accumulated in a former life, while *pūta* means pure from the decay caused by the sins of the present life. Cf, Sāyaṇa on the *ṚV*, 10.18.2.
107. Cf. *ṚV*, 10.18.1-4, tr. by H.H. Wilson *Ṛgveda Saṁhitā*, Vol. 6, p. 58.
108. *apratihata-sarvendriya-vijñānāya iti artham*—Sāyaṇa on *ṚV*, 10.18.1.
109. The adjective *pracetas* means clever, wise, attentive which also qualifies a special aspect of practical knowledge. It is not only applied to Agni, but to a number of other deities like Mitra, Varuṇa and Rudra. The quality was in all probability supposed to be proper for those great gods who excelled in intellectual abilities, cleverness, and resourcefulness in achieving extraordinary deeds. (*Vide* J. Gonda, *Epithets in Ṛgveda*, p. 89).
110. S.D. Satvalakar, *AVSB* Transl. *AV*, 6.28.3.
111. R.T.H. Griffith, *Hymns of Ṛgveda*, Transl. 10.165.4.
112. R.T.H. Griffith, *op. cit.*, Pt. II, p. 599.
113. *tām antako mārtyavo adhok/*—*AV*, 8.10.4(7).

114. *mṛtyoḥ padbīśat paśān mām moci/*—*AV*, 16.8.32
ye te sahasrāyutam pāsā mṛtyo martyāya hantave/
tan yajñasya māyayā sarvān ava yajāmahe//—*TB*, 3.10.8.2
sa mṛtyu-pāśān praṇaudya . . . /—*KatṭhaUp*, 118.
115. *AV*, 16.8.32.
116. *AV*, 12.2.9.
117. *sa sarvān pāśān sarvān sthāṇūn mṛtyoḥ atimucya eva udamucyate/* —*AB*, 12.3.
118. *Mṛtyuḥ prājānām ādhipati sá mām avatu/*—*AV*, 5.24.13.
Yamaḥ pitṛṇām adhipati sa mām avatu/—*AV*, 5.24.14.
119. Cf. N.J. Shende, "Mṛtyu", In *Journal of the University of Bombay*, Vol. 27, September, 1958.
120. *ŚB*, 10.6.5.1 tr. by J. Eggling, *SBE*, Vol. 43, p. 402.
aśanāyā hi mṛtyuḥ — *BṛUp*, 1.2.1.
121. P.V. Kane, *HDS*, Vol. IV, p. 199.
122. Cf. "I errect this circle of stones for the protection of the living" — H.H. Wilson, Transl. *ṚV*, 10.18.4
paridhi has two meanings — (1) three sticks used for fence in a sacrifice (*TS*, 2.5.8.6), (2) as an adjective it means something which obstructs *ṚV*, 9.69.11; VS, 19.53; *TS*, 2.6.12.1 — (*paridhīyate ebhiḥ sarvam iti paridhayo rākṣasāḥ* — Sāyaṇa on *ṚV*, 9.69.11).
123. P.V. Kane, *HDS*, Vol. IV, p. 199 — *antar mṛtyum dadhatām parvatena iti aśmānām uttarato agneḥ kṛtvā . . . . yathāhanyanupurvam bhavanti iti amatyān ikṣeta* — *AGS*, 4.6.10.
amātya here means all members of the family, men and women, except the performer of the sacrifice, P.V. Kane, *op. cit.*, p. 199.
124. *parvatena śiloccayena mṛtyum sarveṣām mārakam etat namakam antuḥ dadhatām antarhitam kurvantu' yathā na āgacchati tathā kurvantām iti* — Sāyaṇa on the *ṚV*, 10.18.14.
125. Mahīdhara on *VS*, 35.15.
126. *KaṭhaUp*, 1.10; 1.13; 1.22; 1.29.
127. *KaṭhaUp*, 1.15.
128. *Śāṅkarabhāṣya* on *KaṭhaUp*, 1.4.
129. *pitā sā u náḥ pipartuḥ* — *AV*, 12.1.12, here Parjanya is addressed.
130. *Vide* S.D. Satvalekar, *AVSB*, p. 105.
131. *Vide* S. Bhattacharji, *Indian Theogony*, p. 79.
132. *Vide* P.V. Kane, *HDS*, Vol. IV, p. 341.
133. *nava vai prāṇāḥ sapta śirṣān avāñco dvau iti* — *ŚB*, 8.4.3.7.
134. *pitṛloka svāmino devātmakāḥ mṛtā santo bhogāt tat lokam prāptāḥ manuṣyātmakāḥ* — Sāyaṇa on *TS*, 1.3.10.4. It is said here that in *piṇḍa-pitṛ-yajña* three *āhutis* with *svadhā*, one each to Soma, Yama and Kavyavāhana Agni are offered and three lumps of rice (*piṇḍa*) are placed. With the three *āhutis* divine Fathers are made happy. After they are pleased human Fathers are made happy by keeping three *piṇḍas* to please them. (*TB*, 1.3.10.4)

135. **See** *supra* 'Yama's abode, and chapter 5. 'Heaven'.
136. Caland, *Die altindischen Todten Bestattungs gebrduche*, p. 174 f. referred to by J. Gonda in *Loka-World and heaven in the Veda*, p. 85.
137. A.A. Macdonell, *The Vedic Reader*, p. 180.
138. *ṚV*, 10.15.6.
139. *ŚB*, 2.4.2.2.
140. A.B. Keith, *RPVU*, Vol. II, p. 425.
141. K.M. Kapadia, *Hindu Kinship*, p. 10.

    A.B. Keith (*op. cit.*, p. 426) holds that the manes are worshipped at weddings because they are interested in the issue of such marriage.
142. *ṚV*, 10.15.6; *AV*, 18.1.52; 4.82.83; *VS*, 19.62.
143. *nakṣatrebhiḥ pitaro dyām apiśan*/—*ṚV*, 10.68.11.
144. Oldenberg, *Religion des Veda*, pp. 372 ff.
145. A.B. Keith, *RPVU*, Vol. II, p. 418.
146. Zimmer, *Altindisches Leben*, p. 402 referred to by A.B. Keith, *op. cit.*, p. 417.
147. *Ibid.*
148. **See** chapter 5 "Transmigration".
149. **See** R.D. Ranade, *A Constructive Survey of Upaniṣadic Philosophy*, p. 161.

3

Yama and Other Gods

On the basis of the statistical classification of the gods (suggested by A.A. Macdonell), Yama cannot be regarded a major god since he belongs to the fifth category of the gods.[1] In the *ṚV* only three hymns are addressed to him (viz. 10.10; 14; 135) and his name appears about fifty times, mostly in the 10th *Maṇḍala*. Yama appears in the other *Maṇḍalas* too e.g., 1.38.5; 85.5; 7.33.9; 9.113.8.[2] These stray and scattered reference are also important for getting a glimpse of the true character of this god.

Yama is seen to be closely associated with other gods. He is mentioned as revelling in the company of other gods (*ṚV*, 7.76.4; 10.135.1). He is also mentioned with individual gods like Varuṇa (*ṚV*, 10.14.7) and Bṛhaspati (*ṚV*, 10.13.4; 14.3). As a conductor of the dead Agni has a close relation with Yama. Agni, Yama and Mātariśvan are mentioned together as different names of the Supreme-being (*ṚV*, 1.164.46).

Yama and Varuṇa

Among all the Vedic gods Varuṇa seems to be closest to Yama. Due to similarities between them in more than one respect, Varuṇa is also considered to be a duplicate of Yama.[3]

Like Yama Varuṇa is also called a king (*ṚV*, 1.24.7, 7.87.5).[4] He is the lord of all beings (*ṚV*, 2.27.10) and of all the universe (*ṚV*, 5.85.3). Varuṇa and Yama are mentioned as two kings, who can be seen in the realm of the dead. A man, who has recently died, is told to hasten to the other world, where he would see both, i.e., Yama and Varuṇa (*ṚV*, 10.14.7; *AV*, 18.34.6). In the *ṚV*, 10.14.7, Varuṇa along with Yama is mentioned as enjoying the *svadhā* oblations which are otherwise exclusively for Yama and the Fathers.

Varuṇa is frequently called *asura*, i.e., one who possesses the largest amount of *asu* (the magical power-substance) and therefore, has the greatest power.[5] He is the magician-creator of the world as well as its 'Supreme Sovereign'.[6]

Varuṇa who is the upholder of the cosmic law (i.e., *ṛta*) is also by logical extension a moral governor who employes his noose and puts the evil-doers in bondage by way of punishment (*ṚV*, 7.84.2,[7] *AV*, 4.166.9). The *TS*, 2.3.13 says that Varuṇa binds with his noose a person who is involved with evil deeds.[8] Similar is the purport of the *TB*, 1.7.2.6 which says that Varuṇa grabs a person doing unlawful deeds.[9] Obviously the noose of Varuṇa, the supreme binder-god, performs a dual function. Varuṇa binds down all the phenomena of the universe with his noose and thereby controls the universe, making it a well-regulated whole.[10] On the other hand, he also uses his noose to punish the sinner. Thus Varuṇa controls with his noose the cosmic as well as the moral order. Varuṇa also watches the sacrificial rites and punishes people for the inaccuracies therein, if any, with his knots and cords which are repeatedly mentioned in the *Brāhmaṇas*.[11]

According to the *ṚV*, 1.122.9 Mitra and Varuṇa inflict disease of the heart on a men who does not offer oblations to them.[12] The *ṚV*, 1.122.9 says

> A man who does you wrong, Mitra and Varuṇa! who injures you in any way or does not present you with oblations, contracts for himself sickness in his heart.[13]

According to H.H. Wilson, *yakṣmā* is a disease in general. V.S. Apte understands it as a pulmonary disease and *yaksma-graha* as "attack of consumption".[14]

can be inferred that diseases are the *pāśa* of Varuṇa. H.H. Wilson observes that a kind of dropsy seems to be referred to as Varuṇa's noose in the *AV*, 4.16.7. The *ṚV*, 7.89.2 refers to this disease[15] (i.e., dropsy) as inflicted by Varuṇa. This disease (also mentioned in the *AB*, 7.15) is supposed to cause water-retention in body resulting in enlargement of the belly and the condition of a man sick with dropsy is vividly expressed here in the following way—

I move along tremulus like a wind-blown skin.[16]

According to a story in the *AB*, 7.13-18 Varuṇa is said to have punished the king Hariścandra for the breach of his promise by making him sick with dropsy. There is no deed, good or bad, of which Varuṇa is ignorant. The all-seeing sun who is the eye of Varuṇa (*ṚV*, 1.115.1; 6.51.1)[17] by which he sees the deeds of a man as well as his truthfulness and falsehood. The sun is mentioned as the 'golden-winged messenger of Varuṇa' (*ṚV*, 10.123.6).[18] In the *ṚV*, 7.34.10 Varuṇa is mentioned as thousand-eyed; he watches everything that is secret, every deed done or to be done (*ṚV*, 1.25.11)[19] the worshippers pray Varuṇa and seek deliverance from his noose (*ṚV*, 1.25.21; 6.74.4).

Varuṇa's function as a punisher brings him close to Yama. Though Yama is not explicitly mentioned as a punisher or as a judge in the *ṚV*, but a parallel to Varuṇa's noose can be seen in Yama's foot-fetter (*padbīśa*). The worshipper prays to be freed from the *pāśa* and *paḍbīśa* of Varuṇa and Yama respectively (*ṚV*, 10.97.16). In the *ŚB* Yama is clearly mentioned as a punisher.

Varuṇa gets the epithets *satya dharman* and *dharmapati*. (*TS*, 1.8.10.1; *TB*, 1.7.10.3). In this connection it may be noted that Yama holds the epithet of *dharmarāja* in the Epics.

The *VS*, 24.28 mentions buffalo as the animal to be sacrificed to Varuṇa.[20] In the Epics Yama has a buffalo as his mount. Varuṇa's emissary, a bird with golden wings, is said to be residing in the region of Yama.[21] The *AV*, 1.14 is addressed to "Varuṇa, or Yama" (*Varuṇo Yamo vā*), thus equating or at least connecting Varuṇa with Yama.

In the *AV*, 6.46.1 the dream or the evil-dream is called Yama's son by Varuṇānī, i.e., Varuṇa's consort. It is significant that Yamī is not stated to be the mother of Yama's son. This is one of the few references which indicate that Yamī was not originally considered to be Yama's wife, and for that matter no wife of Yama is mentioned in the *ṚV*. Yamī is mentioned in the *ṚV* as Yama's twin-sister but she is not mentioned as Yama's wife.[22]

At another place a bad dream is called a son of Grāhī and also of Nirṛti, Abhūti, Nirbhūti, Parābhūti and Deva-jāmi in the subsequent lines *AV* 16.5.

Another connection of Yama and Varuṇa is said to be through Nirṛti.[23] Nirṛti is conceived as a malevolent goddess, who brings diseases and destruction. Varuṇa is the lord of *ṛta* or the cosmic order and Nirṛti, who is the negation of *ṛti* (which is probably another form of *ṛta*)[24] is associated with death and destruction and in this capacity she is considered to be the female counterpart of Yama. At a few places Yama is indentified with death (*ṚV*, 10.165.4,[25] *AV*, 6.28.3; 93.1).[26] In the *MS*, 2.5.6 it is said that Mṛtyu indeed is Yama (*mṛtur vai Yamaḥ* — *MS*, 2.5.6), while *Kauśikasūtra*, 8.23 states that Yama is *mṛtyu*. It is important to note that Varuṇa is also identified with death. The *KS*, 13.2 says that, while practising witchcraft, one should sacrifice a black ram, which belongs to Yama, because 'Varuṇa is death'.[27]

Varuṇa is also said to be the earlier name of Prajāpati, the lord of (pro-)creation.[28] Prajāpati is identified the Primeval Man (*Puruṣa*) who was offered in the first sacrifice and whose dismembered limbs became this universe.[29]

Varuṇa is the greatest *asura* because he possesses the largest amount of *asu* or magical power-substance. With his magical powers he creates the cosmos. He is the magical creator of the world as well as its Supreme Sovereign.[30] Thus it is seen that Yama and Varuṇa both share an important attribute of being the creator of the Universe. The *ṚV*, 10.13.4 gives a vague account of the sacrifice of a divine being for the cause of progeny, in which it is said that Yama sacrificed his body for the cause of progeny. This stanza provides a rudimentary and obscure account of the sacrifice of a Cosmic

Man which find a detailed expression in the *Puruṣasūkta*. On this basis an equation can be formed, i.e., Varuṇa = Prajāpati = Puruṣa = Yama, which equates Varuṇa with yama in the capacity of a creator, but it is difficult to establish an identity between Yama and Varuṇa. Varuṇa is sometimes represented as being identical with the other Vedic deities, but Varuṇa is not identical with any of them. Actually he 'includes and transcends them all'.[31]

Yama and Agni

Agni is called 'a dear friend Yama' *priyo yamasya kāmyo* (*ṚV*, 10.21.5). Yama's connection with Agni is mainly through the funeral rites as well as through the sacrifices to the Fathers. These are three forms of Agni as mentioned in the *ṚV*. They are (1) *Kravyād* (2) *Kravyavāhana* and (3) *Havyavāhana*.

KRAVYĀD AGNI

This form of fire is used for the cremation of the deceased. It consumes the corpse and takes the deceased to the other world, i.e., the world of the Fathers (*ṚV*, 10.16.1-4) which is according to *AV*, 18.3.71 the world of the righteous people. Hence this corpse-burning fire is called *kravyād*, i.e., consumer of flesh. Yama is connected with *kravyād* through its function of consuming the dead body and also of taking the dead to the world of the Fathers which is the realm of Yama. In the *AV*, 12.2.54, *kravyād* Agni is called Yama's fire who belongs to the south direction which is considered to be Yama's direction.

After the cremation, this fire is left at a cross-road in the south direction because it is not used for any other purpose e.g., sacrifices to the gods or to the Fathers.

For obvious reason, the *kravyād* fire is considered inauspicious and unfit for sacrificial purpose. It is also strongly wished that this fire should not come again (i.e., no death should occur in the family). Therefore after the cremation is done, this fire is sent away and another fire is procured for performing the rest of the rites, i.e., the sacrifices to the

Fathers.[32] Compare here "I send away the flesh-devouring Agni to a distance: let him, bearing away sins, repair to the realm of king Yama; but let this other Agni (*itaro jātavedāḥ*) convey the oblation to gods (*ṚV*, 10.16.9).[33] The next stanza states that before performing the worship of the manes, the *kravyād* Agni is turned out (*ṚV*, 10.16.10).[34] The *Sūtras* also instruct that *kravyād* Agni is to be discarded after the cremation. With the recitation of the *ṚV*, 10.16.9 the fire is taken to the south and discarded at a crossing there. Another fire is prepared from the north direction for performing the *śānti-karman* (post-cremation rites) and also the sacrifices to the Fathers (*ĀŚS*, 2.219).[35]

KRAVYAVĀHANA

In the *ṚV* the fire carrying oblations to the manes is called *kravyavāhana* (10.16.11) or the carrier of *kravya*. Commenting on this stanza Sāyaṇa takes *kravya* as *kavya*. *Kavyas* are the offerings made to the Fathers (Sāyaṇa on the *ṚV*, 10.15.9) therefore *kravyavāhana* is explained as *kavyasya voḍha agniḥ*. Udgītha, a predecessor of Sāyaṇa (whose commentary on the *ṚV*, 10.15.9 is available) retains the word *kravya* and explains the word *kravyavāhana* as *kravyāsya voḍha agniḥ*.[36]

Basically *kravya* means flesh. So *kravyavāhana* is a 'fire carrying the flesh-oblations'.[37] S.D. Satvalekar points at the offering of flesh to the Fathers in the *VS*, 35.20.[38]

In the post-Ṛgvedic literature the term *kavyavāhana* instead of *kravyavāhana* is extensively used for the "fire carrying oblations to the Fathers".[39] According to Hillebrandt the word *kavyavāhana* is a new form of the older word *kravyavāhana* caused "probably by a real change in sound or formed for euphemistic reasons".[40] Hillebrandt refers to the views of M. Bloomfield (*Festgabe fur*, Streitberg, p. 13) explaining the word to be "a product of contamination of *kavyavāhana* with much more common *havyavāhana*."[41] A.B. Keith, however believes that *kravyād*, *kravyavāhana* and *kavyavāhana* are different names of one form of Agni. He further comments that the term *kravyād* alternates with *kravyavāhana* and later with *kavyavāhana.*[42]

It should be noted here that the term *Jātavedas* is used as a general name of Agni and that it is used at different places as a name of any of the three forms of Agni. In the *ṚV*, 10.16.9 the priest says, "I drive away this *kravyād* Agni to a distant place. Let this other fire (*itaro jātavedāḥ*) carry oblations to the gods." Verily, here *Jātavedas* stands for the *havyavāhana* Agni, while in an earlier stanza (*ṚV*, 10.16.1) *Jātavedas* stands for the *kravyād* Agni, where he is told to burn the corpse properly.[43]

In the *AV* also the term *Jātavedas* is used to denote various forms of Agni. For example, in the *AV*, 18.3.42 *Jātavedas* stands for the *kavyavāhana* Agni while in the *AV*, 18.3.71 it denotes the *kravyād* Agni.

The *VS*, 1.17 distinguishes the three forms of Agni in the following way:

(1) *Āmāt*

(2) *Kravyād* — corpse-devouring fire

(3) *Devayāja* — sacrificial fire

Āmāt—In the vocable *āmāt*, *āma* means "raw, uncooked". According to A.B. Keith *āmāt* means the 'eater of raw flesh'.[45] Since the Agni who consumes flesh (corpse) is spoken of as *kravyād* here, it is unlikely that *āmāt* also refers to the flesh-devouring Agni. A plausible meaning of *āmāt* can be the fire who consumes the rawness of food (by cooking it). Thus *āmāt* can be the kitchen fire used for cooking the food. Uvvaṭa and Mahīdhara seem to be referring to this meaning of *āmāt* in their commentary of this stanza (i.e., *VS*, 1.17).[46]

In *TS*, VI. 5.9.1 Agni tells Indra imperatively "thou shalt not offer what is raw (*āmaṁ*) in me".[47] 'A consumer of rawness' can, therefore, be a figurative expression for the fire that cooks.

But according to the *MS* Agni has two forms.[48] He carries oblations to gods by one and to the Fathers by the other. Here no separate Agni as the consumer of the corpse is mentioned. It seems that the functions of both these fires have got assimilated here. According to ĀŚS the *kravyād* is left after the cremation and another fire should be prepared for further rites (i.e., *pitṛmedha*). The fire carrying the oblations to Fathers must be other than the eater of corpses which is left aside after the cremation. This confirms that *kravyād* and *kavyavāhana* are two separate forms of Agni performing two separate functions.

The *TS*, 2.5.8.6 mentions the three forms of Agni (1) *Havyavāhana*, (2) *Kavyavāhana* and (3) *Saharākṣas*. According to it *havyavāhana* belongs to the gods, the *kavyavāhana* belongs to the Fathers and the *saharākṣas* is associated with goblins and belongs to the *asuras*.

The *TS*, 3.3.8 tells that Yama is Agni and the fire-altar is Yamī.[49] According to the *TS*, 1.8.5 one can attain Yama's kingdom by perfomring the *Agniṣṭoma* sacrifice.

Yama and Havyavāhana

The *ṚV*, 10.51 contains a legend connected with the *havyavāhana* Agni, Yama and other gods. The story is about the disappearance of Agni who concealed himself in water. Eventually all oblations to the gods came to a stand-still. It was Yama who found out the hidden Agni. The gods implored Agni to come from his hiding place. They told Agni "We all looked for you and it was Yama who recognised you blazing from your ten hiding places".(*ṚV*, 10.51.3) These ten hiding places are, according to Sāyaṇa, the three worlds—(1) heaven, (2) mid-region and (3) earth; three divinities — (4) Agni, (5) Vāyu and (6) Āditya; (7) water, (8) shrubs, (9) trees and (10) bodies of living beings.[50] R.T.H. Griffith observes that the meaning of ten hiding places appears to be that Yama knew that Agni would appear again from the fire-sticks worked out by fingers of both the hands.[51] Gods requested Agni to come out and become the conveyer of the oblations offered to them. Agni expressed his fear and said that his elder brothers were also engaged in this work of oblation bearing and they were killed while performing their duty. On seeing his brothers' fate, Agni, trembling with fear, had concealed himself (*ṚV*, 10.51.6). Sāyaṇa comments that the three brothers of Agni, viz. Bhūpati, Bhuvanapati and Bhūtānāmpati were killed while performing their duty as oblation-bearers of the gods.[52]

The gods assure Agni of a fair deal. They grant him immortality (*ṚV*, 10.51.7) and also a portion in the oblations (*ṚV*, 10.51.8).

W.E. Webster remarks that the legend contained in this hymn was probably invented to account for the triumph of Agni 'the youngest of the gods' over the older deities Mitra and Varuṇa.[53]

This story also occurs in the *TS*, 2.6.6 and the *TB*, 7.13. The *TS*-version tells that three elder brothers of Agni died while carrying oblations to the gods. Afraid of meeting the same fate he escaped and entered the waters. When the gods looking for Agni reached there, the fish told them about his hiding place. At this, Agni cursed the fish that they would be killed by men. The gods requested Agni to come out and become their oblation-bearer. Agni finally agreed when he got the assurance that the offerings which fall outside the altar shall go to his brothers (*TS*, 2.6.6).

Another version, with some variation, is found in the *TB*, 7.13. According to it when Agni fled away from gods, he assumed the form of a mole and entered the earth. The story of Agni's flight also appears in *TS*, 6.2.8; *Bṛhaddevatā* 7.6.1.77 and *ŚB*, 1.2.3.1.

Apart from being called a dear friend of Yama (*ṚV*, 10.21.5) Agni along with Yama is adored with praises (*ṚV*, 10.64.3). The *AV*, 3.31 is addressed to *pāpmahā* Agni and here Agni is prayed to unbind the cords of death from which a *brahmacārin* seeks to be released.

At some places the word *Yama* is used as a name for Agni (*ṚV*, 1.66.8). Sāyaṇa also points out that here Agni is called Yama.[54] Here the word *Yama* which also means 'a twin' is used for Agni, because he and Indra are said to be twins. Agni is also called Yama from $\sqrt{yam}$ ~ *yaccha* = to give, because he grants the worshipper all his cherished desires.[55]

The *ŚB*, 7.1.1.1 even establishes an identity between Yama and Agni and where it is said that king Yama is the same as the *Gārhapatya* fire. The place of the *Gārhapatya* fire is swept with a *palāśa*-branch and *palāśa* is believed to be an emblem of Yama.[56] The *ŚB*, 7.2.1.10 also says that Yama indeed is Agni and according to the *JB* Agni is death (*JB*, 1.332; III. 348).

Yama and Soma

The Fathers are said to belong to Soma and hence Soma comes to be indirectly connected with Yama, the lord of the Fathers. In the *ṚV*, 8.48.15 where Soma is prayed, he is said to be in the company of the Fathers.[57] In the *ŚB*, II.6.1.4 the Fathers are repeatedly called *Somavantaḥ*. Here Soma is called *pitṛmat*. The *TB*, 2.6.16.2 also connects Soma with the Fathers. According to *ŚB*, 2.4.2.12 Soma is the god of the Fathers. The Fathers are also called *somyāsaḥ*, i.e., Soma-loving or connected with Soma[58] (*ṚV*, 10.14.6; 15.1; *AV*, 2.12.5).

In the *ṚV*, 10.57.3-5 Soma-*nārāśaṁsa* and the Fathers are mentioned together in connection with the sacrifice to the Fathers. According to Sāyaṇa the *nārāśaṁsa* Soma is the Soma connected with the Fathers.[59] Soma is always invoked in the rituals for the Fathers and he is especially the deity at the *pitṛmedha* (*VS*, III.56).[60] At the offering of the *piṇḍa-pitṛyajña*, Soma is invoked as *kavyavāhana*.[61] It is to be noted here that the *kavyavāhana* is a form of Agni, especially connected with the Fathers as their oblation-bearer.

The *MS*, 1.10.18 calls Soma as the god of the Fathers. Here, he is also called *pitṛmat*.[62] It is said here that the offering made to Soma are considered as offered to the Fathers because Soma indeed is the god of the Fathers. In the *VS*, 2.29 also Soma is called *pitṛmat*. Thus Soma, who is often spoken of as god of the Fathers, and Yama who is the lord of the Fathers *pitṛṇām adhipatiḥ* — (*AV*, 5.24.14) are connected with each other through the Fathers. Though it is difficult to see an identification between Soma and Yama,[63] there is a distinct relationship between Soma, the god of the Father and Yama, the lord of the Fathers.

Soma, conjointly with Yama, Varuṇa, Aśvins and others

is prayed to save the worshipper from death (*mṛtyu*) (*AV*, 19.20.1). Another verse says that one, who prepares *viṣṭārin brahmodana* for the priest, lives happily with Yama in the company of the *Gandharvas*, who are connected with *Soma* (*AV*, 4.34.3). Soma is believed to be the extract of the *Soma*-plant[64] mixed with milk or honey, which was offered to the gods. The sacrificer too partook this sacrificial drink after offering it to the gods, Soma was deemed as the best offering to the gods (*uttamaṁ haviḥ*, *ṚV*, 9.86.10).

It is quite clear from the Vedic reference that *Soma* is primarily a sacred ritual drink. Gradually it became so closely associated with the moon to have become another name for *Candramas* (moon).

The *ṚV*, 9.41.5 says that Soma fills the earth and sky with its rays.[65] In the *AV*, 11.6.7 the identity of Soma with *candramas* (moon) is established.[66] The *ŚB*, 2.4.2.7 states that this indeed is Soma who is called *Candramas*, the food of the gods.[67] It is clear that the moon came to be regarded as the drink of the gods. It diminishes in size, when it is being consumed and then gradually regains its original size after a given time.

According to Hillebrandt Soma in the *ṚV* always stands for *Candramas*[68] and also that these five gods viz. Varuṇa, Āpāṁnapāt, Bṛhaspati, Yama and Soma are closely connected with *Candramas*.

This view is, however, strongly criticized by many other scholars[69] R.N. Dandekar observes that Varuṇa's apparent identity with Soma which constitutes one of the main planks in Hillebrandt's hypothesis can be more adequately explained by assuming that it was perhaps a conscious attempt on the part of later Soma-priests to glorify Soma by bringing him in contact with Varuṇa, the world-sovereign.[70] Soma is also identified with Viṣṇu, Śiva, Kuber, etc.[71] R.N. Dandekar asserts that *Soma* is primarily the sacred ritual drink which fact would be quite clear from the Vedic references. The identification of Soma with the moon can only be a secondary character and may be regarded as a product of poetical fancy.[72] Thus, according to R.N. Dandekar Hillebrandt's assertion that Soma is essentially identical with the moon (*HVM*, I.282 ff.) is quite unconvincing.

Yama's direct association with Soma (as *candramas*) is seen in *JB*, 1.246 where Yama is said to be residing in the heart of the moon. Also, the *JB*, 1.28 equates the mythological hare in the moon with Yama — "This indeed is a hare in the moon . . . . This indeed is Yama that is seen in the moon. He indeed controls everything" (*JB*, 1.28).

Yama and Nirṛti

A consistent account of Nirṛti's personality and her bearings is found in the *ṚV* down to the *Brāhmaṇas*. She is depicted as a goddess having malevolent qualities and hence is regarded with fear and apprehension. It is prayed that Nirrti should not harm the worshipper or his kith and kin. The *ṚV*, 10.59 is addressed to Nirṛti imploring her to leave the sacrifice alone and depart from the place of the sacrifice so that no harm might come. The refrain of the hymn is a prayer to Nirṛti asking her to leave the sacrifice and go to distant places.

According to Sāyaṇa Nirṛti is *pāpa-devatā*, i.e., an evil-goddess[73] and *rakṣojāti-devatā*.[74] Sāyaṇa has also mentioned her as Mṛtyu-*devatā*, the goddess of death.[75] The *ṚV*, 10.16.1 (*AV*, 3.1.1) is used to bring a patient back from Nirṛti's lap. If one is said to be sleeping in Nirṛti's lap it is meant that he is dead (*ṚV*, 10.95.14). This shows that she is connected with deseases and death. In the *ṚV*, 1.38.6 Nirṛti's name is accompanied by the word *durhaṇā*, which is a substantive for harm or mischief,[76] and also by *durvidātra*,[77] meaning ill-disposed; envious. J. Gonda comments that there is a tendency in the *ṚV* that generally no epithets are given to the words for unfavourable happenings, formidable beings, terrible concepts and subjects; in short, all manifestations of evil are generally speaking left without epithetical attributes. It was considered wise, J. Gonda[78] believes, to conceal the attributes of their qualities and properties, not to ascribe any honour to them and not to add to their powers and influence by using epithets which could be regarded as praise. But one of the exceptions to this tendency is Nirṛti, the goddess of disorder and destruction who is styled as *durvidātra* (*ṚV*, 10.36.2) which is used to typify the inimical behaviour of the injurious or malacious (*arātim durvidātram*— *ṚV*, 10.63.12) and a wicked person (*manyum durvidatrasya*—*ṚV*, 10.35.4).[79]

Nirṛti is also portrayed as terrible (*VS*, 12.64) and wicked (*ŚB*, 7.2.1.3). She is described as black, horrible, holding a noose (*TS*, 4.2.5.3) — an iron-noose (*VS*, 12.63) and also sharp weapons.[80] She is connected with black colour. The *TB*, 1.6.1.4 states that Nirṛti's garments are black and black chaff is her sacrificial fee.[81]

Nirṛti is described as ever-increasing in might (*ṚV*, 1.38.6). She is a great and all-pervading goddess having golden hair (*AV*, 5.7.9) and wearing dark clothes (*TB*, 1.6.1.4). With her connection with black colour it is natural that the factors of chaos and disorderliness are attributed to Nirṛti. When the Vedic Āryans realised that the universe was governed by some definite law and order, owing to which it was a cosmos and not a chaos, this realisation gave birth to the concept of *ṛta*[82] and Varuṇa was conceived as the upholder of *ṛta*.

Later on while applying this cosmic law to a limited sphere, i.e., the world, it was observed that some happenings seem to be breaking the cosmic law and oder (*ṛta*). These happenings of unorderliness are seen in the form of diseases and disasters. Death (i.e., untimely death), difficulties, poverty, barrenness are regarded as abnormal[83] conditions. On the analogy of Varuṇa, who is the upholder of *ṛta*, Nirṛti was conceived as personifying such unorderliness or aberration of order.[84] Thus Nirṛti can be regarded as a linguistic feminine negative counterpart of *ṛta*.

Fatah Singh observes that Nirṛti obviously appears to be the negation of *ṛtiḥ* which is probably another form of *ṛtam* and it would mean cessation or negation of *ṛta*.[85] But S.K. Lal finds no connection between *ṛta* and Nirṛti. According to him "Nirṛti has no connection with Ṛta, not even negatively or as its opposite element. It appears that the concept of Ṛta and Nirṛti developed independently".[86]

Nirṛti is also connected with sudden death. The *AB*, 4.10 states "the *hotṛ* wrests from the hands of Nirṛti her cords and puts them down while repeating the *Dvipadā* verse". The verse says: "May she who is the ruler of all that is born and moves not be angry (with us), not visit us (with destruction)." He does so for attaining his full age. He, who has such a knowledge, attains his full age. This passage shows that Nirṛti's displeasure can cause destruction as well as untimely death.

If the oblation meant for any god gets burnt, it would show that Nirṛti has taken hold of that sacrifice. She takes over the offerings made in that sacrifice. If, therefore, the offering gets burnt, one should suspend the sacrifice and again prepare the offerings for the original deity. The burnt portion of the oblation should be given away, by way of *dakṣiṇā*, to the sacrificer's enemy; thereby Nirṛti seizes the enemy.[87]

Moreover, Nirṛti is said to take possession of a wife, who has no sons (*ŚB*, 5.3.1.13).[88] She also seizes upon that part of soil in which no plants are produced. This shows that Nirṛti is connected with the barrenness of land as well as that of women.

According to another view Nirṛti is not the presiding deity of lawlessness, chaos or disorder. She is "the evil spirit that grapples men when they violate Ṛta. She is nowhere associated with Varuṇa even as a negation of Ṛta".[89]

But Nirṛti cannot be taken as only a punisher, because a punisher inflicts punishment when the person has committed some crime, while Nirṛti is said to be causing harm even otherwise as she brings death, destruction and calamity. Moreover, Nirṛti cannot be regarded as a punisher only, because in that case neither her dark bearings nor the repeated prayers of the sacrificer's imploring her to depart to the distant places can be explained.

Nirṛti is also seen as a goddess of the earth. According to Fatah Singh "Nirṛti derived from *ni* + √*ṛ* is *Pṛthivī*.[90] Yāska gives two derivations of the word Nirṛti.[91] They are:

(1) *ni* + √*ram*, and (2) *ni* + √*ṛ*.

Durgācārya's commentary is helpful in understanding the full derivation from both the roots. According to him Nirṛti is the Earth and it is derived from √*ram* = 'to enjoy', because creatures living on the earth rejoice here. The other derivation of Nirṛti is from √*ṛ* which would mean calamity, pain and sorrow.[92] It has been rightly pointed out that derivation of Nirṛti from √*ram* is loose due to the disregard to the vowels, since *r* in *ram* could have no correspondence to *ṛ* in old Indo-Āryan.[93]

The second derivation of Nirṛti from *ni* + √*ṛ* means misery, absence of prosperity.[94] Mahīdhara in his commentary on the *VS*, 12.63 expresses Nirṛti as calamity and also as Earth.[95] V.K. Rajwade renders Nirṛti as 'piercing poverty'[96] which, according to Siddheshwar Varma, may be corrected into 'degenerating'.[97]

The traditionally handed down meanings of the word Nirṛti show a dichotomy in the nature of Nirṛti as (1) blissful because Nirṛti is 'the earth' on which creatures live happily and (2) as a source of calamity. Thus Nirṛti is said to be blissful as well as a source of misery. This contradiction can be explained in the context of geological calamities. The earth undergoes upheavels due to earthquakes and volcanoes. Due to these events the same blissful earth becomes the cause of death and destruction. Thus the two meanings of Nirṛti (i.e., (1) the earth and (2) calamity) are not contradictory.[98]

Direction of Nirṛti

Nirṛti is connected with the south-west direction of which she is the presiding deity. The *VS*, 9.35 refers to the oblations to be offered to Nirṛti in the south-west and in other direction for their presiding deities. The *TB*, 1.6.1.2 states that the south-west is her quarter where she reigns. A place where the soil is saline by nature (*svakṛta-iriṇa*)[99] or a cleft (*pradara*) is her abode (*TS*, 5.2.33). She is offered oblations in the Nairṛtya (south-west) direction at an *iriṇa* (i.e., a place where the soil in saline) (*ŚB*, 5.2.3.2-3). because the saline land belongs to Nirṛti.[100] The *Kauśika Sūtra*, XIII.28 recommends propitiatory rites in case of sudden cleft in ground in the village, or house, on fire-house or meeting place.[101]

Yamī and Nirṛti

Yamī and Nirṛti are both equated with the Earth. In the *TS*, 3.3.8 it is said Yama is Agni, this earth (i.e., the altar) is Yamī,[102] while the *TS*, 4.2.5 states "As earth men know thee, Nirṛti, I know thee on everyside." But it is difficult to find an identification between Yamī and Nirṛti. The malevolent features of Nirṛti's nature are obvious, while this cannot be said of Yamī. In the *Brāhmaṇas* also Nirṛti is not directly equated with Yamī.[103] It is also noteworthy that Nirṛti does not represent the earth as a whole, but only a part of it which is barren and uncultivable. The *ŚB*, 7.2.1.8 says "on whatever part of earth there is a cleaving or in whatever part of it plants do not grow, indeed, that part of earth is Nirṛti." In the context of the *Rājasūya* sacrifice in the *ŚB*, 5.2.3.3 and 7.2.10.8, the sacrificer takes a fire-brand from the *anvāhārya-pacana* (e.g., the southern) fire and therewith goes southwards. And where he finds a natural cleft, having made up a fire there he offers with the *VS*, 9.35. "This, Nirṛti! is thy portion, accept it gracefully, hail! For Nirṛti is this (earth), whomsoever she seizes upon with evil him she seizes upon with destruction (*nirṛti*), hence whatever part of this (earth) is of Nirṛti nature that he thereby propitiates and thus Nirṛti does not seize upon him while being consecrated. And the reason why he offers in a self-produced hollow or cleft is that, that much of this (earth) is possessed by Nirṛti."[104]

Some element of similarity is noticeable in the personalities of Yama and Nirṛti. The lap of Nirṛti is considered to be death (*ṚV*, 10.161.2; 10.95.14; *AV*, 3.11.2). The *ṚV*, 10.161.2; *AV*, 3.11.2 are used to bring back a sick man from the lap of Nirṛti. Nirṛti is punisher who binds the offender with a rope around his neck (*AV*, 6.63.1). Like Yama she holds a noose (*TS*, 4.2.53) which is an iron-noose (*AV*, 6.63.1). Freedom from the rope of Nirṛti means a long life, strength and vigour (*AV*, 6.63.1).

Nirṛti and Yama are both connected with evil-dreams. In the *ṚV*, 10.164, Yama is the god invoked for dispelling evil-dreams. The *AV*, 6.27-29 are employed for dispelling evil-dreams and they are addressed to Yama and Nirṛti conjointly.

The dove and the owl, who are the messengers of Yama are also said to be Nirṛti's messengers (*AV*, 6.27.1; 6.29.2).

In spite of Nirṛti having attributes like a noose, dove and owl as her messengers and her connection with evil-dreams which are same as Yama's, there is no similarity in the function of the two. Nirṛti is basically a goddess of death, destruction and disorder, while Yama is the ruler of the departed souls. Therefore, Nirṛti cannot be safely called a female counterpart of Yama.[105] It is only in the later Vedic literature and more fully in the Epic and the Purāṇic literature that Yama came to be connected with death, one of his main tasks being that of taking away the lives. This later aspect of Yama is nearer to that of Nirṛti.

In the Vedic literature where Yama is equated with Mṛtyu (he is even called *mārayitre* which means 'destroyer, killer') it is quite possible to connected her with Yama, possibly as a female counterpart from the functional point of view.

Notes

1. For details see 'Classification of the gods' in chapter 1.
2. *mā . . . . pathā Yamasya gād upa* /— ṚV, 1.38.5.
   Yamasya jātam amṛtam yajāmahe /— ṚV, 1.83.5.
   Yaména tatam paridhim /— ṚV, 7.33.9.
   yatra rājā Vaivasvato . . . . tatra mām amṛtam kṛdhi /— ṚV, 9.113.8.
3. Asko Parpola, *The Sky Garment, Studia Orientalia*, Vol. 57, p. 37.
4. ṚV, 1.24.8; 4.1.2; 5.40.7; *AV*, 3.4.5; 6.
5. R.N. Dandekar, *VMT*, p. 54.
6. With his *pāśa* (noose) Varuṇa holds the universe, for he is the binder god (*Ueru - n - OS) and regulates its movements (ṚV, 7.84.2; 10.149.1). Linguistically Varuṇa is best derived from √*Uer = to bind. *Vide* R.N. Dandekar, *op. cit.*, p. 58. Its other derivation, i.e., from √*vṛ*/ to cover (*Nir*, 10.4 *Varuṇo vṛṇotīti sataḥ*, also *yacca vṛtvā atiṣṭha tad Varuṇo abhavat*), does not cover all the important traits of this god's personality. Secondarily, in that case its form would be Varūṇa. . . . . *vide* R.N. Dandekar, *op. cit.*, p. 35.

   Theime (in 'Mitra and Aryaman') combines part of two distant theories viz. Lüuder's equation *ṛta* = truth and Müller's derivation of Varuṇa from IE √*ver* 'to speak' and proposes that Varuṇa means 'true speech' . . . . *vide* R.N. Dandekar, *op. cit.*, p. 319.

7. *yau setṛbhir arajjubhih sinīthaḥ/*— ṚV, 7.84.2.
8. *Varuṇa eva Varuṇapāśena gṛhṇāti yad pāpmana gṛhito bhavati/*— *TS*, 2.3.13.
9. *anṛte khalu kriyamāṇe Varuṇo gṛhṇāti/*— *TB*, 1.7.2.6.
10. ṚV, 7.84.2; 10.149.1.
11. *ŚB*, 1.3.1.16 *Varuṇo vai granthiḥ Vāruṇyā vā eṣā yad rajjuḥ/*— *vide* also *ŚB*, 5.2.5.16; 6.4.3.8, *KB*, 5.3.
12. *svayam sa yakṣmaṁ hṛdaye ni dhatta/*— ṚV, 1.122.9.
13. H.H. Wilson, Tran. ṚV, 1.122.9. "The folk, O Mitra and Varuṇa ! who hate you, who sinfully hating pour you no libations, lay in their heart, themselves a wasting sickness, whereas the righteous gaineth all by worship."

    R.T.H. Griffith, *Hymns of the Ṛgveda*, Vol. 1., p. 168.
14. V.S. Apte, *Student's Practical Dictionary*, Part-III, p. 1297.
15. *yad emi prasphuran iva dṛtiḥ na dhmātaḥ/*— ṚV, 7.89.2.
16. R.T.H. Griffith, *op. cit.*, p. 85.
17. Also ṚV, 7.63.1; 10.37.1.
18. *hiraṇyapakṣam Varuṇasya dūtam/* — ṚV, 10.123.6.
19. *ato viśvāni adbhuta cikitvān abhi paśyati/*

    kṛtāni ya ca kartvā/— ṚV, 1.25.11.
20. *Varuṇāya mahiṣān ā labhate/*— *VS*, 24.28.
21. Satvalekar observes that this messenger of Yama is the sun who shines like gold and helps Varuṇa in bringing rains — S.D. Satvalekar, *AVSB*, 18th *kāṇḍa*, p. 49.
22. See 'Yama and Yami' chapter 4.
23. S. Bhattacharji, *Indian Theogony*, p. 83.
24. Fatah Singh, *Vedic Etymology*, p. 112.

    According to S.K. Lal (*JOIB*, XXXIV p. 310) Nirṛti has no connection with *ṛta* even negatively.
25. *tasmai Yamāya namo astu mṛtyave/*—ṚV, 10.165.4.
26. See "Yama and Mṛtyu" chapter 2.
27. *mṛtyur vai Varuno* — *KS*, 13.2; cf *ŚB*, 12.7.2.17.
28. Asko Parpola, *op. cit.*, p. 65; cf. J. Eggeling, *ŚB*, *SBE*, Vol. 44, p. XVIII ff.
29. ṚV, 10.90.
30. R.N. Dandekar, *VMT*, p. 29.
31. *Ibid.*, p. 62.
32. ṚV, 10.16.9.
33. H.H. Wilson, *Ṛgveda Saṁhitā*, Trans. Vol. 6, p. 52.
34. *tam harāmi pitṛyajñāya/*— ṚV, 10.16.10.
35. *dakṣinasyām diśi catuṣpathādau aupāsanāgnim nirasyati. uttareṇa śanti karmārthaṁ ādatte*, *ĀŚS*, 22.19.
36. Udgītha's Commentary on ṚV, 10.15.9, *Ṛgveda Saṁhitā*, Vol. IV,

Vaidika Saṁsodhana Maṇḍala, p.327.

37. *kravis — n rohes flaisch kravya-vahana — Leichname (kravya) for fuhrend (vahana von vah)*", Grassmann, *Wörterbuch*, p. 359.
38. S.D. Satvalekar, *AVSB*, Part IV, 18th *kāṇḍa*, p. 94.
39. *TS*, II. 5.8.6.

    VS, 19.64-66, *TB*, 1.6.9.6.
40. A. Hillebrandt, *Vedic Mythology*, tr. by S.R. Sarma, Pt. I, p. 76.
41. A. Hillebrandt, *op. cit.*, p. 387, fn. 196.
42. A.B. Keith, *RPVU*, p. 160.
43. *ayam itaro Jataveda devebhyo havyam vahatu prajānan/— ṚV*, 10.16.9.
44. A.B. Keith, *op. cit.*, p. 160.
45. *āmam apakvaṁ atti iti laukiko aganiḥ/*— Mahīdhara on the *VS*, 1.17.

    yenedaṁ manuṣyāḥ apakvam annam aśyanti sa ucyate — Uvvaṭa on *VS*, 1.17

    āmāt = raw, uncooked — Suryakanta, *Vedic Dictionary*, p. 142.
46. *dve vā agneḥ tanvau havyavāhanyā devebhyo havyaṁ vahati kavyavāhanyā pitṛbhyaḥ — MS*, 10.18.
47. A.B. Keith, Trans. *TS*, *HOS*, p. 544.
48. Sāyaṇa explain that Agni is called Yama because the place of sacrifice is fixed (*niyata*) and the earth which is prepared as the altar is Yami *Yamo agniḥ tasya eva homādhāra niyatatvāt. iyaṁ vedi rupā bhūmiḥ Yamī* — Sāyaṇa on *TS*, 3.3.8.
49 *Vide* Sāyaṇa on the *ṚV*, 10.51.3.
50. R.T.H. Griffith, *The Hymns of Ṛgveda*, trans. Vol. II, p. 453.
51. *Vide* Sāyaṇa on the *ṚV*, 10.51.6.
52. *Ṛg-veda Saṁhitā*, tr. by H.H. Wilson, Vol. 6, p. 172.
53. *Agniratra yama ucyate* — Sāyaṇa on *ṚV*, 1.66.8.
54. *Indrāgnyor yugapat utpannatvāt Agner yamatvam*— Sāyaṇa on *ṚV*, 1.66.8.

    Yamo ha jāto Indreṇa saha saṁgataḥ — *Nir*, 10.21.

    yacchati stotṛbhyaḥ kamān iti Yamo agnir ucyate/— Nir, 10.21.
55. S. Bhattacharji, *Indian Theogony*, p. 105.
56. *tvam Soma pitṛbhih saṁvidānaḥ/— ṚV*, 8.43.13.
57. Suryakanta, *Vedic Dictionary*, p. 721.
58. 10.57.3—*naraiḥ śansyante iti nārāśaṁsah pitaraḥ teṣām camasām kampanam eva homaḥ tathā vidhena somena* — Sāyaṇa on the *ṚV*, 10.57.3.
59. *atra pitṛyajñe somanāmako devo asti*—Mahīdhara on the *VS*, III.56.
60. S. Bhattacharji, *Indian Theogony*, p. 106.
61. *Somo vai pitṛṇām devatā pitṛdevatyam Soma yat Soma pitṛmantam yajati somapāṁs/ tān pitṛn yajati/— MS*, 1.10.18.
62. Hillebrandt strongly asserts that Soma is essentially identical with

moon (*HVM*, p. 202). He also takes Yama to be a moon-god (*HVM*, p. 227). Following this equation Yama comes to be identified with Soma.

63. Some scholars entertain a different view.
64. *sa pavasva vicarṣaṇa ā mahī rodasī pṛṇa/ Uṣāḥ Sūryo na raśmibhiḥ/* — *ṚV*, 9.41.5. In such passages as this where Soma is mentioned as filling heaven and earth with light, it is temping to identify him with *candramas*.

    S.S. Bhawe, translates it as follows: "Such thou active one! flow on well, fill in the great heaven and earth with rays like sun and the dawn" — *Soma Hymns in ṚV*, Pt. II, p. 81.
65. *Somo mā devo muñcatu yamāhuḥ candramā iti/*— *AV*, 11.6.7.
66. *eṣa vai Somo devānām annaṁ yat Candramāḥ/*— *ŚB*, 2.4.2.7.
67. A. Hillebrandt, *HVM*, tr. by S. Rajeswar Sarma, Pt. I, p. 202.
68. A.A. Macdonell, *VM*, p. 113.
69. E.W. Hopkins, *The Religions of India*; A.B. Keith, *RPVU*, vol. I, p. 117.
70. R.N. Dandekar, *VMT*, p. 50.
71. Williams Monier, *The Sanskrit-English Dictionary*, p. 53.
72. R.N. Dandekar, *VMT*, p. 50.
73. Sāyaṇa's commentary on the *ṚV*, 7.104.9.
74. Sāyaṇa on the *ṚV*, 1.38.6.
75. Sāyaṇa on the *ṚV*, 10.36.2.
76. J. Gonda, *Epithets in the Ṛgveda*, p. 131.

    Sāyaṇa however, takes *durhaṇā* as 'hard to be killed'.
77. *ṚV*, 10.36.2; (Commentary on *ṚV*, 1.38.6) and Griffith as 'hard to be conquered'.
78. J. Gonda, *op. cit.*, p. 32 f.
79. *Vide* J. Gonda, *op. cit.*, p. 131.
80. *ŚB*, 7.2.1.1; 7.2.1.10-11; *AB*, 2.15; *Nir*, 2.28.
81. *kṛṣṇam vāsaḥ, kṛṣṇa tūṣam dakṣiṇā etat vai nirṛtyai rūpam/*— *TB*, 1.6.1.9.
82. Cf. J.R. Joshi, *Some Minor Divinities in Vedic Mythology and Ritual*, p. 152.
83. J.R. Joshi, *op. cit.*, p. 152.
84. *Ibid.*
85. Fatah Singh, *Vedic Etymology*, p. 112.
86. S.K. Lal, "Nirṛti", *JOIB*, XXIV (3-4) 1975, p. 301.
87. *ĀŚS*, 9.15.6-9.
88. *yā vā aputrā patnī sā Nirṛti-gṛhītā/*— *ŚB*, 5.3.1.13.
89. S. Bhattacharji, *Indian Theogony*, pp. 82-83.
90. Fatah Singh, *Vedic Etymology*, p. 151.
91. *tatra nirṛtir niramaṇāt ṛcchateḥ kṛcchāpattir itarā* — *Nir*, 2.7.
92. *niviṣṭāni ramante asyām bhūtāni iti nirṛti pṛthivī ram dhātoḥ, ṛcchateḥ itarā kṛcchāpattir duḥkha saṁjñikā nirṛtiḥ pāpmā/*— Durgācārya on *Nir*, 2.7.

. . . *nirṛtiḥ* (earth) *is* (so-called) from giving enjoyment; the other word (*nirṛtiḥ*), which signifies calamity, is derived from (the root) √ṛ (to befall) . . . ."

Lakshman Sarup, Trans. *Nir*, 2.7.

93. S. Varma, *Etymologies of Yāska*, p. 110.
94. √ṛ = to go, to = injure — Suryakanta, *Vedic Dictionary*, p. 220.
95. *nirṛtiḥ kṛcchāpattiḥ/ syād alakṣmīstu nirṛtiriti abhidhānāt bhūmir vā nirṛti digabhimāninī devatā/*— Mahīdhara on the *VS*, 12.63.
96. V.K. Rajwade, *Yāska's Nirukta, Text and Exegetical notes*, p. 334.
97. S. Varma, *op. cit.*, p. 137.
98. Cf. P.V. Pathak and J.P. Nayak, *Tectonic Upheavals in the Indus-region and some Ṛgvedic humns* (Part-III); Nirṛti and significance of oblations to Nirṛti at Iriṇa, *ABORI*, LXVII, 1986, pp. 265-69.
99. Sāyaṇa takes *iriṇa* here in the sense of *ūṣara* a place with barren (or saline) soil.
100. Cf. *ŚB*, 7.2.18 — "in whatever part of it the plants are not produced, verily, that part of it Nirṛti seizes upon."
101. A. Weber, *Omina Und Portenta*, p. 386 — referred to by J. Eggeling trans. *ŚB*, *SBE*, Vol. 41, p. 43.
102. Sāyaṇa comments that this earth in the form of altar is Yamī. also, *ŚB*, 5.2.3.3 — *iyam pṛthivī vai nirṛtiḥ*.
103. Cf. S. Bhattacharji, *op. cit.*, p. 93.
104. J. Eggeling, trans. *ŚB*, *SBE*, Vol. 41, p. 43.
105. Cf. S. Bhattacharji, *op. cit.*, p. 80.

4

Yama's Personality and His Functions

Yama's Sovereignty

In the *ṚV* as well as in later Vedic texts Yama is constantly called *rājan* (a king). This suggests that he was the king of a particular region (*ṚV*, 9.113.8; 10.14.1). This region is situated in *parame vyoman* (*ṚV*, 10.14.8) and according to Sāyaṇa *parame vyoman* refers to *svarga* (heaven). Yama's region is the abode of the Fathers too, where they live blissfully in the company of their lord Yama (*AV*, 5.2.14; *ŚB*, 7.1.14). Thus Yama is the king of the dead who reach his kingdom after death.

Yama is fondly remembered as the 'first to die' (*AV*, 18.3.13). After passing through death himself, he found out a new path and finally secured a settlement for all the people who died (*ṚV*, 10.14.2). The concept of a pioneer of a new path and finder of a new realm has its natural extension in the concept of his sovereignty over that newly found region.

Yama's association with Varuṇa is significant for establishing the former's own sovereignty, when the deceased reaches the highest heaven, he finds king Yama and Varuṇa rejoicing in the *svadhā* oblations offered to them (*ṚV*, 10.14.7). Varuṇa, the typical sovereign in the Vedic mythology, guards the cosmic order (*ṚV*, 7.86.1; 6.70.1; 5.69.4). It is said that by the law of Varuṇa heaven and earth are held apart (*ṚV*,

7.86.1; 6.70.1); he made a path for sun (*Ṛ*V, 1.24.8); he (with Mitra) supports heaven and earth (*ṚV*, 5.69.4). As a righteous king Varuṇa punishes the evil-doers (*ṚV*, 7.85.3). Yama's association with Varuṇa suggests his equally high status of a sovereign. Yama is mentioned as holding a *padbīśa* (*ṚV*, 10.97.16) which can be regarded as a symbol of his sovereignty just as the *pāśa* is of Varuṇa (*ṚV*, 1.24.15; 6.74.4; 10.85.24). A.A. Macdonell observes that Yama's foot-fetter (*padbīśa*) is spoken of as parallel to the bond of Varuṇa.[1]

It is said that Varuṇa grabs a person who breaks the sacred order (*TB*, 1.7.2.6)[2] and it is earnestly prayed: "May I be retrieved from the *pāśa* of Varuṇa and the *paḍbīśa* of Yama" (*ṚV*, 10.97.16, also *VS*, 7.112.2; 9.96.2). This suggests that Yama too punished the defaulters with his *paḍbīśa* as Varuṇa did with the *pāśa*. In the capacity of a punisher he is close to Varuṇa. Punishing the guilty, being one of the most important duties of a sovereign, Yama's sovereignty is evident. R.N. Dandekar observes that the possession by Yama of *paḍbīsa* corresponds to the *pāśa* of Varuṇa. This may be regarded as a symbol of sovereignty and seems to be one of the remnants of Yama's kingship.[3]

A *paḍbīśa* is a *pāda-bandhanam*,[4] i.e., something by which one of confined by foot. The *paḍbīśa* is mentioned more frequently in connection with the trying of a horse (*ṚV*, 1.162.14; *VS*, 25.28) and it may presumably be a rope/ chain/noose mentioned in the *Purāṇas* with which Yama or his assistants binds/bind the evil-doers for taking them away to Yama's region.[5] In the *Purāṇas* Yama is described as holding a *pāśa* which he or (on some occasions) his *dūtas*[6] use for binding the people, whose period of life on earth is over, and taking them to Yama's kingdom.

Lord of the Earth

Yama, who is basically the king of the other world where the Fathers are his subject, is also mentioned as the overlord of the earth. Some scattered pieces of evidence surely suggest his original sovereignty over earth.

According to the *ṚV*, 10.14.9, Yama grants the required

piece of land for performing the cremation of the deceased. (*ṚV*, 10.14.9, *VS*, 35.1, *TS*, 4.2.3), because he is the overlord of the earth. The *AGS*, 4.2.10 states that for preparing the place for cremation, the Adhvaryu priest sweeps the cremation place with a branch of *śamī* tree, while reciting *apeta vīta* (*ṚV*, 10.14.7). This *ṛc* is addressed to the fiends, etc. who might be residing at that place. They are told to leave the ground and move to far-off places since that ground is given to the deceased by Yama himself.

This stanza (i.e., 10.14.9) also appears in the *VS* with a slight variation (*VA*, 35.1). The second hemistich of the *VS*, 35.1 is same as the *ṛc* with only one change of *dadāti* to *dadātu*. The first hemistich begins with *apeta vīta* as the *ṚV*, 10.14.9 with the rest part of it being variant. With the recitation of this *VS*-stanza the Paṇis who are the enemies of the gods (*devapīyavaḥ*) are told to leave the place which is being prepared for the *pitṛmedha*. According to the *Kātyāyana-Śrauta-Sūtra*, 21.2.32, the ground is to be swept with a *palāśa* branch or with *śamī* branch according to *AGS*, 4.2.10, with the recitation of *apeta vīta*.

The *VS*, 35.1 and following stanzas are in connection with the '*pitṛmedha* rites' and according to Mahīdhara this ritual is called *varṣā-smaraṇam* (Mahīdhara's comm. on *VS*, 35.1). Commenting on this group of *mantras* Mahīdhara quotes the *Kātyāyana-Śrauta-Sūtra* and the *Yajus-pariśiṣṭa*. He explains the details of the ritual connected with the making of a *samādhi* of the deceased, in which a pot containing the bones of the deceased is deposited in a pit specially prepared, in accordance with the prescribed measurement, for the purpose and these *mantras* are recited during this ritual. The *VS*, 35.1, *apeta vīta* is recited at the time of cleaning the place for funeral rites, but Mahīdhara explains it in a different context. While the *ṛc* is for the cremation of a dead body, the *VS*, 35.1 is according to Mahīdhara, for preparing a *samādhi* by placing the bones of the deceased in a special pit prepared for this purpose, according to the prescription of the *śūlva-sūtra*.

Thus it is seen that the stanza *apeta vīta* (*ṚV*, 10.14.9 as well as *VS*, 35.1) is recited at the time of the ritual-cleaning of the place of cremation-rites. It is interesting to note that this stanza also occurs in the *VS* (12.45) with a different background. The context here, i.e., *VS*, 12.45 is that of preparation of the *Gārhapatya* fire and the stanza is as under:

> *apeta vīta vi ca sarpatāta ye atrā sthā purāṇā ye ca nūtanāḥ/*
>
> *adāt yamo avasānaṁ pṛthivya akrḥ imaṁ pitaro lokaṁ asmai/*
>
> — *VS*, 12.45

The similarity of this stanza with the *ṚV*, 10.14.9 and *VS*, 35.1 apparent, and even where the words are different, the purport is more or less the same as that of the aforesaid stanzas. But it is important to note that the context is absolutely different here. While the *ṚV*, 10.14.9 and the *VS*, 35.1 both are in connection with the cremation rites, the present stanza *VS*, 12.45 is connected with the preparation for a sacrifice. This shows that Yama grants permission for using the required portion of land, be it for the cremation of the dead or for the sacrificial purposes. The *VS*, 12.45 is recited at the *gārhapatya-cayana* (*Kātyāyana-Śrauta-Sūtra*, 17.1.1).[7]

Mahīdhara comments that this stanza is addressed to the servants of Yama who might be present there. According to him Yama being the lord of the whole earth, his servants move at every place[8] and with this stanza they are told to move away, because Yama gave this place to the *yajamāna* (sacrificer).

Yama's overlordship over the earth is mentioned at several places. The *TS*, 3.45.1 mentions that Yama is the overlord of the earth just as Agni is of the creatures, Indra of the *lokapālas*, Vāyu of the atmosphere and Sūrya of the sky.[9]

The *MS*, 3.2.3 states that Yama is the god of this terrestrial region.[10] Thus the whole expanse of earth belongs to Yama. So his permission is necessary for performing any rites in which a section of earth would be used: be it the cremation of a dead person, or the preparation of the fire-altar for performing sacrifices. One, who performs sacrifice without taking Yama's permission, is not entitled to get the fruit of that sacrifice. If a negligent sacrificer piles up the fire-altar without seeking Yama's permission, he piles it up for Yama. Only after reciting the *mantra*—*apeta vīta* (*VS*, 12.45) and having asked Yama's permission thereby to use that portion for the sacrificial purpose, a sacrificer piles the altar for himself (*TS*, 5.3.2; *MS*, 3.2.3; *ŚB*, 7.1.1.2-33). Furthermore by granting his permission Yama grants a debt to the sacrificer. If a sacrificer, therefore, occupies a place for the sacrifice and prepares a fire-altar there, he owes a debt to Yama. This debt can be repaid by completing the sacrifice properly. If he fails to do so, and leaves altar without kindling the fire, Yama's assistants bind him by neck and take him away to the other world (*TS*, 3.3.8.3-4).

Strife for Supremacy

The *TS*, 2.4.2 gives an account of a strife, for gaining supremacy, between the gods and Yama. Yama deprived the gods of their power and he himself gained supremacy. The gods reflected that Yama has become here what we are. From this account it can be deduced that Yama, who was till then the lord of the yonder world only, gained the overlordship of the earth too after the struggle with the gods which Yama won.

In the *ṚV* there is no record of such a strife. S. Bhattacharji observes that Yama was not initially immortal like other gods, but after some struggle with the established gods he wrested power and was raised to the rank of a god.[11] But there is nothing to suggest here (*TS*, 2.4.2) that initially Yama was not a god and he gained the godhood after defeating the gods. This account only tells that Yama gained more power after defeating the gods. It is possible that his gaining the overlordship is suggested here. Thus it can be said that a god who was already the lord of the yonder world and the king of the Fathers defeated other gods and gained the overlordship of the earth too.

The *MS*, 25.11 records Yama's attainment of the overlordship of the earth.[12] The *Brāhmaṇa*-texts highlight the fruit of the sacrifices. The supremacy attained by Yama is attributed to the sacrifice. The *TMB*, 11.10.20 states that by this (sacrifice) Yama inconquerably won the overlordship of the world.[13]

Thus Yama's gaining supremacy is attributed to two factors:

(1) the struggle which he faught with the gods and won, and

(2) by performing some special sacrifice.

Lord of the South Direction

The *ṚV* contains no clear record of Yama's connection with the southern quarter; but in the *AV* he is explicitly connected with the south (*AV*, 9.7.20) of which he is the lord. His abode is also said to be in the southern direction from where he is invited along with the Fathers to receive the oblations offered to them.

But at a few places Indra is mentioned as the lord of the southern quarter, of which at other places Yama is mentioned as the lord (*AV*, 3.27.2, *ŚB*, 3.1.1.7). In the *TS*, 5.5.10 Indra is called the lord of the south and Yama of the *vaśinī*. Sāyaṇa explains *vaśinī* as the down-direction (*adho dik*)[14] which he interprets as *bhūmi*—the earth. According to this explanation Yama is here regarded as the lord of the earth.

In *AV*, 6.28.3 Yama is mentioned as the master of all two-footed and four-footed creatures; here Yama is identified with Mṛtyu (death).

In the *Brāhmaṇas* too, as noted earlier, Yama rules over the settlements of the earth and he grants it to the sacrificer (*ŚB*, 7.1.1.1). Seeking his permission before preparing the fire-altar is obligatory.

According to the *ŚB*, 13.8.2.4 Yama rules over the earth and grants abode to the creatures. The *ŚB*, 2.3.2.1 states that Yama is the ruler of the dead, as well as one of the deities that, 'reside in him that exists'.

Thus it is seen that Yama, who was a lord of the yonder world (heaven), became the lord of earth also. Later he is the lord of southern direction only. Thus a god who is regarded as the lord of the earth, gradually became the lord of south quarter only.

Yama's Connection with Sacrifice

Yama is connected with sacrifice in a special way. Though Manu is called the first sacrificer (*Ṛ*V, 8.43.13; 10.63.7), the *Ṛ*V, 10.13.4 contains an account of Yama having performed a sacrifice and, having offered in it, for the cause of progeny, his own body as the final offering.[15]

In the *Ṛ*V, 10.14.16 Yama is mentioned in connection with the three special Soma-sacrifices, which according to Sāyaṇa are *Jyotiṣṭoma, Gauṣṭoma* and *Āyuṣṭoma* sacrifices. This stanza is translated in the following way — "Yama acquires the three *Trikadruka* sacrifices, the six earths, the one great (moving world); the Triṣṭubh, Gāyatrī, all the sacred metres converge in Yama."[16]

The expression *patati* in this *ṛc* signifies that Yama reaches these sacrifices to protect them. A.A. Macdonell takes the vocable *trikadruka* to mean the 'three Soma-vats' and Soma is described as flying through the three Soma-vats. The subject of the verb *patati* here is Soma according to A.A. Macdonell, Yama according to Sāyaṇa and the dead according to Geldner.

S.S. Dange[17] observes that the idea of Yama being invoked to rush to protect the *trikadruka* does not seem quite convincing, because Yama does not figure at all in other places where the word *trikadruka* occurs (i.e., *Ṛ*V, 1.32.2; 2.11.7; 2.55.1; 22.1; 8.13.18; 92.21). In taking Yama as the subject of the verb *patati*, Sāyaṇa appears to be influenced by the reference of Yama in the previous stanzas of this hymn (i.e., *Ṛ*V, 10.14). Furthermore this verse clearly shows two different ideas contained in the first and the second hemistich. The second hemistich states that the metres are established in (the abode of) Yama. With this also goes the second part of the first hemistich which describes the way to Yama's world and it is said here that the unit of the six worlds[18] has to be crossed to reach the abode of Yama.

In the *AV*, 18.1.32 Yama is said to have entered the sacrifice. This Sāyaṇa explains as "the sacrifice pleased Yama", while Whitney translates it as 'this sacrifice of mine is based on Yama'.[19]

Yama the Judge

In the *ṚV* Yama is mentioned as holding a *paḍbīśa*[20] (foot-fetter) which like the *pāśa* of Varuṇa can be regarded as a means of according punishment. A worshipper prays to be retrieved from the noose of Varuṇa and the fetters of Yama (*ṚV*, 10.97.16; *VS*, 12.90). Here is an indication that Yama, like Varuṇa punished the evil-doers. Yama is prayed to make the worshippers free from sins (*AV*, 3.2.11). The nature of this punishment, however, is not clear. The Vedic texts do not provide anything to suggest that Yama used his foot-fetters for binding people at the hour of death for carrying their lives away. This idea is expressed in the *Purāṇas* and there a rope or chain (*nigaḍa—GP*, 2.23.38) is mentioned. With this rope Yama or his assistant binds (the soul of) a dying person.

In the *Vedas* Yama is principally the king of the Fathers and not the judge of good of evil deeds of men. However, the *ŚB*, 11.2.7.33 says that after his death a man's deeds are mounted on a balance in the yonder world and he attains a good or bad region according to his deeds.[21] It further says that one who realises this fact mounts the balance even in this world; i.e., he is careful about doing good deeds only, and is thus saved from being mounted on balance in the yonder world. The yonder world mentioned here refers to the region of Yama. The *ŚB*, 11.7.3.3 says that the separation of good and evil deeds is done by fire.

The *TA*, 6.5.13[21] has the first clear statement that people are classified as truthful and untruthful in front of Yama. But here too, Yama's role in separating them or judging their actions and awarding punishments accordingly is not very clear. It is significant that the *TA*, 6.5.13 states that the truthful and the liars are separated in the presence of Yama, the king. This may be considered as the earliest reference where Yama is depicted as supervising the separation of the good and the evil. Here the development from the *ŚB*, 11.2.7.33 is clear. In the *tulādhāna* (mounting on a balance), i.e., judging people as good or bad on the basis of their good or evil deeds, Yama's involvement is absent, which is suggested in this later reference (*TA*, 6.5.13). Here it is said that the truthful and the liars (i.e., pious and the evil-doers) are separated before Yama; it can be assumed that this separation is done in order to punish the guilty (sinner) and reward the pious. It may be inferred here that since Yama watches the separation, he also pronounces the reward and punishment to people according to their good or bad deeds. This seems to be a precursor of Yama's role as a judge of the dead, which is well established in the Epics and the *Purāṇas*.

Yama's Benevolence

Like any other Vedic god Yama too is prayed to grant various things to the people. Though Yama is connected with the dead, of whom he is the king, it is significant that he is not considered to be a fearful god. The prayers to him are not offered out of fear as to Rudra.[23] On the contrary Yama is considered to be a kind and benevolent god who himself passed through death, i.e., surrendered his immortality for the cause of progeny and became immortal in a new region. He grants longevity to the living beings; and to the dead a proper place in his kingdom.

In the *ṚV*, 10.14.14 Yama is besought for happiness and long life and also for prosperity and good health (*ṚV*, 10.14.11). The same idea is also found in the *ṚV*, 9.113.7.

In the *AV*, 19.20.1 Yama along with Soma, Varuṇa, Aśvins and Pūṣan is prayed to grant immortality. In the *AV*, 18.3.63; 18.4.54 Yama is prayed for an abundant life. A person praying to become immortal actuality wishes to enjoy a long life on earth[24] and after death, a permanent place in Yama's region (*ṚV*, 9.113.7).[25]

In the *AV*, 16.4.4 Yama is prayed for protection against the difficulties caused by men. In the *AV*, 3.2.11 Yama is prayed for the safe conduct, apparently from this life to the next, and also for deliverance from sins. According to the *TS*, 6.5.13 the righteous and evil-doers are separated under the supervision of Yama. It is, therefore justified that the worshipper prays Yama to free him from the sins. Death is also sought to be warded off with Yama's help. Yama is also a protector of the sacrifices. It is stated in the *AV*, 12.3.8 that Yama and the Fathers protect the vessel of food cooked for the sacrificial purpose.

In the Vedic literature Yama is mainly a king of the departed souls and he is not directly connected with the phenomenon of death. Hence, hardly any element of fear is seen in the hymns addressed to Yama. He is considered to be a king, a protector and a well-wisher of all the dead who reach his region. Though the occasion of death is of profound sadness, and though there are frequent prayers to Yama requesting him to grant a long life, even then Yama is not a feared-god simply because he has no direct connection with death. Though people reach his region after death, he does not cause death. He takes under his wings the soul who reaches his region. Yama announces that by reaching there the dead had became his own. Yama grants him a place in his region and announces that then onwards he, i.e., the dead would receive a portion from the oblations which are offered to him (i.e., Yama) (*AV*, 18.2.37).[26]

The *KaṭhaUp* also provides the details of Yama's personality which is far from fearful. He exhibits extreme politeness and reverence towards a guest by offering him, here Naciketas, three boons for the three nights he had spent at Yama's palace-gate,[27] waiting for him.

It is also significant that when Naciketas' father angrily told him that he had given him (Naciketas) to Mṛtyu, Naciketas was not at all afraid of an encounter with Yama. This proves the point that since Yama does not cause death; he is not a feared god. He is regarded with high esteem and reverence, because he is the lord and protector of people after their death, which is considered to be the surest reality in the earthly life.

Yama: The Creator

According to the *Ṛ*V, 10.10.4 Yamī is a twin-sister of Yama and they are the offsprings of a Gandharva and *apyā-yoṣā*. Sāyaṇa, Udgītha and Mahīdhara take Gandharva and *apyā-yoṣā* to be Vivasvat and Saraṇyū. F. Max Müller holds a similar view.[28]

In the *ṚV* Yamī appears only in the 10th *Maṇḍala*. The *ṚV*, 10.10 contains a dialogue between Yama and Yamī, which appears also in the *AV*, 18.1.1-16. In this dialogue-hymn Yamī, with a desire to procreate asks Yama to oblige her by uniting with her as with a wife. Yama refuses saying that he does not want such relation, since they are brother and sister. Yamī persuades him and says that gods take pleasure in a union like this which is forbidden for the mortals (*ṚV*, 10.10.3).[29] She further adds that no one would know of it (*ṚV*, 10.10.6). Yama, not the least influenced by these arguments, asks her that it is not proper for them to do something which was never done before (*ṚV*, 10.10.4).[30] He further states that no one can escape the watchful eyes of the spies of the gods (*ṚV*, 10.10.8) and that the gods would be offended by such an immoral act. In the *AV*, 18.1.14 Yama says that the idea of a brother and a sister sleeping together is something to which his mind revolts. Yamī argues that they have lain together once in the mother's womb (it would not be a sin to do so again), since the gods have created them to make a conjugal pair even in their mother's womb. (*ṚV*, 10.10.5; *AV*, 18.1.1). But Yama remains unfaltered and rebuffs her saying that such intimacy is considered immoral in which a *salakṣmā* (i.e., akin, a sister) becomes *viṣurūpā* (i.e., non-akin), i.e., a sister becomes a wife.[31] The subsequent ages would come when such deeds would be done. She should, therefore, approach some other man (*ṚV*, 10.10.10). Yamī speaks comtemptuously, when Yama rejects her suit altogether.

The theme of this dialogue has led to an assumption that Yama and Yamī were the parents of humanity and Yamī is thus considered both, 'a sister and a wife of Yama'.[32] In this hymn Yamī, though a *jāmi* to Yama wants to behave like an *ajāmi* and approaches Yama, the only *martya* (i.e., mortal), with a desire for sexual union in order to procreate and start a human progeny.[33] Yamī says, that the gods also desire off-springs from one alone of mankind.[34] Yama gently but firmly turns down this proposal calling such a relation between a brother and a sister as an highly immoral act. Yama's firm and strong denial here gives a glimpse of an important aspect of Yama's character, which later developed in the *Purāṇas* where he is called Dharmarāja, i.e., the upholder of the moral and ethical order. In spite of Yamī's various arguments Yama rejects her request on moral grounds and suggests her to approach some other man; therefore, this hymn does not imply that the incest actually took place, and the humanity originated from it, making Yama and Yamī the parents of the humen race. Furthermore, there is no other reference connecting Yamī with the creation of humanity. Though *ṚV*, 7.33.9; 10.13.4 suggest Yama's role as a procreator, Yamī has no place there. Had the incest actually taken place, the Vedic poets would not have left it without mentioning or suggesting. The hypothesis that the two formed the first human couple whence came the whole race of humans[35] has been rightly challenged by Max Müller and has been discarded.[36]

R.N. Dandekar holds the view that the idea of the origin of the mankind through an incest was very offending to the morality of that age. The poet-seers did not mention it and even left the hymn (*ṚV*, 10.10) incomplete, because if completed, it would have nullified their purpose. "This hymn is evidently a protest against a union that was unobjectionable to the older generation."[37]

The assumption of Yama and Yamī as the parents of humanity is mainly based on similar myths in other primitive mythologies which record an incest and the origin of mankind through it.[38] There is nothing in the *Vedas* to support it.[39]

Though Yama is an Indo-Iranian divinity, there is no warranty for saying that Yamī is also the same, because Yimak who is considered to be the Iranian counterpart of Yamī appears only in the post-Avestan writings.[40] The part of a myth which developed in later writings cannot be foisted upon the earlier writings.[41] Hence the myth of an incest and the origin of the human race, therefrom cannot be considered Indo-Iranian. it seems to have developed independently in the later Iranian literature.

The *Ṛ̣V*, 10.10 and the *AV*, 18.1.1-16 close without giving the slightest indication of Yamī's success in accomplishing her desire. But the hymn looks complete even without it and conveys its meaning emphatically. It depicts Yama speaking again and again against the immoral act in spite of receiving contemptuous remarks from Yamī; so the hymn looks complete and not a torso. The hymn would appear to have ended abruptly and inconclusively only if read with a prejudiced concept of the incest virtually having taken place, as is found in other primitive mythologies. But the Vedic text does not provide any such hint. In the *AV* also this hymn, which occurs there with slight variations, ends at the same juncture as in the *Ṛ̣V*.

The interpretation of myths dealing with incest or awkward sex relations demand extreme care. There are a number of such myths other than that of Yama and Yamī like, the myth of Vṛṣākapi, or Brahmā and Sarasvatī, etc. They do not necessarily indicate a social behaviour.[42] In many cases already floating myths go enacted for rain and prosperity getting Vedic names. On the other hand many such rituals get turned into awkward myths. According to Ulrisch Schneider,[43] in olden times the birth of a twin of opposite sexes was considered evil. Since they although being brother and sister were laid together in the mother's womb (cf. *Ṛ̣V*, 10.10.5, 7). It may, therefore, be said that the *Ṛ̣V*, 10.10 was considered as a part of the ritual to avert the inauspiciousness believed to be brought by the birth of the twins, especially the twins of the opposite sex. Thus this hymn had a ritual application of being recited for the expiation on the birth of such a twin. S.A. Dange observes that an important aspect of the Vedic ritual accounts is the element of sex in it. When such rituals fell back, the mere account that was a word frame for the ritual lost its meaning. According to him the Yama-Yamī or Vṛṣākapi and other such myths were developed from original rituals and these are the cases where ritual produced wrong myths. Hence what appears to be a mythical account was never a myth but only a description and the guidelines to the ritualists and "though somewhat elliptical to later generations it was a formula — like indication for the ancient people." These ritual accounts became myths at a stage when the original tradition was lost, as in the case of Yama-Yamī hymn (*ṚV*, 10.10). In some cases the ritual was not completely lost, e.g. the *Ṛgvidhāna* (3.119.127) enjoins the two verses from the Vṛṣākapi hymn (*ṚV*, X.86.16-17) to be recited at the special bath to be administered to an issueless women, or to one who is not happy with her husband. In the case of Yama-Yamī hymn the ritual is forgotten, only the account of the rituals is preserved in this hymn.[44]

In the introduction to the *AV*, 3.28.4, which is used to avert the evil effect of a twin's birth, Sāyaṇa remarks that the birth of a twin to a cow, a mare, a she-donkey or a woman is an unusual occurrence, and this hymn is used as an expiatory recitation for averting the evil.[45]

The *ṚV*, 10.13.4 contains an account of Yama having performed a sacrifice in which he, as the chief priest and the sacrificer offered his own body as the sacrificial oblation. This sacrifice was performed for an onset of progeny and it can be called the primeval sacrifice. Out of the self-immolation of Yama in this sacrifice the human progeny originated. The ṛc under consideration is as follows:

devebhyaḥ kaṃ avṛṇīta mṛtyuṁ,
prajāyai kam amṛtaṁ nāvṛṇīta/
bṛhaspatiṁ yajñam akṛṇvata ṛṣiṁ,
priyāṁ yamas tanvaṁ prārirecīt./
(*ṚV*, 10.13.4)

According to Sāyaṇa this *ṛc* can be rendered as follows:

> Whom has he (i.e., Yama) selected as the killer of the gods? Whom has he not selected as the non-slayer of the human beings? (Yama does not send a killer at a time when the process of *havir-dhāraṇa* is taking place). The priests performed the sacrifice with the *mantras*. Yama saves our dear body from death.

Sāyaṇa's interpretation does not help to get a clear import of the stanza. Following Sāyaṇa H.H. Wilson translates —

> Whom has he selected as the slayer of the gods? Whom has he not selected as the non-slayer of the human race? They have made *ṛṣi* Bṛhaspati the sacrifice. Yama preserves our dear bodies.[46]

According to Geldner's interpretation, which holds a diversity, a portion of the *ṛc* can be translated as —

> for gods (Yama) took death, for the progeny he did not take immortality. The gods made *ṛṣi* Bṛhaspati the offering.[47]

An altogether different interpretation is suggested by N.G. Chapekar —

> Yama has taken away the dear body (of this dead man). Why did he choose mortality for the people? Why did he kill this man in spite of his having performed the sacrifice with *mantras* (bṛhaspati).[48]

The present *ṛc* is considered to be exceedingly obscure,[49] but it surely contains one of those few stray and scattered references connected with a Vedic god which have escaped priestly revision and, therefore, retain the traces of the original character of that god.[50] It also contains one of the two versions of the mythological motif of the primeval sacrifice, the other version is found in the *Puruṣa-Sūkta* (*ṚV*, 10.90).

Strictly following the text this *ṛc* (*ṚV*, 10.13.4) may be rendered as follows:

> For the sake of the gods indeed (he) chose death; (he) did not choose indeed in the interest of the progeny a life immortal. They made Bṛhaspati, the *ṛṣi*, a sacrificial offering. Yama gave up (his) dear body.[51]

The middle voice of $\sqrt{}$*vṛ* in the first hemistich suggests that

Yama chose mortality for himself[52] and he did not prefer immortality for himself. According to the first hemistich of the *ṛc* the gods had arranged this sacrifice for (the birth of) the human progeny. The second hemistich concluded that Bṛhaspati, the *ṛṣi* was offered as the oblation and Yama gave up his dear body. This indicates that Yama was himself the *bṛhaspati* , i.e., the principal priest and the sacrificer. The chief priest is also called *bṛhaspati*, because he is the representative of the Bṛhaspati, the divine priest. In the *VS*, 2.12 the *Brahman* priest is called *bṛhaspati*. Commenting on the *VS*, 2.12 Uvvaṭa and Mahīdhara state that *Bṛhaspati* is designated as *Brahman* priest in the sacrifice performed by the gods, and even men attain this title by taking resort to Bṛhaspati.[53]

Here in the *ṛc* under discussion (*ṚV*, 10.13.4) they (i.e., the gods) made the priest (i.e., the *bṛhaspati*) the offering (*yajña*).[54] In the light of this study the purport of the *ṚV*, 10.13.4 is intelligible. It is referring to a primeval sacrifice arranged by the gods with the definite purpose, i.e., beginning of a progeny. In the sacrifice they offered the sacrificer, i.e., Yama as the oblation because he chose to give up his body in order to accomplish the desire of the gods. Thus, this *ṛc* records the immolation of a divine being who was immortal like other gods. This explains why Yama is called a mortal in spite of his divine birth.

The *Puruṣa-Sūkta* (*ṚV*, 10.90) gives a detailed account of a sacrifice in which a cosmic man *Puruṣa* is sacrificed. The basic motif in the case of Yama (*ṚV*, 10.13.4) and *Puruṣa* (*ṚV*, 10.90) is thus the same, i.e., the immolation of a divine being for the sake of creations.[55] On this basis Yama is considered to be Father of the mankind.[56]

According to the *Puruṣa-Sūkta* the sacrifice is arranged by the gods (*ṚV*, 10.90.6) in which a Cosmic Man *Puruṣa* is sacrificed (*ṚV*, 10.90.15) and the creation originated from the different parts of his body.[57] The *ṚV*, 10.13.4 presents a similar account, though very vague and incomplete, of a sacrifice and the self-immolation of a divine being, i.e., Yama, for the cause of the gods and progeny. It is, however, not mentioned how Yama's sacrifice helped in starting the human progeny, a point which is mentioned in the *Puruṣa-sūkta*. It can be said that the *ṚV*, 10.13.4 and *ṚV*, 10.90 are two versions of mythological cosmogonic motif of the primeval sacrifice.

R.N. Dandekar also notices similarity in the character and Yama and *Puruṣa*. According to him, both of them are hermophrodites. *Puruṣa* creates Virāj out of his own self (*ṚV*, 10.90.2). Though Yama is not directly expressed as a bisexual being, Güntert has pointed out that his name 'Yama' can be linguistically connected with Lat. *Geminus*, *Gemullus*, and GK *didumos* which mean both the twin and a hermophrodite.[58] From the similarity of sacrifices mentioned in the *ṚV*, 10.13.4 and the *ṚV*, 10.90, and also on the basis of the similarity in the character and the functions of Yama and *Puruṣa*, it can be concluded that the *Puruṣa* of the *Puruṣa-sūkta* is only a more detailed priestly modification of the original mythical conception of Yama.[59]

It is suggested in the *ṚV* 10.13.4 that out of the primeval sacrifice in which Yama immolated himself the progeny originated. On this basis Yama is considered to be the father of mankind. It is also important to note that Yama is said to have started progeny through a primeval sacrifice and Yamī plays no part in it. The idea of incest is not supported by the text.[60] Yama and *Puruṣa* are similar in character as divine beings sacrificed in the primeval sacrifice, but *Puruṣa* not only started a human progeny, he is also the creator of the universe. Origin of the various kinds of creatures as well as the sun, moon, sky, ether, air, fire and earth is attributed to *Puruṣa* (*ṚV*, 10.90.8, 10, 13, 14).

Manu too is called the progenitor of mankind (*ṚV*, 1.80.16) and the first sacrificer (*ṚV*, 8.43.13; 10.63.7). He is also a son of Vivasvat. Due to these aspects Manu is a 'double' of Yama. He came to be regarded as the father of mankind when Yama was allocated the kingdom of the dead. Yama's role as the first sacrificer was also transferred to Manu.

R.N. Dandekar holds the view that the incestuous union of Yama and Yamī produced the mankind, but the idea of humanity having originated from an incest was highly objectionable to the morality of that age and so the Yama-*Yamī-Sūkta* is left incomplete. This motif of incest in Yama-mythology seems to have been particularly responsible for the withdrawal of Yama from the Vedic cosmogonic mythology and the priestly emphasis laid on Yama's double, Manu. There was a considerable interaction between the Yama-myth and the Manu-myth and Manu-myth overshadowed the Yama-myth. Yama's character as the progenitor of human race was forgotten and only a few stray references reveal it. The parallels between the Yama-myth and the *Puruṣa*-myth helped to bring the Manu-myth and *Puruṣa*-myth together. Yama and *Puruṣa* having indentical characters, while *Puruṣa* and Manu, both signifying 'man' being more or less synonyms, there was a considerable intermixture of these three—Yama, *Puruṣa* and Manu-myths.[61]

The idea of Yama having created the human progeny also finds expression in the *ṚV*, 7.33.9; 12 where it is said that Yama spread out the 'garment of creation'.[62] The theory which is very vaguely and indirectly mentioned in the *ṚV*, 10.13.6, that Yama created a progeny, is explicitly mentioned here in the *ṚV*, 7.33.9.

> *te it niṇyam hṛdayasya praketaiḥ,*
> *sahasra-valśaṁ abhi saṁ caranti/*
>
> *Yamena tataṃ paridhiṃ vayantaḥ*
> *apsarasaḥ upaseduḥ Vasiṣṭhāḥ.*[63]
>
> They alone move about fearlessly owing to the innate knowledge of their heart, in that secreṭ of the thousand branches intending to weave that garment, first woven by Yama, Vasiṣṭha approaches the celestial nymph (for birth).[64]

According to this *ṛc* Vasiṣṭha approached the celestial nymph for being born from her. It was due to a strong urge to extend the garment which was (first) woven by Yama, that Vasiṣṭha wanted to be born.[65] He desired to enter the thousand-branched and thousand-threaded secret namely the mundane existence which was started by Yama. *Saṁsāra* is conceived here as a tree of a thousand branches (like the *aśvattha* of the *BG*, 15.1b) and a garment of a thousand threads in the *Ṛ V*, 7.33.9c.[66]

The vocable *paridhi* in this stanza is taken to be a cloth, a garment.[67] But *paridhi* also denoted a sacrifice since *tantu* stands for *yajña* at several places. In the *Ṛ V*, 10.53.6; 9.22.6; 7, Sāyaṇa takes *tantu* in the sense of 'a sacrifice'. Following Sāyaṇa, Wilson translates *tantum tanvan rajaso bhānum anvihi* as "spreading out the sacrifice follow the illuminator of the world".[68]

On the other hand the word *tantu* is also used to denote a thread, which can also metaphorically denote the thread of progeny, continuation of the family line. The *Ṛ V*, 10.56.6 has *tantum ātatam* which Sāyaṇa translates as — *prajām vitata kṛtavantaḥ iti śeṣaḥ putra-pautrādi rupeṇa anavacchinnām prajām ityarthaḥ*. The *AB*, 3.38 says *prajā vai tantuḥ*. In the *TA*, 7.11.1 also *tantu* signifies the continuity of progeny and it is said here *prajā tantum mā vyavachhetsīḥ*; thus *tantu* signifies the continuity of progeny. It is interesting to note that the word *tanaya* denoting 'son' also, like the word *tantu*, is derived from √*tan*.

The two views regarding the meaning of *tantu* are discussed by Sāyaṇa in his commentary on the *Ṛ V*, 6.92. Here he presents both the views. According to *saṁpradāya-vidaḥ*, ie., the knowers of the tradition, here is a figurative allusion to the mysteries of the sacrifice where the threads of warp, (*tantu*) are the metres of the *Vedas*, and those of the woof, (*otu*) are the *Yajus* (i.e., liturgic prayers and rituals and the combination of the two is the cloth, i.e., the sacrifice.) *Tantus* are the various threads of the cloth which it is made up of. The Vedic metres, e.g., *Gāyatrī*, etc. are also *tantus* of a sacrifice which it is made up of. The other view is of the *ātmavidaḥ* or the *Vedāntins* who understand *tantu* as alluding to the mystery of creation. Thus 'spreading out the garment' denotes creation of the progeny, which, the *Ṛ V*, 7.33.9; 12 state, was started by Yama. It is clear that *Yamena tatam paridhim* highlights Yama's function as a creator which is only vaguely suggested in the *Ṛ V*, 10.13.4.

Notes

1. A.A. Macdonell, *Vedic Reader*, p. 212.
2. *anṛte khalu kriyamāṇe Varuṇo gṛhṇāti/*— *TS*, 1.7.2.6.
3. R.N. Dandekar, *VMT*, p. 136.
4. Sāyaṇa on *AV*, 8.1.4.
5. In *GP* the term used is *nigaḍa*, i.e., metallic chain. *kecit nigaḍa-pāśaiśca baddhāḥ* — *GP*, II. 23.38.
6. In the Ajāmila story in the *BhāgP*, 6.1.28 the servants of Yama are mentioned as holding a *pāśa*. In the *BhāgP*, 6.2.30 Ajāmila states that the servants of Yama caught him with a noose and dragged. However, it does not suggest that he was bound by *padbīśa*, i.e., foot-fetter and was dragged by his feet.
7. *atha gārhyapatya-cayanam ucyate. palāśaśākhayā gārhapatyam vyūdūhati apeta vīta iti pucchaḥ pratidiśam purastāt prathamam/*— *KāŚS*, 17.1.1.
8. *Yamasya sarva-bhūmi-adhipatitvāt bhṛtyāh sarvatra caranti tān prati ucyate/*— Mahīdhara on *VS*, 12.45.
9. *Agnir bhūtānāṁ adhipatiḥ . . . Indro jyeṣṭhānām, Yamaḥ pṛthivyāḥ Vāyurantarikṣasya/*— *TS*, 3.4.51.
10. *Yamadevatyo vā ayaṁ pṛthivīlokaḥ/*— *MS*, 3.2.3.
11. S. Bhattacharji, *Indian Theogony*, p. 48.
12. *Yama amuṣya lokasya ādhīpatyam ānaśe/*— *MS*, 25.11.
13. *etena vai Yamo'napajayyaṁ amuṣya lokasya ādhipatyaṁ ānaśe/* — *TMB*, 11.10.21.
14. *etac ca bhūmirūpāyā adho diśo nāma/*— Sāyaṇa on *TS*, 5.5.10.
15. See under "Yama: The Creator".
16. H.H. Wilson,*Ṛgveda Samhitā*, pt. 6; p. 43.
17. S.S. Dange, *A lost (?) Funeral Custom from the Ṛgveda* (10.135), *Proceedings & Transactions of AIOC* no. 28, 1976. Darwad, pp. 219-25.
18. The concept of six worlds is clear in the Ṛgvedic tradition and Sāyaṇa in his commentary on the *ṚV*, 10.14.6 gives the names of the six worlds as *dyaus*, earth, waters, herbs, the sun and good speech.

    '*Ekaṁ bṛhat*' may, according to Macdonell signify the universe — A.A. Macdonell, *Vedic Reader*, p. 175.
19. W.D. Whitney, Transl., *Atharvaveda*, 18.1.32.
20. Cf. also *AV*, 6.96.2; 7.112.2; 8.7.28; *vide* Chapter 3: 'Yama & Varuṇa'.
21. *tulāyām ha vā amuṣmin loke ādadhati yataradya syati tad anveṣyati yadi vā sādhu asādhu vā iti atha yan eyam veda asmin ha eva loke tulām ārohati amuṣmin loke tulādhānaṁ mucyate sādhukṛtyā ha eva asya yacchati na pāpa kṛtyā/*— *ŚB*, 11.2.7.33.

    Weighing of the deeds of a dead man in the presence of Yama has a parallel in Egyptian mythology where the heart of the dead is weighed before. Thoth, the lord of the nether world—*Vide* Epilogue.

22. *vaivasvate vivicyante Yama-rājani te janāḥ/*
ye ceha satyena icchante ye u ca anṛtavādinaḥ//— *TA*, 6.5.11.

23. *ṚV*, 2.33.4; *vide* R.C. Hazra, "Ṛgvedic Rudra, an extremely unsocial and non-cooperating god", *JOIB* 25 (3-4), 1976, pp. 213-22.

24. *antakāya mṛtyave te namaḥ prāṇa apāna iha te ramantāṁ/*
ihāyamastu puruṣaḥ sahāsunā sūryasya bhāge amṛtasya loke//
— *AV*, 8.1.1.

25. *Vide* Chapter 2 — 'Yama's Abode'.
sa no yamaḥ prataram jīvase dhāt/— *AV*, 18.3.63.
Whitney translates — "He who maintains himself by his might, like (birds) in the atmosphere poet of the Fathers, favourer of prayers (*mati*) — him praise ye all befriended, with oblations. May that Yama give (*dha*) us to live further on" W.D. Whitney, Transl. *Atharvaveda*, p. 865.

26. *dadāmi asmā avasānam etad ya eṣa āgan mama ched abūt iha/*
Yama's cikitvān pratyetadāha mamaiṣa rāya upa tiṣṭhatām iha//—
AV, 18.2.37.

27. *Vide* chapter 5 — "Yama — the Preacher of Philosophy".

28. F. Max-Müller, *Lectures on the Science of Language*, II, p. 483.

29. *Vide* H.H. Wilson, Transl. *Ṛgveda Saṁhitā*, Vol. VI, p. 26.

30. Cf. H.H. Wilson, "We have not done what was done formerly", Transl. *Ṛgveda Saṁhitā*, pt. 6, p. 27.

31. *salakṣma yad viṣurūpā bhavāti/*— *ṚV*, 10.10.2.

32. E.W. Hopkins, *Religion of India*, p. 131.

33. R.N. Dandekar, *VMT*. R.N. Dandekar holds the view that this incest took place and records it as the second stage in the evolution of Yama mythology.

34. H.H. Wilson, *op. cit.*, p. 27.

35. A. Macdonell, *History of Sanskrit Literature*, p. 118.

36. F. Max-Müller, *Lecture on the Science of Language*, Second Series, pp. 510, 521.

37. R.N. Dandekar, *VMT*, p. 120.

38. "From Yima and Yimak, who was his sister was born a pair, a man and a woman, and they became husband and wife together . . . . and the lineage went on."
— E.W. West, *Pahalavi Texts*, pt. I, *SBE*, 5.87.

39. "There is not single word in the Vedas pointing to Yama and Yamī as the first couple of mortals, as Indian Adam and Eve." — J. Muir, *OST*, Vol. V, p. 288.

40. Cf. A.A. Macdonell, *VM*, p. 173 — "The myth of the primeval twins that produced the human race . . . . seems to be Indo-Iranian."
— E.H. Meyer takes Yamī to be a later creation like Indrāṇī and others, *Vide* A.A. Macdonell, *op. cit.*, p. 173.

41. *Vide* P.V. Kane, *HDS*, Vol. I, p. 209.

42. Awkward Sex Couples was the necessity of a new agricultural stage of fertility — S.A. Dange, *Vedic Myths, in Social Perspective*, p. 43.

    S.G. Kantawala provides a symbolic interpretation of the Brahmā-Sarasvatī myth — *Vide* "Two legends from the Purāṇas: a study in upabṛṁhaṇa", *Indo-logica Taurinensi*, Vol. 8-9, pp. 980-81, 219-22.

43. Ulrisch Schneider, *Indo Iranian Journal* (Hague, Holland) pt. 10, 1967, pp. 1-32, referred to by Gayacharan Tripathi, *Vedic Devatā*, p. ii, 609.

44. S.A. Dange, *Vedic Myths in Social Perspective*, p. 41.

45. "*gavāśvā gardabhī-mānuṣīṇām yamalajananaṁ adbhutaṁ tad śāntyartham*" — Śāyaṇa on *AV*, 3.28.4.

46. H.H. Wilson, *Ṛgveda Saṁhitā*, pt. 6, p. 37.

47. K.F. Geldner, *Der Ṛgveda, HOS*, Vol. 35, p. 141.

48. N.G. Chapekar, *Yama and Pitar, Belvalkar felicitation Volume*, pp. 36-42.

49. R.T.H. Griffith, *The Hymns of Ṛgveda Saṁhitā*, Vol. II, p. 397; H.H. Wilson, *op. cit.*, p. 37.

50. R.N. Dandekar, *op. cit.*, p. 128.

51. *Vide* R.N. Dandekar, *op. cit.*, p. 128.

52. V.S. Apte, *Practical Sanskrit-English Dictionary*, pt. 3, p. 1448.

    On this use of the middle voice, T. Burrow comments that the middle is used when the subject is in some way or other specially implicated in the result of the action. (*The Sanskrit Language*, p. 293).

53. *devanām yajne yo brahmā tasmai brahmaṇe bṛhaspataye ca prāhuḥ Bṛhaspatir vai devānām brahmā tad adhīṣṭhita evāyaṁ manuṣyo brahmatvam karoti* — Mahīdhara on the *VS*, 2.12.

    Mahīdhara, while commenting on the *VS*, 8.9 also deals with the word *bṛhaspati-sutasya* and gives two interpretations of the word *bṛhaspati* — (1) squeezed by *bṛhaspati*, the *yajamāna* who has performed great sacrificial deeds — *bṛhato mahato yajñakarmaṇaḥ patiḥ bṛhaspatiḥ yajamānaḥ*

    (2) impelled by *bṛhaspati*, the *Ṛtvij* brāhmaṇa *yad vā bṛhaspatayo brāhmaṇāḥ ṛtvijaḥ*.

54. *Yajnā* = offering, oblation — V.S. Apte, *op. cit.*, p. 1298.

    Here also the middle voice *akṛṇvata* confirms that this act was done by the gods for themselves. *Vide* ante fn. 8.

55. R.N. Dandekar, *op. cit.*, p. 131.

56. In this connection Yamī has no role to play since the progeny originated from a sacrifice. It must be noted that there is nothing in the text to support the idea of the birth of a human progeny through the supposed incest of Yama and Yamī.

    Vide chapter 4 — 'Yama and Yamī.

57. Similar myths of the origin of the different aspects of creation out of the different parts of a divine character possessing a human form are also found in other primitive mythologies, e.g., the creation of

heaven and earth from the two halves of the Goddess Tiamat. In Edda (II) in the ancient Germanic mythology of Tuisto and Ymir lived, there was neither land nor sea, neither earth nor heaven above. From Ymir's flesh the earth was created, out of his blood the oceans, mountains from his bones and trees from his hair, from this skull the heaven originated. Cf. *ṚV*, 10.90.13.14.

Vide R.N. Dandekar, *op. cit.*, p. 130.

58. Güntert, *Der arische Weltkönig and heiland*, p. 334 referred to by R.N. Dandekar, *op.cit.*, p. 132.

59. *Vide* R.N. Dandekar, op. cit., p. 132.

60. In the later writings of the Iranian mythology where Yima and Yimak are paired, they are mentioned as the parents of mankind and also of various other species of animals.

61. *Vide* R.N. Dandekar, *op. cit.*, pp. 137-38.

62. H.D. Velankar, *Ṛgveda Maṇḍala*, VII, p. 82.

63. According to Sāyaṇa's interpretation the *apsaras*, wearing the garment of Yama, approached Vasiṣṭha like a mother. But the next stanza states that Vasiṣṭha has decided to be born. Hence he must have approached the *apsaras*, not the *vice versa*. Evidently the subject of *upaseduḥ* should be Vasiṣṭha and not the *apsaras*.

64. H.D. Velankar, *op. cit.*, p. 86.

65. This was regarded as one of the three obligation to be fulfilled by men:

The obligation to gods by performing sacrifices, that to the *ṛṣis* by celebacy and that to the Fathers by progeny.

This third obligation is referred to in the *ṚV*, 10.56.6 (*tṛtīyena karmaṇā*). "It is a kind of cosmic-ethical obligation which developed in the course of time into the concept of *pitṛ-ṛṇa*.

— R.N. Dandekar, *VMT*, p. 336.

66. H.D. Velankar, *op. cit.*, p. 86.

67. The words *tatam* and *paridhi* show that *paridhi* means a garment. — H.D. Velankar, *op. cit.*, p. 86.

68. H.H. Wilson, *Ṛgveda Saṁhitā*, Vol. IV, p. 175.

5

Yama: The Preacher and Eschatology

IN the *Upaniṣads* Yama's connection with death is clearly expressed. At several places he is even identified with *mṛtyu* (death). In the *KaṭhaUp* Yama emerges as a preacher of the *Brahman*-philosophy. He imparts the knowledge of the highest principle to Naciketas, who chose it as the third boon which Yama had promised him. It is only after testing Naciketas for the firmness of his determination as against all allurements of worldly pleasures (*KaṭhaUp*, 1.22; 1.29; 1.23-25) and being satisfied with the worthiness of this recipient, Yama happily disclosed to young Naciketas the knowledge which is difficult to be obtained even for the gods.

According to the *KaṭhaUp* Naciketas, the son of Vājaśravas was deeply troubled on seeing his father giving away old cows as the sacrificial gifts which he offered after the completion of a sacrifice. Those cows were no longer able to drink, to eat, to give milk or to calve (*KaṭhaUp*, 1.37) Naciketas, truthful as he was, could not reconcile himself to this deception which he thought was the path to a joyless hellish existence. He approached his father and asked 'whom will you give me?' In asking this he revealed his boldness proceeding from the innate virtue of *śraddhā*. When he repeated his question a second and then a third time, the father got infuriated and said, 'I give you over to Death'. Young Naciketas was neither disturbed nor angry. With his passion for truth and fearlessness he reached the doors of Yama. Yama was away from his abode and Naciketas waited there for his return. Yama returned after three nights and considered it a lapse on his part for having kept a holy guest waiting. He decided to make amends and asked Naciketas to choose three boons.

With the first boon Naciketas secured his return to his father who with his anger bygone, would welcome him back. As the second boon he learnt from Yama the details of a fire (i.e., sacrifice) which leads to heaven. At this juncture Yama conferred an additional boon that that fire would thenceforth bear Naciketas' name. As the third boon, Naciketas, with utmost preciseness, asked for the secret of the life after death to be disclosed to him. He said that there was a doubt in regard to a man who had died. Some said he existed, while others said he did not exist. Yama reflected that the mystery of the life after death was difficult to be understood. Even the gods had not been sure on that subject and Naciketas was too young to assimilate that knowledge; therefore Yama offered various attractive gifts, i.e., centenarian sons and grandsons, beautiful women, herds of cattle, elephants, horses, gold, a very long life for himself and told him not to ask about the existence of man after death. But Naciketas insisted on his boon because where else he could get a better instructor than Yama on a subject regarding the life after death. Naciketas was not lured by wealth and long life or other-worldly pleasures and he refused to choose something else as a boon. He wanted the secret of death to be revealed to him by the Lord of Death himself. Here Yama was pleased that between the 'good' (*śreyas*) and the 'pleasant' (*preyas*) Naciketas had chosen the 'good'. He was now convinced that Naciketas was a true seeker of knowledge. He expressed a desire, viz. "May there be for us an inquirer like you, Naciketas" (1.2.9). Ignorant men under delusion of wealth think that "there is nothing beyond this world and they came again and again under my (i.e., death's) way" (1.2.6).

Yama spoke to Naciketas on the mystic symbol *Oṁ* as synonymous with *Brahman*. He also preached the doctrine of the immortality of the soul (i.e., the Self, the *Ātman*) — The

fig. 5.1

Self is not born, nor does it die, it sprang from nothing and nothing sprang from it; it is unborn, constant, eternal and primeval; it is not slain when the body is slain. If a killer thinks that he kills, or if the killed thinks that he is killed, both of them do not understand that this Self neither slays, nor is slain (1.2.19). This self cannot be obtained by mere academic pursuits, nor by intellect. He is to be obtained only by the one whom he chooses (1.2.23).

Narrating a parable of the chariot, Yama further explains the body to be a chariot and Self to be sitting in it. In this chariot intelligence (*buddhi*) is the charioteer and the mind the reins, while the senses are the horses (1.3.3-4). A wise man's mind (i.e., the reins) are firmly held and therefore his senses (i.e., the horses) are under his total control (1.3.3-5).

Though Yama's objective is to answer Naciketas' query about the life beyond death, he now teaches about the Supreme Self, of which the Individual Self is a part. While instructing about the survival of the finite Self, Yama dilates on *Brahman* solely with an object of enabling Naciketas see that the finite Self is non-different from the infinite Self.

The non-difference of *jīva* and *Brahman* forms the central teaching of all the *Upaniṣads*. The five *Mahāvākyas* (1) *ahaṁ brahmāsmi* — *BṛUp*, 1.4.10, (2) *tat tvam asi* — *ChāUp*, 6.87, (3) *sarvam khalu idaṁ brahma* — *ChāUp*, 3.14.1 (4) *ayaṁ ātmā brahma* — *MāUp*, 1.2, (5) *satyaṁ jñānam anantaṁ brahma* — *TaitUp*, 2.1.1 occurring in different *Upaniṣads* affirm this identity in a direct and forthright manner.

After explaining to Naciketas the real nature of *jīva*, Yama takes up the original question and tells about the survival of the Self after death. According to their deeds and knowledge some enter a womb in order to be born again and some get insentient form and go into inorganic matter. The Self is one but takes different forms, just as the fire takes different forms according to whatever it burns; in a similar way one Self within all things becomes different according to whatever it enters (2.5.9). Yama declares that one gets liberated from the clutches of death by discerning that Supreme Self.

ESCHATOLOGY

Admission in the realm of Yama is considered to be the highest fate for the dead. He joins there the category of the Fathers, who are not only worshipped like gods but are also believed to possess powers to influence the life of those on earth. In the rites offered to the dead the main idea is to secure for him, the dignity of *pitṛ* (Fathers) (*ṚV*, 10.16.1; 2) and thus make him immortal in Yama's region.[1]

Heaven

According to the Vedic thought the kingdom of Yama is heaven where the Fathers reside and revel in the company of their king Yama; therefore, Yama is called *saṅgamanaṁ janānām* (*ṚV*, 10.14.1) 'the gatherer of the people'. At the cremation the dead is told to go to Yama who collects all the dead in his realm, because that is the place which he discovered for all the dead to live in (*ṚV*, 10.14.2) [2]

Ritual Heaven

There are some references in the later texts like the *Brāhmaṇas* which seem to speak of *svarga* (heaven) as explicitly distinguished from the abode of the dead. There are references of a sacrificer reaching heaven immediately after completing a sacrifice, i.e., even without dying. It will be an error if it is interpreted that the sacrificer died immediately after completing the sacrifice, and went to heaven. This shows that *svarga* was not always identical with the abode of the blessed dead. As observed by J. Gonda, such statements where the sacrificer is said to have attained heaven without having died refer to the ritual heaven, and the sacrificer's ritual birth therein.[3] The idea of the ritual heaven, i.e., the earthly heaven, is made clear by such identification as in *ŚB*, 9.3.4.13 where the *āhavanīya* fire is said to be the *svargaloka* and when they annoint the sacrificer there it is said that they annoint him in the world of heaven. The *ŚB*, 13.2.8.5, quoted also by Mahīdhara at the *VS*, 23.20 states that 'heaven is where they immolate the victim'.[4] Mahīdhara adds that the term *svarga-loka* is synonymous with *yajñabhūmi*, i.e., the sacrificial place.

According to the *PB*, 10.4.5 the sacrificer after having reached the *svarga-loka* (heavenly abode) remains resplendent until old age and eats food suitable for brahmins. As the sacrificer here is said to have (ideally) reached heaven and he is wished to live here on earth until old age, it is evident that the real heaven and the bliss of that world are not meant here, but the earthly welfare of the sacrificer after he has reached the ritual-heaven and has returned to this world.[5]

Location of Heaven

Yama's kingdom is situated in the midst of the sky (*ṚV*, 10.15.14), in the highest heaven (*ṚV*, 10.14.8). The worshipper earnestly desires to become immortal in Yama's kingdom which is a place of eternal light (*ṚV*, 9.113.7,9). According to the *AV* also Yama's region is in the highest (6.63.3) and luminous world (18.1.57), situated in the third firmament called *pradyau* and which is the dwelling-place of the Fathers (18.2.48). The other two firmaments are mentioned as *undanvatī* (watery) and *pīḷumatī* (starry). At the funeral the dead is told to acquire a place among Fathers and prosper in their company (18.2.25).[6] The dead find rest in the third heaven. Heaven is said to be the world of light brightened by sun (*AV*, 9.5.18).[7]

In the *Yama-loka* the *pitṛs* are said to enjoy in the company of Yama (*ṚV*, 10.14.10; 10.15.8); they eat the offerings made to them with *svadhā* (*ṚV*, 10.14.7). The pious drink *soma* with Yama (1.35.6). In the *ṚV*, 1.154.5b a place where all god-seeking people delight[8] is also said to be the "favourite region of Viṣṇu, who is a friend of the pious".[9]

Heaven/Yama-loka

Yama's region bears the name *Yama-loka* (*TB*, 3.9.20.1, *JB*, 1.167, *PB*, 9.8.4, etc.). It is also called *Yamasya-sādanam*, i.e., 'the abode of Yama' (*AV*, 18.2.56). In the kingdom of Yama the pious dead live in the companionship of the gods. In the *AV*, 18.2.55 Savitṛ is prayed to take the dead to the region where the pious dwell. The next stanza (*AV*, 18.2.56) states that this region is *Yamasya sādanam*, i.e., 'abode of Yama' where the dead is being carried to.[10] This shows that *Yamasya sādanam* or the region of Yama is considered to be heaven, i.e., the region of the pious. The dead is told to go to the region where his ancestors have gone before; it is said that there he would see Yama and Varuṇa (*ṚV*, 10.14.6). The *Jātavedas* Agni is urged to take the deceased to the Fathers (*ṚV*, 10.16.1-2), to the region of the pious (*sukṛtām lokam*—*ṚV*, 10.16.4).

On the basis of these statements and other similar references viz. *ṚV*, 10.14.14,[11] etc., it may be concluded that Yama's region was considered to be the highest heaven which is the ultimate goal of all god-seeking people.

It may be noted that in the *Brāhmaṇas* Yama's region also bears the name *pitṛ-loka*. One who performs sacrifices cherishes a hope; "May there be a place for me in Yama's world" (*ŚB*, 4.3.4.27).

Life of the dead in this region, which is brightened by in — exhaustible light is full of joy. It is to be noted here that in the Vedic thought the ideas of sun, sunlight, celestial, light are inextricably mixed up with those of well-being, good fortune, happiness and glory; the light of the sun means the possibility of life,[12] of activity and of human existence and 'to see the sun' means 'to live' (cf. *ṚV*, 10.14.12; 10.57.4[13]).

The most detailed Ṛgvedic account of the pleasures of the life in heaven is found in the *ṚV*, 9.113.7-11. According to it the eternal light illuminates this region; abundant waters flow; all desires are fulfilled and people are satiated. There is joy and merriment everywhere and the place resounds with the music of flutes and songs (*ṚV*, 10.135.7). This region of eternal bliss can only be attained by those who perform meritorious deeds and hence it is called *sukṛtāṁ lokaḥ*[14] (*ṚV*, 10.16.4, *VS*, 15.50). Here the pious dead get whatever they had sacrificed and had offered as gifts to the priests (*ṚV*, 10.154.3, etc.). They are also united with the fruit of their *iṣṭāpūrta* (the merits acquired by sacrifices and charitable acts); therefore, the sacrificers, who performed religious rites in conformity with the approved norms, expected their post-mortem existence to be happy. Here we have possibly the germ of the later doctrine of *karma*. In the *ṚV* the term *karman* means 'work' in general and specificially 'the sacrificial work'. Such work constitute the merit which wins the pleasures of heaven for the departed souls.

In the heaven the dead unites with the Fathers and assumes a shining body (*ṚV*, 10.14.8). This body is free from diseases, frailties and imperfections (*ṚV*, 10.16.6). The *AV* also states that the dead assumes a special body in heaven which is free from imperfections. His limbs are not lame or crooked any longer (*AV*, 3.28.5; 6.120.3). He is said to assume a complete body (*AV*, 18.2.21). In the heaven the deity carrying his life (i.e.,*asunīti*) shapes his body (*AV*, 18.3.59). Yama makes his body free from diseases (*AV*, 18.2.12). In the heaven the new body is joined with mind, life and limbs (*AV*, 18.2.24). Similar ideas are expressed elsewhere in the *AV* (*AV*, 6.120.3).[15]

According to this description heaven is a bright world where pious people live in joy and harmony. They cast aside their ailments and physical deformities like lameness and deformed limbs. They acquire a luminous body and meet their relatives. The *AV* describes, quite explicitly, the pleasures of heaven enjoyed by one who offers *bṛhmodana*. In the realm of Yama he enjoys the company of the Gandharvas, he moves on a chariot (*AV*, 4.34.4). He also finds sexual pleasures there. Lakes full of *ghṛta*, honey, wine, milk, water and curds are seen here (*AV*, 4.34.2-6).

On reaching heaven with their new faultless bodies the pious dead are welcomed by the gods and are loved by them (*ṚV*, 10.56.1). The dead beholds both Yama and Varuṇa there (*ṚV*, 10.14.7). Yama recognises him as his own and offers him a resting place (*AV*, 18.2.37). Here are divine cows who yield all the desired objects (*AV*, 4.34.8). Here the dead souls get food and water offerings bestowed by their descendants on the earth (*AV*, 18.4.36; *ŚB*, 13.8.1.4).

According to the *KaṭhaUp*, 1.12.13,18 the *svarga-loka* is a place of delight. Here people with all their sorrows gone enjoy themselves.[16] The *KaṭhaUp*, 1.3 mentions several *lokas*, i.e., the worlds of different gods such as that of Agni, Vāyu, Varuṇa, Āditya, Indra, Prajāpati, and Brahmā. Śaṅkarācārya on the *Vedānta-Sūtra*, 4.3.4 comments that the word *loka* means a place for enjoying the fruit of one's actions.[17] A gradation of the higher worlds is described in the *BṛUp*, 3.6 like this: *Deva-loka, Prajāpati-loka, Brahma-loka*. A combination of blissful human condition, bodily happiness, power, well-being, etc. with an attempt at systemizing in a certain order, the *lokas* of the Fathers, Gandharvas, Prajāpati, etc. is presented by the author of *BṛUp*, 4.3.33.[18]

Though there are references in the *ṚV* to heaven, the kingdom of Yama where all blessed souls of those who had performed meritorious acts live happily, the doctrine of reward and punishment, according to which all actions of the people are evaluated, was not yet formulated. It is clear that the seers of the *ṚV* intended on a happy life on earth, where they wished to live for a hundred autumns and even more (*ṚV*, 7.66.16).

The general idea behind various *mantras* of the *AV* is also to enhance the happiness of this life by removing death, diseases and other difficulties and subduing the enemies. The thoughts of the Vedic seers rarely dwell upon the life after death; therefore, the reference to the pleasures enjoyed in the heaven are very few and those of the punishments and sufferings of hells are fewer. And the dead are said to be receiving in the heaven the reward of their *iṣṭāpūrta*, i.e., the religious merit earned by performing the sacrifices and by charitable acts.

Though in the *ṚV* heaven is repeatedly referred to as *sukṛtāṁ lokaḥ* (i.e., the region of the pious), which these people attain by their religious merit, but the germs of the doctrine of *karman* can also be seen in the *ṚV*. There is a clear reference that in heaven the dead is united with the fruit of his sacrificial and charitable acts (*ṚV*, 10.34.8).

It is also to be noted here that in the *ṚV* heaven is a place of permanent stay for a person who is granted entry into it. This is made clear by the expressions contained in the *ṚV*, 10.107.2; and *ṚV*, 9.113.7-11, etc. where the man is said to become immortal in Yama's region. The concept of the religious merit being exhausted by enjoying pleasures in heaven was not yet developed. The religious merit is thus never exhausted and, therefore, he does not have to be born again on earth.[19]

Thus heaven in the *ṚV* is more like *mokṣa*, i.e., the place of emancipation rather than a place for enjoying the heavenly pleasures for the given time which a man earns by performing meritorious deeds on the earth. According to the *PB*, 6.8.15 (also *ŚB*, 2.4.2.9) the 'yonder world', (heaven) is granted once and for all away from here.[20] The *ŚB*, 2.4.29 also states that "people going to heaven do not return" (*sakṛt parāñcaḥ pitaraḥ*— *ŚB*, 2.4.29); such passages do not contemplate the idea of exhaustion of *sukṛta*. On the other hand people living in this world are born again and again. The *ŚB*, 13.2.4.1 clearly identifies *asau lokaḥ*, (yonder world) and the sphere of the gods. It also identifies this world as *manuṣya-lokaḥ*.[21]

Passage to Heaven

For reaching heaven (the abode of Yama) the spirit of the dead takes up the path which was found by Yama. It is a steep path leading to the highest heaven (*ṚV*, 10.14.1-2). The Fathers are said to have taken up this path (for reaching Yama's abode) (*ṚV*, 10.14.7). By this path the dead goes to the realm of eternal light (*ṚV*, 9.113.7). There he meets the Fathers who revel with Yama and Varuṇa in the yonder world where there is no hunger or thurst. He goes there in a divine car or on wings.

At the cremation of the dead Agni is urged to burn the corpse properly and carry the souls of the dead to *sukṛtāṁ lokaḥ*, (world of the pious).[22] In the *AV* also, as in the *ṚV*, *sukṛta* generally means the merit a sacrificer gains by performing the sacrificial duties correctly. For one who performs good acts, i.e., the sacrifices an entry in heaven becomes his prerogative. Performance of certain sacrifices precisely and faultlessly enables the sacrificer to ascend to heaven by following the *devayāna*, i.e., the path of the gods (*AV*, 18.4.2).[23] This luminous path of the gods is revealed to the man who performs good deeds (*AV*, 18.4.14).[24] The sacrificers who performed the religious rites expected a happy post-mortem existence in heaven.

Punishment

As gods rewarded the pious souls by granting a permanent stay in heaven, they also punished the guilty by causing sufferings. The irregularity and inaccuracy in performing the sacrifices brought the wrath of the gods. There are earnest prayers to the concerned gods with which men want to be spared from being punished for their wrong actions. Sometimes the gods are requested to direct their anger towards the enemies. Rudra is prayed not to get angry over the faults which the worshippers might have done (*ṚV*, 10.15.6).

Unlike the rewards which are said to be received in heaven, punishment can be imposed on the guilty even in his present birth. This punishment came in the form of diseases and other sufferings.

Varuṇa's displeasure is said to cause dropsy. The *ṚV*, 7.89.2 refers to dropsy as the disease inflicted upon by Varuṇa. In the *AB*, 7.13-18, Varuṇa is said to have punished king Hariścandra by making him sick with dropsy. It is significant to note here that the cause of Varuṇa's wrath was king's failures in keeping his promise made to him. Besides, as the promise was made to Varuṇa, Hariścandra incurred Varuṇa's wrath also because this god is also the protector of *ṛta*, i.e., the moral order. By breaking his promise the king had also broken a moral rule. Mitra and Varuṇa punish the guilty by inflicting a heart disease on him (*ṚV*, 1.122.9).

Concept of Hell

As the term *sukṛtāṁ lokaḥ* clearly indicates a place where the virtuous go after death, it is natural that some kind of place was thought for the *duṣkṛt*, i.e., evil-doer, and that place was a natural compliment to heaven.

Regarding the fate of the wicked, obscure indications only are found in the *ṚV*. The *ṚV* contains a reference to a place where the evil-doers are punished. A deep place *gabhīraṁ padam* is for the evil, false and untruthful (*ṚV*, 4.5.5). Indra and Soma are urged to hurl the evil-doers into the abyss of bottomless darkness so that none of them may get out from there (*ṚV*, 7.104.3), and that the robbers and enemies may lie below all the three earths (*ṚV*, 7.104.11).[25] Indra is prayed to consign to the lower darkness a man who injures a worshipper (*ṚV*, 10.152.4). These passages present an idea of the Ṛgvedic seers' belief in the existence of a place where the wicked are punished by gods. According to H. Oldenberg *gabhīraṁ padam* refers to hell.[26] The *ṚV*, however, does not mention the tortures of hells as found in the later literature, but the sages of the *ṚV* had some faint glimmerings of a dark deep pit below earth to which the wicked persons were relegated by the gods.

According to the early Ṛgvedic belief it was the destiny of the wicked to fall into the dark depths and disappear.[27] As the heaven was a permanent abode for the pious dead, this dark pit is for the sinners where they remained for ever. The concept of the sins being exhausted by undergoing the prescribed punishment came much later and which, in contrast with the earlier belief, holds that man is subjected to punishments in hells and rewarded with the pleasures in heaven and after that he has to be reborn on earth. However the germs of the doctrine of *karma* and rebirth can be seen in 1st and 10th *Maṇḍala* of the *ṚV*.

In the idea of a dark pit for punishing the guilty, the germs can be seen of the later concept of *naraka* (hell) as a place for the sinners. It is to be noted here that this pit is also said to be situated below the three earths.

An early reference to man's soul, (*jīvātman*) attaining a higher or lower region according to his own good or evil deeds is found in the *ṚV*, 1.164.38. According to it the Self (*ātman*) is immortal but cognates with a mortal body doing various good or bad deeds and consequently moves to higher or lower regions to bear the fruit of those actions. By doing evil deeds he goes to the lower regions while the meritorious deeds take him to higher regions. These rewards or punishments granted to him are for ever. The pious, therefore, have no fear of falling down on earth after all their merits get exhausted by enjoying the pleasures of heaven. Similarly the evil-doers also do not exhaust their sins by undergoing the punishment which is, therefore, never over. Thus heaven or hell, whatever is granted once, is final and permanent.

The *AV* mentions *naraka-loka* as a place of female goblins and sorceresses. This place is said to be located in the lowest region and darkness (*AV*, 2.14.3), black darkness (*AV*, 5.30.11). It is also a place where a murderer has to go (*VS*, 30.5).

Torments of Hell

The torments of hell are described in the *AV*, 5.19 where it is said that those who insult a brahmin or take away his money have to sit in the stream of blood and eat hair (*AV*, 5.19.3). It is further said that if people injure a brahmin their country falls into calamities and sinks down like a broken boat in water (*AV*, 5.19.8).

In the *ŚB*, 11.6.1 a reference to the torments of hell is found. According to it and *JB*, 1.42.44, Bhṛgu thought very high of himself. He considered himself to be more learned than his father, Varuṇa.

When Varuṇa came to know this he asked Bhṛgu to go in each direction one by one, see whatever he finds there and report everything to Varuṇa. Thus, due to his pride, Bhṛgu was sent to see these directions. He saw there horrible scenes of torture. He saw men being cut into pieces and being eaten by others. Horrified Bhṛgu asked them as to why they were doing this gruesome act of cutting a human being and eating him up. The answer he was given here is significant. They said that this man had done the same to them during his earthly life. Now, they, the victims, settle the score by cutting him into pieces. Bhṛgu also saw the lord of that place as a yellow-eyed and black-complexioned man holding a staff,[28] beside two maidens — one of them fair and the other described as *atikalyāṇī*, i.e., either 'very fair' or 'past her beauty'.[29]

Another picture of hell is found in the *KausBr*, 11.2 where a man is, in the next world, eaten up by the animals which he had devoured during his life. Certain rituals are also suggested to save one from getting into such predicament.

The idea of reward or punishment awarded according to one's own deeds is found in *ŚB*, 6.2.2.27; 10.6.3.1. The *ŚB*, 1.9.3 states that the dead pass between two fires which burn the evil-doers but allow the virtuous go by. Moreover all the actions of a dead are weighed on a balance and he receives award or punishment according to his good or evil deeds (*ŚB*, 11.2.7.33). It is to be noted here that in the Brāhmaṇic thought the good deeds were more often of the nature of sacrificial duties than ordinary good-work. One who reads the *Veda* in a particular way is said to be freed from dying again and attains oneness with *Brahman* (*ŚB*, 10.5.6.9). If the sacrifice is performed properly, it secures for the sacrificer a place in heaven (*ŚB*, 11.4.4.12).

The *TA*, 1.19 refers to four hells in four directions. They are:

(1) *Visarpin* in the south-east;

(2) *Avisarpin* in the south-west;

(3) *Viṣādi* in the north-east;

(4) *Aviṣādi* in the north-west.

People fall in these hells as the result of their own bad actions. In the *Viṣādi* hell people are tormented by dejection due to repentence. *Visarpī* is the hell where people move here and there walking under tremendous pain, while *Avisarpī* is a hell where the dead are unable to move at all and in *Aviṣādi* the people live always under fear. The *KaṭhaUp*, mentions the pleasureless regions which Naciketas fears that his father would get for giving away useless cows as gifts. The *KaṭhaUp* says nothing about the torments of the hells.

The *BṛUp*, 4.4.11 speaks about an extremely dark region where there is no happiness. People who are ignorant and unenlightened go to these regions after their death.[30] On the other hand the *BṛUp* also tells about a man attaining the merger of his soul in *Brahman*. The *BṛUp*, 4.9.9.7 says that when a man becomes free from all desires, he, though a mortal, becomes immortal and obtains *Brahman*. It further says that the vital air of a man with all his desires centered only in the Self, do not depart and such a man being *Brahman* (while he lives) goes to *Brahman* after his death and becomes pure light. The *BṛUp*, 4.4.11 and *IśaUp*, 3 both tell about a dark region where there is no sun-light. Demonic (*asuryā*)[31] are the regions, covered with darkness where those who have destroyed their souls are obliged to go (*IśaUp*, 3).

Taking into account these scattered but clear references to a dark, pleasureless place are sufficient to conclude that the Vedic people entertained the idea of the existence of a place like hell where the guilty were punished after death. However, the lack of detailed descriptions of hell, as seen in the *Purāṇas*, indicate that these ideas developed extensively only in the time of the Epics and the *Purāṇas*.[32]

Transmigration

In the major part of the *ṚV* the idea of the transmigration is conspicuously absent. The Vedic Āryans did not give much thought to death or the existence of man after death. The *ṚV* hymns are primarily prayers to the different gods and reference to death and post-mortem existence is only casual. Even then some glimmering of the Vedic seers' thoughts on transmigration can be seen in the *ṚV* also.

It is often said that the idea of transmigration is of a very late origin and it did not exist in the time of the *ṚV*. It is also said that it was an un-Āryan belief.[33] R.D. Ranade strongly refutes the idea of A.A. Macdonell that the Āryan settlers might have received the first impulse in this direction from the aboriginal inhabitants of India, which later developed into a theory of chain of existences intimately connected with the moral principal of requital.[34]

Though the idea of transmigration is not very explicit in the greater part of the *Ṛ*V*, but that an approach is being made is not hard to discover. According to the Ṛgvedic belief death was not the ultimate end of one's existence and that the living beings continue to exist even after their carnal death. The worshippers wish to enjoy a life of one hundred years and after the fall of their bodies want to become immortal in the realm of Yama. This confirms their belief in the continued existence of man even after his death.

The first stage in the evolution of the Ṛgvedic idea of transmigration consists in taking an animistic or hylozoistic view of the world. At the cremation of the dead his eye is asked to go to the sun, his vital breath to the wind, the spirit has been directed to go to heaven or earth in accordance to its *dharma* (merits),[35] or even to move to waters or trees as it suited it (*ṚV*, 10.16.3). The word *dharma* in this stanza is very significant because the soul is asked to go to heaven or to earth according to its merit. This confirms that this stanza is definitely expressing transmigration and not just putting forth certain hints towards the animistic or hylozoistic view of the world. There is one more passage definitely connected with the idea of transmigration. In *ṚV*, 10.58.1-12 the poet says that he is going to recall the departed soul (of an apparently dead-man) so that the dead may get back his soul and continue to live. The departed sould is said to have gone to distant places. The seer calls back this soul which, he says, might have gone to heaven or earth, to the four-cornered globe, which may have diffused in the various quarters, which may have gone to the oceans or the beams of light, to waters or herbs, to the sun or to the dawn, to the mountains or which may have spread through the whole world. This hymn surely suggests that the soul does not perish along with the body in which it existed. It can separate itself from that body because it has an independent existence.[36]

Sufficient evidence as to prove the existence of the idea of transmigration in the *ṚV* is also provided by the *ṚV*, 1.164.30 and 1.164.38. According to Roth, Böhtlingk and Geldner also these stanzas contain the early thoughts on transmigration.[37] They tell that the soul is a moving, speedful life-principle which comes and goes, moves backward and forward, comes in the contact with the body and then moves from it in the opposite direction.[38]

The culminating point of this doctrine is reached in the *ṚV*, 1.164.31 where poet claims to have seen (probably with his mind's eyes) the *gopa*, i.e., the guardian of the body moving unerringly by forward and backward paths, clothed in collected and diffusive splendour and it kept on "returning frequently inside the mundane region" (*varīvarte bhuvaneṣu antarā iti* — *ṚV*, 1.164.31). This interpretation leaves no place for doubt that it is referring to the repeated transmigrations of the soul. To support his point that *gopā*, i.e., 'guardian' mentioned in this stanza is the 'soul', R.D. Ranade refers to the preceding stanza, (i.e., 1.164.30) and comments that *gopa* in the *ṚV*, 1.164.31 is no other than the soul may be seen from the manner in which the previous stanza mentions the "breathing, speedful, moving life-principle". Moreover the frequentative *varwarti* tells about the soul's frequent returns to the world.[39]

It is important to note here that Sāyaṇa takes *gopā* to be the sun whose reappearance every morning is here expressed as his frequent visits. In this sense the frequentative *varīvartī* denotes the frequent (here daily) appearance of the sun in the morning, and not of the rebirth of the soul.

On the basis of this reference it can be said that the ideas of transmigration are implicitly found in the *ṚV*. They mention the passage of the soul from the body, souls inhabiting various forms of existence like water and plants and also the soul acquiring several births and thus present the early thought on transmigration as contained in the *ṚV*.

The *ṚV*, 10.16.6 states that after his death man gets a new body which is free from its previous imperfections. According to the *ṚV*, 10.14.8 the dead takes up a new luminous body. Following Sāyaṇa's interpretation this stanza can be seen as suggesting the rebirth of a dead by saying: "leave your imperfections and come back again with a new shining body".[40]

The soul of the dead is here asked to return to its chosen home "when the soul of the dead returns, he is said to go back home, as it were returning to his true home".[41]

H.D. Velankar interprets the term *asta* figuring in the *ṚV*, 7.12.10 as 'in the home of man'; here the gods have sent Agni to the *asta* for men's protection, whereas Agni's home is called *dama*.[42] Thus the *ṚV*, 10.14.8 does not suggest the rebirth of the dead.

On the basis of these references found in the first and tenth *Maṇḍalas* of the *ṚV* it can be derived that the ideas of transmigration are implicitly found in the *ṚV*. This ultimately proves that the idea of transmigration existed in the Vedic thought and it was not borrowed from the non-Āryan aboriginals of India. As R.D. Ranade puts: "whenever there is recognised the possibility of the soul coming to inhabit a body as a godlike principle from without, wherever, it is supposed that they could likewise part from the body, wherever it is thought that the soul after parting from the body could lead a life of disembodied existence, and wherever, it is supposed to return again to the earth and inhabit any form of existence, there is a kind of undying life conceived for the soul from which the step to actual transmigration is not far removed."[43]

Transmigration and Karma

Recurrent births are mentioned at several places in the *Brāhmaṇas*. It is said that one who lacks in the knowledge of a sacrifice and performs it in a wrong way, i.e., making faulty fire-altar, etc., is born again and becomes the food of death again. On the other hand, one who performs sacrifices with the correct knowledge gains immortality (*ŚB*, 10.4.3.10). Pin-pointing the possible error which an ignorant or negligent sacrificer commits the *ŚB*, 10.2.6.19 and 10.5.1.4) states that the recurrent death is the destiny of man who does not prepare the fire-altar in a correct way. Here in the reply to a question as to who conquers the recurrent birth it is said that those who make the altar correctly become the deity Agni and as Agni, i.e., the Fire-element is immortal, he too becomes immortal.

These and other such statements suggest that only the defaulters in performing sacrifices are born again in this world in order to suffer from recurrent deaths, while others who perform it correctly become immortal after death.

According to another Brāhmaṇic view all are born again after death to recompense for their good or bad actions. The type of their next birth is based on the type of actions performed by a man during his life. It is said that after his death a man is born in the world which he has worked for (*ŚB*, 6.2.2.27).[44] Thus man (or the personal principle in him) is born into the existence he made for himself.

According to the Brāhmaṇic transmigration theory the *karman* (i.e., good or bad actions of man) result in happiness or sufferings in his earthly life as well as in the hereafter life. The performance of the religious rites according to the prescribed norms and the knowledge of their import brings for the sacrificer an abundance of food in this life and imperishable *sukṛt* in the yonder world (*ŚB*, 1.6.4.16). At another instance the reward includes good eyesight till old age in this world and in the beyond (*ŚB*, 1.6.3.41).

In the *ŚB* every man is said to have three births, i.e., a man is born thrice (*ŚB*, 11.2.1.1). His first birth is when he is born as a child of his parents, the second by spiritual education when he begins performing sacrifices and the third after his death. The passage under reference is translated as follows:

> Verily, man is born thrice, namely in this way: first he is born from his mother and father, then when to whom the sacrifice inclines performs offering he is born a second time; and when he dies, and they place him on the fire, and when he thereupon comes into existence he is born a third time.[45]

According to the *ŚB*, 1.5.3.14 the rebirth in this world is a reward for some special knowledge. It is, therefore, looked upon as a blessing and not something wished to be

> spared from. The same text states that as the spring assuredly comes into life again out of winter, for out of one other is born again; therefore, he who knows this is indeed born again in this world.[46]

Ritual Rebirth and Death

At more than one place in the *Brāhmaṇas* there are statements about a sacrificer reaching heaven even without dying. Such statements suggest that *svarga-loka* or 'heaven' was not or not always, or not explicitly identified with the abode of the blessed dead, and therefore it would be an error to read the statements about *svarga* along with an un-expressed 'after death'.[47] The earliest reference to this notion is seen in the *TS*, 6.9.9.2 that a man, by performing certain rites can reach heaven without dying. The *PB*, 21.4.3 states that the performer of the *Aśvamedha* reaches the yonder world with his body (*saśarīraḥ*) and elsewhere (*PB*, 11.8.14) it tells about a definite Sāman for 'beholding the world of heaven'. That this ritual enables a sacrificer to see the heaven straightaway (*añjasā*), the inference that the sacrificer died at once to go to the abode of the dead is not probable.

According to the *ŚB*, 7.3.1.12 the officiant priest causes the sacrificer to be reborn in the *svarga-loka* (i.e., heaven); but he does not cause his sudden death or his post-mortem transference to heaven. In the *ŚB* it is said that Mṛtyu was assured by *Brahman* that all will have to pass through death in order to attain heaven. In this light, the rebirth without having to die indicates the ritual-rebirth of the sacrificer and the world which is said to be gained by singing certain hymn is certainly the ritual heaven (*AB*, 3.19.4; cf. *AB*, 6.4.11; 6.20.2).

In the *Upaniṣads* the doctrine of transmigration is seen well established. The idea of recompense in the other world is also combined with the doctrine of rebirth.

The *BṛUp*, 5.10.1 can be considered to contain the oldest Upaniṣadic thought on eschatology. According to it a soul, after death, ascends through the regions of wind, the sun, the moon and then reaches a region which is sorrowless and snowless (*ahiman*) and lives there for ever.[48] The passage however, does not tell whether this is the fate of all the souls or of the virtuous souls only. No such distinctions are made as virtuous and sinful.

The *ChāUp*, (5.10.3.6) speaks about two types of fate for the dead. The two paths, i.e., the *devayāna* and the *pitṛyāṇa* also called *arci-mārga* and *dhūma-mārga* respectively are also described. It is believed that those who perfom charitable deeds follow the *pitṛyāṇa* after their death. On this path the soul enters successively into smoke, night, dark fortnight, six months when the sun has southern inclination, the *pitṛ-loka* (region of the Fathers), sky and from sky to the moon. After having stayed in the moon for a specific length of time, i.e., till the effect of his actions lasts, the soul undertakes the return-journey. Heading towards the earth the soul moves from moon to sky from sky to wind, from wind it becomes smoke from smoke the cloud is formed and from that it becomes the rain cloud. The rain produces rice, corn, etc. Those, who eat these grains, procreate and the dead is thus reborn on the earth as the soul takes up a new body.

The other path is the *devayana* or the path of the gods. The final destination of this path is *Brahman*. Those, who cultivate faith and penance enter, successively, after their death, in the regions of light, day, bright fortnight, six months when the sun has northern inclination. From there the soul enters the region of year (*saṁvatsara*), sun, moon and the light and ultimately enters *Brahman*, never to return (*ChāUp*. 5.10.1-2).

Thus it is clear that in contrast with the *devayāna* the *pitṛyāṇa* is a path to rebirth. Those who take up *pitṛyāṇa* are finally reborn on earth.

In the *KaṭhaUp* (1.1.6) the fate of man is described as a cornfield, where the crop is grown and cut again and again. In a similar way man also takes birth and dies again and again. The germ of the theory of *karman* which later developed fully in the *Purāṇas* can be seen in the *ChāUp*, 5.10.7.

According to it the next life of man as well as his fate and circumstances in that life solely depend upon his good or evil actions performed during the present life. The *ChāUp*, 5.10.7 remarks that those whose conduct has been good will attain some good birth, i.e., the birth of a brahmin, a kṣatriya, a vaiśya, but those whose conduct has been evil get a low birth, i.e., the birth of a dog, a hog, a cāṇḍāla (a low-caste).

In the *KauUp*, 1.2 it is clearly stated that the soul gets different bodies in accordance to his *karman* or knowledge. A variety of bodies are mentioned here which a soul may get. They are a worm or a moth, a fish or a bird, a leopard or a lion, a serpent or a man or any of the other creatures.

The *BṛUp* describes in details the manner in which a man dies and is reborn (*BṛUp*, 4.3.37-38; 4.4.1-2). It also says that the knowledge, the works and the former consciousness of the dead follow him after his death.[49]

The manner in which the soul leaves the present body and takes up another is very explicitly related with the example of a caterpillar. When a caterpillar moving on a blade of grass reaches the end of it, it looks for another support, and then draws itself towards this new support. Such is the transition of soul from one body to another. Giving another example the text states that as a goldsmith takes a piece of gold and out of that he frames another form which is newer and more beautiful. In a similar way the Self after having thrown off this body and dispelled ignorance, takes on another newer and more beautiful form. The law of *karman* is also seen here. *BṛUp*, 4.4 further says that the soul gets a holy body if his actions have been good and a sinful body if his actions have been bad.[50] Ultimately it can be said that the germs of transmigration which are found in the *ṚV* have developed fully in the *Upaniṣads*.

The Two Paths **(*ChāUp* 5.10.1-6)**

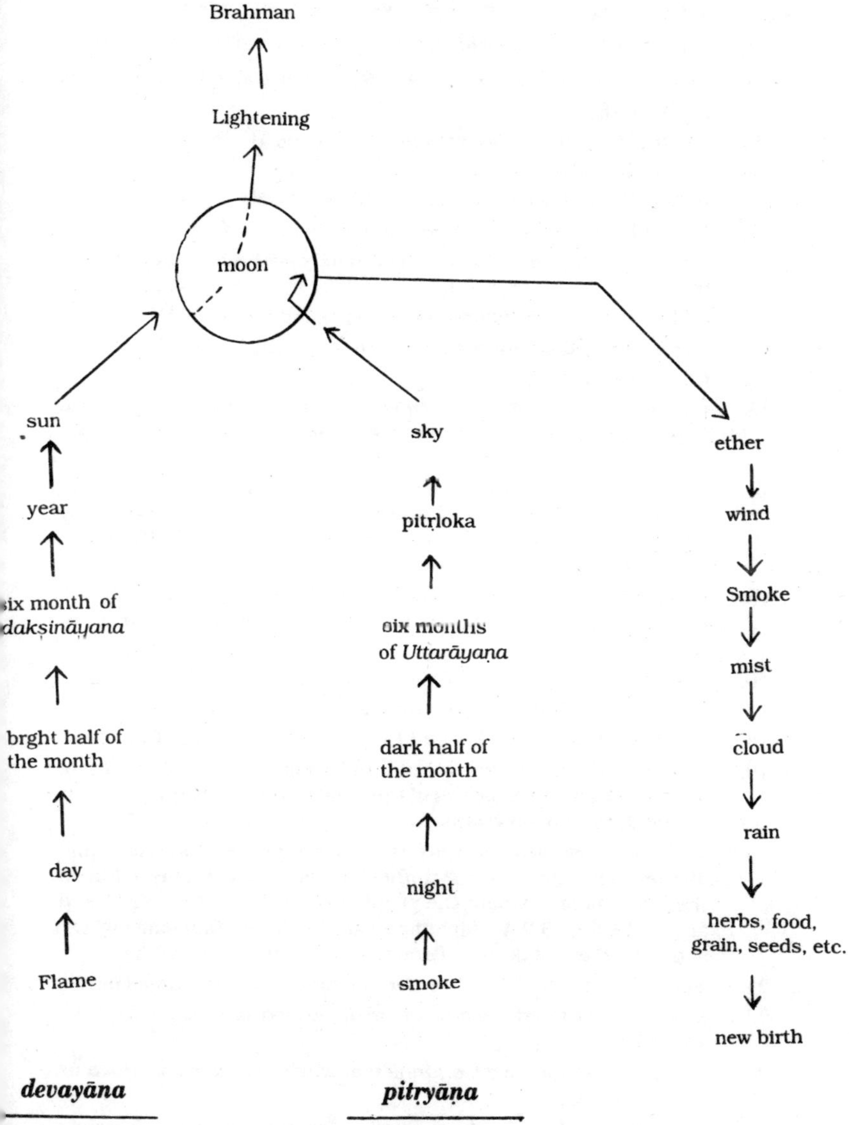

fig. 5.2

Notes

1 *martyo yam amṛtattvam eti* — *AV*, 18.4.37.
lokam pitṛṣu vitvā edhasva yamarājasu — *AV*, 18.2.25.

2. See "Yama's abode", chapter 2.
3. J. Gonda, *Loka — World & Heaven in the Veda*, p. 89.
4. *eṣa vai svargo loko yatra paśum saṁjñapayanti*/— *ŚB*, 13.2.8.5.
5. *Vide* J. Gonda, *op. cit.*, p. 90: ***See also*** Caland, *Pañcaviṁśa Brāhmaṇa*, p. 235.
6. *lokam pitṛṣu vitvā edhasva yamarājasu*/ — *AV*, 18.2.25.
7. *tena lokān sūryavato jayema*/ — *AV*, 9.5.18.
8. *naro yatra devayavo madanti*/ — *ṚV*, 1.154.5b.
9. *Vide* H.H. Wilson, *Ṛgveda Saṁhitā*, transl., Vol. 6, p. 80.
10. *yatra āsate sukṛto yatra ta īyuḥ tatrā tvā devaḥ savitā dadhātu*/ — (*ṚV*, 10.17.4, *AV*, 18.2.55).
tābhyām yamasya sādanam samitiscāv gacchatāt/ — *AV*, 18.2.56.
11. *sa no deveṣu ā yamat dīrgham āyuḥ prajīvase*/ — *ṚV*, 10.14.14.
12. Cf. Renou, *EVP*, VIII, p. 901.
13. *tau asmabhyam dṛśaye sūryāya punar dātām asum adya iha bhadram*/ — *ṚV*, 10.14.2; *AV*, 18.2.13. *jīvase jyok ca sūryam dṛśe*/ — *ṚV*, 10.57.4.
14. The idea of a post-mortem existence in the sense of a definate place, which is the abode of the blessed dead is indeed often rejected by later authorities. For a short survey, *vide* P.V. Kane, *HDS*, Vol. V, pt. II, pp. 1212 ff.
15. *yatrā suhārdah sukṛto madanti, vihāya rogam tanvaḥ svāyāḥ*/ *aślonā angairahrutāḥ svarge, tatra paśyema pitarau ca putrāh*/ — *AV*, 6.120.3.
16. *sokātiko modate svarga-lokam*/ — *KaṭhaUp*, 1.13.
17. *bhogāyatana, Śāṅkarbhāṣya* on *Vedānta Sūtra*, 4.3.4.
18. J. Gonda, *Loka — Worlds and Heaven in the Veda*, p. 109.
19. **See** *infra* 'rebirth' for the 'doctrine of *karman*'. In later *Maṇḍalas* of the *ṚV*, however, the germs of the idea of transmigration are seen — ***see*** *infra* 'transmigration'.
20. W. Caland observes "there is no return from yonder world, once and all they depart from hence thither"; cf. *ŚB*, 2.4.2.9. This world on the other hand is where the people lying in it are born again and again. The *ŚB*, 13.2.4.1 identifies *asau lokaḥ*, i.e., 'the yonder world' and the sphere of gods — *Pañcaviṃśa Brāhmaṇa*, p. 122.
21. **See** J. Gonda, *op. cit.*, p. 84 (for sphere of gods; *svarga-loka*).
22. *śarīram asya saṁdaha atha enam dhehi sukṛtāṁ loke*/ — 18.3.71 also 18.4.11.
23. *tebhir yahi pathībhīh devayānair yair ījānāḥ svargaṁ yānti lokam*/ — *AV*, 18.4.2.
24. *tasmai pra bhāti nabhaso jyotiṣīmān svargaḥ panthā sukṛte*

devayānaḥ/ — *AV*, 18.4.14.

25. *ṚV*, 7.87.5 refers to 'three heavens' and 'three earths' and thus arranged it is 'sixfold'.
26. H. Oldenberg, *Vedic Hymns*, *SBE*, Vol. 46, p. 337.
27. *Vide* S. Radhakrishnan, *Indian Philosophy*, Vol. I, p. 115.
28. That this man is Yama is unproved. A.B. Keith, *RPVU*, II, p. 410 fn.
29. A.B. Keith, *ibid.*
30. *anandā nāma te lokā andhena tamasāvṛtāḥ/*
    tāṁs te pretya abhigacchanti avidvāṅso' budhojanāḥ /
    — *BṛUp*, 4.4.11.
31. R.D. Ranade refers to an interesting suggestion made by R.G. Bhandarkar in *BBRAS* Journal. According to it the Sanskrit equivalent of the word *asurya* may here refer to the Assyrian country. Assyrian and Asuryan being philologically identical, the *Y* and *U* are interchangeable as in Greek, *A Constructive Survey of Upaniṣadic Philosophy*, p. 157.
32. For various views and description of the life after death in the celestial region, heaven, *lokas*, ***see*** S.G. Kantawala, *A Cultural History of Matsya-Purāṇa*, p. 227 f.
33. Macdonell, A.A., *History of Sanskrit Literature*, p. 387.
34. R.D. Ranade, *A Constructive Survey of Upaniṣadic Philosophy*, pp. 146-47.
35. *dharmeṇa sukṛtena* — Sāyaṇa on the *ṚV*, 10.16.3.
36. *Vide* R.D. Ranade, *op. cit.*, p. 148.
37. *Op.cit.*, p. 151.
38. *Ibid.*
39. *Op.cit.*, p. 152.
40. *hitvā avadyam punarastam ehi/* — *ṚV*, 10.14.8.

    Sāyaṇa comments — *tataḥ iṣṭāpūrtena saha āgamya avadyam pāpam hitvā parityajya vriyamānākhyam gṛham ehi āgaccha.* The *pada* text reads the verb *ehi* as *a/ihi* and Sāyaṇa renders it as *ā gaccha.*
41. M. Bloomfield, *PV*, p. 251.
42. H.D. Velankar, *ṚV Maṇḍala* VII, Transl. & Notes, p. 3.
43. *Vide* R.D. Ranade, *op. cit.*, p. 153.
44. *kṛtaṁ lokaṁ puruṣo'bhi jāyate/* — *ŚB*, 6.2.2.27.
45. J. Eggeling, *ŚB*, *SBE*, Vol. 44, p. 23.
46. *Op.cit.*, Vol. 12, p. 148.
47. J. Gonda, *Loka — World & Heaven in the Vedas*, p. 89; ***see*** 'Ritual Heaven', chapter 5.
48. *sa lokam āgacchati aśokaṃ ahimaṃ tasmin vasati śāśvatīḥ samāḥ/* — *BṛUp*, 5.10.1.

    It may be noted here that the region of the blessed is spoken of as a snowless region. He suggests that the Upaniṣadic philosophers were tormented by too much cold and snow in the region where they lived.

49. *tam vidyā karmāṇi samanvārabhete pūrvā prajñā ca* — BṛUp, 4.4.2.

50. *sa vā ayamātmā yathākārī yathācārī tathā bhavati.*
sādhukārī sādhu bhavati pāpakārī pāpo bhavati. / — BṛUp, 4.4.

PART II

Yama in the Purāṇas

6

Parentage, Abode, Companions and Messengers

THE Epics and the *Purāṇas* constitute a link between the Vedic and the classical literature. The Epic literature comprises of *Rāmāyaṇa* (the *Ādi-kāvya*) and *Mahābhārata.* Eighteen *Mahā-Purāṇas* and several *Upa-Purāṇas* constitute the Purāṇic literature. Unlike the *Vedas* they could be read by common people which has added to their popularity. The importance of Purāṇic literature can never be over-estimated. In fact the *Purāṇas* "occupy a unique position in the sacred and secular literature of the Hindus, their importance being regarded as next to the *Vedas* only".[1] The *Mbh* and the *Purāṇas* are also regarded as the fifth *Veda.*[2]

The study of Epics and *Purāṇas* has been stressed as necessary for the interpretation of the *Vedas*. Apart from forming a link between the Vedic and the classical literature, they are also an important source of the cultural history of India. They are useful for a historical study of Indian society in general as well as for comparative studies in the field of religion, philosophy and mythology. The epics and the *Purāṇas* particularly serve as the chief source of information about the Indian mythology. Many a legend, already familiar from the Ṛgvedic hymns and from the *Brāhmaṇas* reappear in the *Purāṇas.*[3] The stories/legends which are nothing more than rudimentary sketches get a better deal in the *Purāṇas* where they are narrated in great details. Some stories appear in more than one *Purāṇa* and in a *Purāṇa* devoted to the praise of a particular deity, the same myths are shown to highlight the supremacy or benevolence of that god. Numerous classical poets and dramatists have found in the Epics and the *Purāṇas*, the themes and plots for their literary works. *Purāṇas* are extremely valuable for the history of philosophy and religion. "Taken collectively they may be described as popular encyclopaedia of ancient and medieval Hinduism religious, philosophical, historical, personal, social and political."[4]

Yāska gives the etymology of the vocable *Purāṇa* as *purā navaṁ bhavati*, i.e., that which is always new in spite of being old (*Nir*, 3.19). According to the *VāyuP*, 1.203, again on the basis of its etymology, the term *purāṇa* means "that which lives from ancient times".[5] The *MatsyaP* describes the *Purāṇas* as containing record of the past events.[6] "Originally the term *purāṇa* signified 'ancient tales' or 'old narratives' in the *Brāhmaṇa* literature, as compared with *Itihāsa* or *Nārāsaṁsa* before it became associated with *Purāṇas* as a class of literature.[7]

Date of the Purāṇas

It is very difficult to determine the exact date of the *Purāṇas*. They "undoubtedly reach back to great antiquity and are rooted in Vedic literature."[8] Though in the *AV* there are references to the *Purāṇas* as independent form of literature it cannot be said that the term *purāṇa* meant actual books at the time of the *AV*.[9] The *ChāUp* however, indicates that the term *purāṇa* denoted a particular work which is mentioned along with the four *Vedas* (*ṚV*, *YV*, *SV* and *AV*) and it is called the 'fifth *Veda*'.

Most of the *Purāṇas* consist of portions which were written at different period of time. While dealing with the age of the *Purāṇas*, therefore, the date of the earliest portion should be considered and not the latest. The earlier versions of the *Purāṇas* existed even at the time of the *Mbh*, while the extant *Purāṇas*, however, can be assigned to the early centuries of the Christian era on the testimony of epigraphy and literature.[10] As noted earlier "it is no doubt true that the *Purāṇas* as they exist cannot be assigned to any particular age, even the component parts of individual *Purāṇas* belonging to different periods, as the process of inflation, omission contamination, etc. have been continuously going on."[11]

According to the popular belief all the *Purāṇas* were the work of the great sage Vedavyāsa, the arranger of the *Vedas* and the author of the *Mbh.*

Characteristics of Purāṇas

The characteristics of the *Purāṇas* have been mentioned in several *Purāṇas* where they are defined as *pañcalakṣaṇa.*[12] These five characteristics are *sarga* (creation), *pratisarga* (dissolution and recreation), *vaṁśa* (divine genealogy), *manvantara* (the ages of Manu) and *vaṁśānucaritam* (genealogy of kings). These characteristics indicate the real nature of the *Purāṇas* in their early, if not the earliest, form. Most of the *Purāṇas* contain much more than these topics, while some scarcely deal with those mentioned in it. Since the *Pañcalakṣaṇa* occupied a very insignificant part in the bulk of a *Purāṇa*, "It appears that the religious instructions was not one of their primary aims".[13] The *dāna* (gifts), *vratas* (religious observance) *tīrthas* (sacred places), *śrāddha* (rites in honour of the Manes) etc. constitute a major portion of the extant *Purāṇas* rendering the *pañcalakṣaṇa* definition only a theoretical definition.

Number of Purāṇas

There are 18 *Mahā-Purāṇas* and 18 *Upa-Purāṇas* according to the traditional view. The names of these 18 *Purāṇas* are enumerated in many *Purāṇas*. R.C. Hazra divided these 18 *Purāṇas* in two categories (i) Major, (ii) Minor. He takes seven *Purāṇas*, i.e., the *MāP, VāyuP, BrahmāṇḍaP, ViP, MP, Bhāg. P; KūrmaP* as major *Purāṇas* and the other eleven (i.e., *VāmanP, LiṅgaP, VarāhaP, PP, Nāradīya, Agni, Garuḍa, Brahma, Skanda, BVP* and *Bhaviṣya*) as the minor *Purāṇas.*[14]

In the *ViṣṇuP*, 3.6.20.29 and *BhāgP*, 12.13.3-8, the

eighteen *Mahā-Purāṇas* are mentioned in a particular order which is maintained in the other *Purāṇas* also. They are *Brahma, Padma, Viṣṇu, Śiva, Bhāg, Nāradīya, Mārk, Agni, Bhaviṣya, Brahma-Vaivarta, Liṅga, Varāha, Skanda, Vāmana, Kūrma, Matsya, Garuḍa* and *Brahmāṇḍa*. In some places the *ŚivaP* is substituted by *VāyuP*.[15]

There is no uniformity in the enumeration of the *Upa-Purāṇas*. They are more sectarian in character, comparatively late and of composite nature. They are *Sanatkumāra, Narasiṁha, Nanda, Śivadharma, Durvāsā, Naradīya, Kapila, Vāmana, Uśanas, Mānava, Varuṇa, Kāli, Maheśvara, Śāmba, Saura Parāśara, Marīca* and *Bhārgava*.[16]

Classification

The *Purāṇas* are classified into ancient and later on the basis of their conformity to the *Pañcalakṣaṇa* definition. Less the number of addition which are foreign to the nature of *Purāṇas*, older is the *Purāṇa*. On this basis *Vāyu, Brahmāṇḍa, Matsya* and *Viṣṇu* are considered ancient *Purāṇas*.

The *Purāṇas* are also divided on the basis of their preferential treatment to the particular deities. The *PP*, 163.81.84 divides them, evidently on the Vaiṣṇava stand-point, as *Sāttvika, Rājasika*, and *Tāmasika Purāṇas* —

(1) *Sāttvika* — *ViṣṇuP, Nāradīya, Bhāg, GP, PP*, and *VarāhaP*.

(2) *Tāmasika*—*MP, Kūrma, Liṅga, Śiva, Agni* and *Skanda*.

(3) *Rājasika* — *Brahmāṇḍa, Brahma-Vaivarta, MāP, BrahmaP, VāmanaP* and *BhaviṣyaP*.

Basing his division on later Tamil works, Dikshitar classifies the *Purāṇas* into five groups.[17]

Deity	Name of the *Purāṇa*
Brahmā	*BrahmaP* and *PP*
Sūrya	*Brahma-VaivartaP*
Agni	*AgniP*

Śiva	*Śiva, SkandaP, LiṅgaP, KūrmaP, VāmanaP, VarāhaP, BhaviṣyaP, MP, MārkaṇḍeyaP, BrahmāṇḍaP*
Viṣṇu	*NāradaP, BhāgP, GP* and *ViP*

On the basis of the contents of the *Purāṇas*, they are divided in six groups. This classification is attempted by Haraprasad Shastri who divided them in the following six groups:

(1) The *Purāṇas* in the first group are encyclopaedia of literature. They deal in addition to the usual Purāṇic material, with medicine, grammar, dramaturgy, music, astrology etc. *GP, AgniP* and *NāradiyaP* fall in this category.

(2) The second group deals mainly with *tīrthas* and *vratas*. These *Purāṇas* have undergone drastic changes and revision resulting in their original matter being lost e.g., *SkandaP, BrahmaP.*

(3) The third group has *BrahmaP, BhāgP* and *BrVaiP.* These *Purāṇas* have undergone revision and the additional matter is added at both the ends of the original matter.

(4) The fourth group, this group is called the historical group. *BrahmāṇḍaP* and *VāyuP* fall in this category.

(5) Sectarian works form the fifth group which consists of *LiṅgaP, VāmanP* and *MāP.*

(6) *Purāṇas* of the sixth group had been revised out of existence. They include *Varāha, Kūrma* and *Matsya.*

The study of the post-Vedic literature has its own importance from the point of view of comparative mythology and the *Purāṇas* are said to be a store-house of religion and mythology. In the *Purāṇas* some Vedic diety have gained importance while some lost their prominence or even relegated to oblivion. Yama is one of those Vedic deities whose personality and character have undergone tremendous change in the Purāṇic pantheon and Purāṇic Hindu religion.

Yama's Parentage

The account of Yama's parentage is found in many *Purāṇas* viz. *ViP, MP, VāP, MārkP, LiṅgaP, BP.* Its different versions are as follows.

MĀRKAṆḌEYA PURĀṆA VERSION

According to the *MārkP* chapter 74, Viśvakarman's daughter Saṁjñā was the wife of Mārtaṇḍa (also mentioned as Sūrya Vivasvat).[18] After the birth of Manu, Saṁjñā found it difficult to bear the radiance of Vivasvat and once he saw her as she closed her eyes on seeing him. He became infuriated and pronounced a curse on Saṁjñā, "you control your eyes from me, O fool! so may you give birth to Yama, the controller of mankind!" He further cursed her to bear a river as a daughter (*MārkP*, 74.4). After the birth of Yama and Yamunā it became impossible for Saṁjñā to bear the lustre of the Sun any more. She asked her own shadow, i.e., Chāyā to take her place and care for her children. Saṁjñā told Chāyā to act as Sūrya's wife and never to disclose her identity to anybody. Chāyā agreed to do so but clarified that if Sūrya became angry and was about to curse her, she would disclose her identity. Agreeing to this Saṁjñā left her father's house leaving Chāyā behind to look after her home and children. Sūrya could not know this change. Three children — Sāvarṇi Manu, Śani and Tapatī were born to Chāyā. Chāyā started giving more attention and love to her own children than to those of Saṁjñā. Manu tolerated her behaviour but Yama could not and on one occasion he lifted his leg to strike her. Though he controlled himself in time and did not hit her, Chāyā was furious. She cursed Yama that as he had lifted his leg for hitting her, his leg would be eaten up by worms. A worried Yama went to Vivasvat and said, "It is surprising that a mother should curse her son. As Manu has said before, "this lady indeed is not our mother, because even if a son is wicked, the mother is never cruel to him" (*MārkP*, 74.32). When questioned by Sūrya, Chāyā maintained that she was Saṁjñā, the daughter of Tvaṣṭṛ, wife of Sūrya and mother of his children. When she did not tell the truth and repeated the same statement, Sūrya got angry and was about to pronounce a curse. At this, Chāyā disclosed the truth and said that Saṁjñā has left for her father's place. Sūrya went to Viśvakarman and learnt from him that Saṁjñā had stayed there for some time but had left when she was told that it was not morally good for a married woman to stay at her father's place for long and therefore, she must return to her husband's house. Sūrya through meditation saw that Saṁjñā, in the form of a mare, was practising penance in Uttara-Kuru.

He also knew the reason for her distress and the aim of her penance. She wanted to make his lustre bearable. Sūrya requested Viśvakarman to reduce his dazzle and make it bearable for others. Viśvakarman reduced Sun's lustre to one-eighth. Out of the pared off lustre of Sūrya he made the trident of Śiva, discuss of Viṣṇu, Śakti of Agni and many other weapons (*MārkP*, 75.17-18). With his diminished lustre Sūrya assumed the form of a horse and went to the Uttara-Kuru region and found Saṁjñā in the form of a mare. She could not recognise her husband. On meeting, their noses united and the mare gave birth to two sons through her nose. Another son Revanta was also born to them after some time.

Vivasvat lessened the severity of the curse to Yama by adding that when the worms from his foot would fall on the earth, it would be alright again. Seeing Yama as possessing a righteous vision[19] and equal bearing towards friends and foes, Sūrya also granted him the authority of the controller (*MārkP*, 75.28; also 105.16-18).

VĀYU PURĀṆA VERSION

According to the *VāP*, 84.24, the daughter of Viśvakarman was Sareṇu. She was married to Vivasvat and then she was named Saṁjñā. The further story has no significant difference from the other versions. But here Śrutaśravas and Śrutakarman are mentioned as two sons of Chāyā who elsewhere are named as Sāvarṇi Manu and Śani respectively. When Yama got angry due to the ill-treatment meted out by Chāyā and was about to kick her, Chāyā cursed that Yama would lose his leg (*VāP*, 84.56-61).

VIṢṆU PURĀṆA VERSION

In the *ViP*, 3.2.1 ff. Pārāsara, on being inquired by Maitreya about the forthcoming *Manvantaras*, states the story of Vivasvat's progeny. According to it Saṁjñā, the daughter of Viśvakarman, was the wife of Sūrya who bore him three children — viz. Manu, Yama and Yamunā. Unable to bear the dazzling lustre of Sūrya any more, Saṁjñā placed her shadow (*chāyā*)[20] in the service of her husband Sūrya and repaired to the forest for practising penance. Due to the similarity of Chāyā's appearance with that of Saṁjñā, Sūrya took her as Saṁjñā and begot in her three more children — viz. Śanaiścara, Sāvarṇi Manu and Tapatī. On one occasion Chāyā got angry with Yama and pronounced an imprecation upon him and thereby revealed to him and Sūrya that she was not Saṁjñā, the real mother of the former.[21] On being further informed by Chāyā that Saṁjñā had gone to the wilderness, Sūrya by meditation beheld her engaged in austerities in the form of a mare in the Uttara-Kuru region. Metamorphosing himself into a horse, he rejoined Saṁjñā and begot three other children — the two Aśvins and Revanta. He then brought Saṁjñā back to his house. To diminish the intensity of his lustre Viśvakarman placed Sūrya on his lathe to grind off some of his (i.e., Sūrya's) effulgence, and in this manner he reduced it by one-eighth, since more than that was inseparable.[22] From the filed off parts of Sūrya he fashioned the discus of Viṣṇu, trident of Śiva, the lance of Kārttikeya and other weapons.

Yama was the fifth descendant of Mahāviṣṇu. From Mahāviṣṇu descended, in the following order, Brahmā, Marīci, Kāśyapa, Sūrya, Yama (*ViP*, 1.13).

MATSYA PURĀṆA VERSION

According to the *MP*, 11.2-3 Vivasvat had three wives (1) Rājñī by whom he had a son named Revanta, (2) Prabhā — by whom he had Prabhāta, (3) Saṁjñā, the daughter of Tvaṣṭṛ by whom he had Manu, Yama and Yamunā. It also says that the latter two were twins.[23] When Saṁjñā found herself unable to bear the dazzle of Sūrya she produced a lady from her own body who resembled her. Saṁjñā asked this lady named Chāyā, to serve her husband and take motherly care of her children, and went away.[24] In due course Chāyā gave birth to Sāvarṇi Manu,[25] Śani, Tapatī and Viṣṭi. Chāyā was partial towards her own children and showered all her love on them. Manu endured this unfair treatment but Yama could not. One day he threatened her by raising his leg. At this Chāyā cursed that his leg would be eaten up by worms and would suffer from wounds emissing pus and blood. Yama got angry and reported this incident to his father, i.e., Vivasvat (*MP*, 11.13). Yama said that he had been cursed by the mother for no fault of his. In a childish freak he lifted up his foot at her at which in spite of the entreaties of Manu she pronounced a course on him. Yama further said that such an attitude of Chāyā showed that she was not his real mother. Vivasvat listened to Yama and expressed his inability to do anything in this matter. He further said that one has to bear the fruit of one's folly and also of the deeds done in the previous births and that even Lord Śiva had to reap the fruit of his action. Thus, Sun expressed his inability to do away with the effect of a mother's curse[26] even when Yama told him that she could not be his real mother. He however, gave him a cock who would eat up all the worms and clean the impurities of the wound.

Thereafter Sūrya frightened Chāyā and made her disclose her identity. Chāyā narrated what had happened and also that Saṁjñā had gone to her father's house. Yama, on the other hand, after getting the effect of the curse minimized went to Gokarṇa-tīrtha where he performed penance for several years. By the grace of Śiva he got the overlordship of the Fathers.[27] He also gained the faculty of distinguishing the good and bad deads of man (*MP*, 11.18).

When Saṁjñā reached her father's house, he reprimanded her for running away from her husband's house. She was denied admittance in the house. From there Saṁjñā went to the Marudeśa where she roamed in the form of a mare (*MP*, 11.26). Viśvakarman reported this to Sun when the latter approached him to inquire about Saṁjñā. Viśvakarman offered to reduce Sūrya's lustre and make him bearable. With his permission, Viśvakarman sliced off, by his instrument *Bhramī* (the wheel), some portion of Sūrya's unbearable lustre. After getting his lustre reduced by Viśvakarman, Sūrya went out in the form of a horse and enjoyed himself in the company of Saṁjñā, who not recognising him as her husband was terrified but helpless. She ejected the semen virile through her nostrils out of which the two Aśvinīkumāras, also called Nāsatya and Dasra, were born. Afterwards Saṁjñā recognised Sūrya and went with him.

LIṄGA PURĀṆA VERSION

The *LP* (1.65.10) provides similar story as that in the *MP*. After being cursed by Chāyā Yama went to Gokarṇa region and there he practised penance for thousands of years. At last, by the grace of Lord Śiva he became a guardian of the region (*lokapāla*) and the overlord of the Fathers. Being a Śaivite *Purāṇa* the *LP* highlights the glory of Lord Śiva who freed Yama from the terrible curse too. Sūrya, on knowing that the woman whom he took as Saṁjñā was not Saṁjñā but Chāyā, set out to look for Saṁjñā. However, how he could know this is not given in the *LP* version. Sūrya found her in the form of a mare. He himself took the form of a horse and Aśvinīkumāras were born to them. Viśvakarman pared off one-eighth part of Sūrya's lustre to make it bearable.

BRAHMA VAIVARTA PURĀṆA VERSION

The *BVP*, 1.47.12 relates that while the Sūrya called Mārtaṇḍa was yet in the cosmic egg, Dakṣa gave him his beautiful daughter Arūpā, as wife.[28] Yama and Yamī were born to her. Arūpā was dazzled by Sūrya's brilliance. Even her golden complexion turned dark due to Sūrya's rays. Deeply dejected she left her shadow, i.e., Chāyā in the house and went to the Northern Kuru for practising penance. She lived there in the form of a mare. Sūrya got two children viz. Śani and Tapatī by Chāyā. Once Yamī and Tapatī quarrelled and turned into rivers by mutual curse. Yama was beaten severely by Chāyā and he angrily lifted his foot (for hitting her). Enraged at this Chāyā cursed, "You, fool! have raised your leg towards me;

therefore, as long as there will be the sun and the moon, the gruesome task of taking away lives of creatures will undoubtedly be yours. If you place your foot on earth, worms will consume it polluted as it is with my curse." Meanwhile Sūrya came there and Yama intimated Chāyā's unfair treatment and added that she was only a 'Chāyā', i.e., 'shadow'-image of his mother. Yama also informed him the unhappy incident concerning Yamunā and Tapatī. In order to reduce the severity of the curse Sūrya said that the river Yamunā would be considered as holy as the Gaṅgā into which she would ultimately flow. Tapatī would be considered equal to the Narmadā in respect of sanctity. He also said that Yama would become a *lokapāla* and that Chāyā would thenceforth live in her own body.

VARĀHA PURĀṆA VERSION

According to the *VP* version Yama and Yamunā were children of Vivasvat whom he got as a boon from Lord Viṣṇu. In the *VP*, 137.281, Varāha tells Vasundharā about the sanctity of the Vaivasvata-*tīrtha* where Vivasvat (Āditya) himself practised penance. Vivasvat was desirous of having a son by the grace of Lord Keśava. He practised severe austerities for thousands of years with the desire of getting a son. At last the Lord was pleased and asked Vivasvat about his desire which should be fulfilled. Vivasvat replied that he wanted a son by Lord's grace (137.285). The Lord granted this and said that Yama and Yamunā would be born to him (137.287).

Discussion

COMMON FEATURES OF THE STORY

Saṁjñā, the daughter of Viśvakarman

Sūrya's[29] wife was the daughter of Viśvakarman.[30] In most of the *Purāṇas* her name is given as Saṁjñā (*ViP, MāP, MP, LP*). She bore three children; Manu, Yama and Yamunā of which the latter two were twins.

Saṁjñā's Departure

Unable to bear Sūrya's radiance any longer, she fashioned a woman from her body who was exactly like herself. This woman was named 'Chāyā'. Saṁjñā asked Chāyā to take care of her husband and children without disclosing her real identity. After this Saṁjñā left for her father's place in the form of a mare. Here it may be presumed that she transformed herself into a mare in order to be able to run away fast from the house before her husband Sūrya could know about her plan.

Saṁjñā's Penance

Saṁjñā went to her father's place first. From there she, in the form of a mare, proceeded to the Uttara-Kuru region for practising penance.

Chāyā's Children

Saṁjñā had left the house after engaging her substitute there. This substitute was 'Chāyā', literally, her own 'shadow'. Sūrya could not discern this replacement and from Chāyā he begot three children — Sāvarṇī Manu, Śani and Tapatī.

Chāyā's Curse

After the birth of her own children Chāyā ill-treated Saṁjñā's children. On one occasion Yama could not endure her behaviour and lifted his leg in order to strike her. This made Chāyā furious and she pronounced a curse upon Yama that he would lose his leg.

Father's Reaction

On being cursed by Chāyā Yama was very unhappy. He reported this incident to Sūrya. Sūrya expressed his inability to do away with the curse of a mother (it is noteworthy that in this case she is not even Yama's real mother), but minimised the effect of her curse.

The Reunion

Sūrya forced Chāyā to disclose the whereabouts of Saṁjñā and he then set out to look for her. Finding her in the form of a mare, Sūrya transformed himself into a horse. A pair of twins, i.e., the two Aśvinīkumāras and Revanta were born to them.

The different versions of this story in different *Purāṇas* are very similar in their details; with some points of dissimilarity.

POINTS OF DISSIMILARITY IN DIFFERENT VERSIONS

While most of the versions record the name of Sūrya's wife as Saṁjñā,[31] the *VāP* provides that the daughter of Viśvakarman was Sareṇu and she was called Saṁjñā after her marriage to Vivasvat. It is significant to note that this name, i.e., Sareṇu is very near to her Vedic name Saraṇyū. It is a possible development, having undergone a phonetic change, from the Vedic word 'Saraṇyū', ('a' becoming 'e' here and 'y' being dropped. This change may be ascribed to a tendency for easy pronunciation). The *BVP* gives the name of Sūrya's wife as Arūpā.

Children of Saṁjñā

Manu was the eldest son of Saṁjñā and Sūrya.[32] The two other children were Yama and Yamunā and they were twins. According to the *VāyuP*, Sūrya in a fit of anger cursed Saṁjñā that she would give birth to the 'controller of mankind', and also that she would bear a river as a daughter. The birth of Yama and Yamunā followed these curses.[33]

Saṅjñā's Secret Department

Leaving Chāyā in her place, Saṁjñā left her husband's house. According to the *MāP* she went to her father, i.e., Viśvakarman's house and stayed there for many days. Then Viśvakarman advised her to return to her husband's house, since it was against the *dharma* of a married woman to stay at her relatives' house for a long time. At this Saṁjñā left her father's house. Reluctant to return to Sūrya she went to the

Uttara-Kuru region and practised penance in the form of a mare.

Chāyā's Children

The *VāyuP* gives the names of the two sons of Chāyā as Śrutaśravas and Śrutakarman, who are called Sāvarṇi Manu and Śani respectively in all other versions. In the *BVP* there is no mention of either Manu or Sāvarṇi Manu (i.e., Śrutaśravas or Śrutakarman) among the sons of Sūrya. Furthermore, Yamunā and Tapatī are said to have quarrelled and turned into rivers by cursing each other. It may be recalled here that according to *MāP* Sūrya cursed his wife Saṁjñā that a river would be born to her and then she gave birth to Yamunā.

Chāyā's Curse

Chāyā ill-treated Saṁjñā's children. On one of such occasions Yama did not conceal his anger and spontaneously revolted by lifting his leg. The added fuel to Chāyā's anger and she pronounced a curse on him. The target was Yama's leg only, but a slight difference is seen in some *Purāṇas*. According to the *MāP* Chāyā cursed Yama that his leg would be eaten up by worms, that it would also suffer from wounds emissing pus and blood (*MP*); that he would lose his leg (*VāyuP*). According to the *BVP* Chāyā cursed Yama that the cruel task of killing people would be his. Thus Yama became a killer-god due to Chāyā's curse to him. It can be compared here that in the *MāP* Sūrya cursed Saṁjñā to bear a conrtroller of mankind and then Yama was born. Furthermore, when Sūrya lessened the severity of Chāyā's curse he also granted him the authority of a controller, pleased as he was due to Yama's righteous vision[34] and equal bearing towards friends and foes (*MaP*, 105, 15-19) : The *ViP* records Chāyā's curse but does not mention as to why she got angry.

On learning from Yama about Chāyā's curse to him Sūrya felt that he was wrongfully cursed. Yet, according to the *MP*, Sūrya showed his inability to do way with the effect of a mother's curse but gave him a cock who would eat up all the worms and clean the wound. According to the *MāP* the sun minimised the severity of the curse by adding that when the worms from his leg would fall on earth, it would be alright again (*MāP*).

Yama's Penance

According to the *MP* Yama retreated to Gokarṇa-tīrtha[35] to practise penance and to please Lord Śiva. At last, Lord Śiva was pleased and Yama asked for (1) the power of protecting the world; (2) the kingdom of the Fathers[36] and (3) the faculty of distinguishing virtue from vice. Śiva granted these to him (*MP*). According to the *LP* also Lord Śiva made Yama a *lokapāla*, but in the *BVP* it was Sūrya who made him a *lokapāla*.

In the *MāP* Sūrya cursed his wife Saṁjñā to bear a river as a daughter, and Yamunā was born to her, while the *BVP* version of this story provides that Yamunā and Tapatī had turned into rivers due to mutual curses. Yamunā became a river in the northern region, while Tapatī in the western region. Thus the story has travelled from North to West, where Tapatī becomes a river in the western part of India (presently in Gujarat) now known as Tāpī.

A skeleton sketch of this story is found in the *ṚV*, 10.17.1-2. It informs that:

(1) Vivasvat's wife was Tvaṣṭṛ's daughter and that her name was Saraṇyū.

(2) Saraṇyū was the mother of Yama. She also bore Aśvins. It further says that she had given birth to two pairs of twins. The *Nirukta* explains that these two pairs of twins were (i) Yama and Yamī, and (ii) Aśvins (dual deities).

(3) Vivasvat's wife, Saraṇyū was hidden by the gods. They fashioned another woman who resembled Saraṇyū. This woman, called Savarṇā was given to Vivasvat as his wife.

The Ṛgvedic account has travelled to the *Purāṇas* retaining some original features and introducing further developments.

The names of most of the characters of this story are seen changed in the *Purāṇas* :

Vedic name	*Purāṇic name*
Tvaṣṭṛ	Viśvakarman
Vivasvat	Sūrya/Mārtaṇḍa/Vivasvat/Āditya[37]
Saraṇyū	Saṁjñā/Sareṇu/Arūpā
Savarṇā	Chāyā (the name of her son is Sāvarṇi Manu which reminds of her Vedic name Savarṇā)
Yamī	Yamunā

According to the Vedic versions Saraṇyū was hidden by the gods. After hiding Saraṇyū they made another woman resembling her. This woman called Savarṇā was given to Vivasvat. Thus Saraṇyū's disappearance was planned by the gods for the sake of the mortals. They hid this immortal bride, i.e., Saraṇyū in order to serve a special purpose which was beneficial to the mortals.

The Purāṇic version has a major diversity here. Here, she was not hidden by the gods. She left the house at her own will. She found it extremely difficult to bear Sūrya's radiance. She had incurred Sūrya's wrath due to her inability to look up in front of him. Sūrya's wrath resulted in a curse to his wife Saṁjñā that she would give birth to the controller of mankind.

In the Vedic version gods hid Saraṇyū and made a similar woman for Vivasvat, but here Saṁjñā herself decided to leave the house. She fashioned a woman from her own body who resembled herself (*MP*). According to *VP*, *MāP*, *BVP* versions Saraṇyū called her own shadow (*chāyā*) and asked her to task care of her family in her absence. It is curious that in *ṚV*, 10.17.1-2 Manu is not mentioned as a son of Saraṇyū or of Savarṇā[38] while *Nir*, 12.10 and *Bṛhaddevatā*, 6.162.7 say that Manu was born to Savarṇā (who is Chāyā in the *Purāṇas*). Max Müller comments that "the fable of Manu might have come at a later stage".[39] In the *Purāṇas* Manu is the eldest son of Saṁjñā and Sūrya. The twin Yama-Yamī were born after him.

V.S. Agrawala gives a symbolic interpretation of this

story and associated the two wives of Sūrya with mortal and immortal creation. He takes Sūrya as a symbol of both immortality and death. Saraṇyū and Chāyā both are wives of Sūrya, the former is immortal or light and the latter is death or shadow or darkness. That which is light is called Saṁjñā (consciousness) and that which is Savarṇā or Chāyā is matter. He further comments that once Sūrya is conceived as *aśva*, the imagery of the Cosmic Tree as *Aśvattha* and its dynamic energy as *aśvā* (mare) is easy. The cosmos is called *Aśvattha*, because a horse (the sun) is at its centre, or because it stands like a horse on three legs and is free on the fourth or because it itself depends on the power or movement of the archetypical horse, that is Sūrya. Thus the conception of Sūrya and Sūryā or *Aśva* and *Aśvā* as the parent of Yama[41] and Yamī on one hand and of the twin Aśvins on the other is consistent in the Vedic thought.

According to V.S. Agrawala it is the doctrine of light and shade (*ātapa* and *chāyā* — *KaṭhaUp*, 3.5.1) which is put into this story. Light corresponds to the immortal creation of *Puruṣa* and shadow to the mortal creation of *Prakṛti*. Sūrya is the symbol of immortality and death, that which is beyond or on the other side of Sūrya is *amṛta*, and that which is on this side is *mṛtyu* (cf. *tad yad kiñca arvācīnām Ādityād sarvam tad mṛtyunā āptam atha ya enam at ūrdhvāṁ cinute sa punar mṛtyum apajayati* — *ŚB*, 10.5.1.4).

Yama's Family

According to the details found in different *Purāṇas*[42] Manu was the eldest son of Sūrya. He was a co-uterine brother of Yama and Yamunā. Yama and Yamunā were twins.[43] They had two more brothers and two more sisters who were born to Chāyā, the substitute of Saṁjñā. They were Sāvarṇi Manu, Śani,[44] Tapatī and Viṣṭi. Aśvinīkumāras and Revanta were also Yama's brothers.[45]

The Yama-Yamī dialogue in *ṚV*, 10.10 has led to an apprehension that Yamī was a sister-wife of Yama.[46] A later version of this hymn is found in the thirteen chapter of *Narasiṁha Purāṇa*. It contains a dialogue between Yama and

Yamī. The purport of this dialogue is similar to that of the *ṚV*, 10.10. It begins with an introduction and the fruit of reading it is stated at the end of the dialogue. It is to be noted that the dialogue in the *ṚV*, 10.10 has no introduction and it ends as abruptly as it begins.

The chapter 12 of the *NP* ends with *Mārkaṇḍeya-Carita* and Śukra requests Vyāsa to narrate to him another *Puṇyā, pāpaharā kathā* (*NP*, 13.1; 3,4). He also wants to know about the merit (*puṇya*) a man of firm mind gets on his not doing a condemned deed. Here Vyāsa tells him the dialogue of high-souled Yama and his sister Yamī. Yama and Yamī were the children of Vivasvat, the son of Aditi, Yamī was younger of the two. Once Yamī approached Yama and spoke like this :

A brother is not a brother if he does not become the husband of his spouseless sister. A man, who turns down the passionate appeal of his sister to become her husband, is not worthy of being called a brother. It is a pity if the brother takes another girl as his wife while his own sister is tormented by passion. Therefore, he (Yama) should wish to do what she is wishing otherwise she would die.

She goes on to the extent of saying that he should unite his body with hers. (*NP*, 13.17). At this Yama gets annoyed and reprimands her for talking about something which is hated in the society. Anybody in this sense would not do such a sin of co-habiting with his own sister. It is a great sin (*mahāpātaka*) which is practised only by animals (13, 19). Here Yamī is ready with the argument that since their former union in their mother's womb was not defiling, it would not be a sin then (13.20). Yama argues that Svayambhū would condemn such an act. The high personage of society should not do contemptible deeds because people tend to follow them. Not doing the condemned deed is a characteristic of *dharma*, and since Yamī's proposal was highly sinful, it was against *dharma*. He points out that the sages call it a sin if one draws one's sister unto oneself. Therefore, she should choose some other partner. Yamī wanted to lure him by referring to her beauty and youthful age. But Yama displays that he was really a *dṛḍhavrata* and *dharmacitta* who wished not to get involved in any sinful act (13.35).

Yamī persisted, but Yama did not succumb to the allurement. As a reward for his firmness and not doing the condemned deed, he attained the godhood (13.36). The following verses state the greatness (*māhātmya*) of this dialogue and the fruit of reading it. It destroys all the sins of the listener. It further says that whoever reads this dialogue, his ancestors are satiated and do not enter the abode of Yama.

As stated in earlier stanzas of the *NP* chapter 13, this dialogue is narrated to Śuka by Vyāsa in reply to his query about the merit (*puṇya*) earned by a man who is firm in his mind and never does any condemnable deed. Thus this dialogue is a laudatory of Yama's who is not only firm-minded (*dṛḍhacitta*), a high soul (*mahātman*) but also upholder of morality and righteousness. Thus this story has an ethical and didactic message.[47]

Although no wife of Yama is mentioned in the *Vedas*, there are some references to his wife and offsprings in the *Mbh* and the *Purāṇas*. According to the *Mbh*, 5.117.81; 13.165.11, Yama's wife is Dhumorṇā. Another wife of Yama is Vijayā.[48]

According to the *BVP*, 1.15.21-22, Yama's consort is the daughter of Mṛtyu (*mṛtyu-kanyā*) who is styled as beautiful, dark-complexioned and *mahāsatī*. She wears red clothes and has six arms. In an icon of Yama she is made standing, along with her sixty-four sons, on the left side of her husband Yama.[49] In the *BVP* a legend connected with Yama's marriage is found.[50] Yama was exceeding pleased with Vijayā the daughter of a brahmin. When she first saw him, she was greatly terrified at his appearance and more so on knowing his identity. Yama allayed her fears and she consented to become his wife.

After their marriage Yama brought Vijayā to his abode. He cautioned her against going to the southern quarter of his kingdom. But after some days, overpowered by curiosity she went to the forbidden region. There she saw people being tormented for their sins.

Sunīthā is the eldest daughter of Yama. Aṅga married her

and the famous king Vena was their son (*ViP*, 1.13). However, according to the *Mbh*, 59.93 and the *PP Bhūmi-Khaṇḍa*, 30.36, Sunīthā was the mind-born daughter of Mṛtyu. She was famous in the three worlds for her beauty and virtues. Here too she is mentioned as the wife of the king Aṅga and the mother of Vena. The *MP* describes her as a daughter of Mṛtyu and as having a ferocious countenance. Other details are similar to those found in the *ViP* and *PP*.

Yama is also said to be the father of Upadānavī and Himā.[51] The *MP*, 49.9 mentions Ilinā as Yama's daughter.

Yama's Kingdom

Since Yama is the lord of the dead, his realm is called *preta-pateḥ puram*, i.e., the city of the lord of the dead (*VarāhaP.*, 194.2).

The *Rāmāyaṇa* provides a lengthy description of the material splendour of Yama's vast kingdom. Beyond his capital is great darkness. His capital is resplendent with golden pillars and seats of diamonds and cat's-eyes, surrounded by bowers is Yama's palace. On the judgement-seat sits lord Vaivasvata, the king (*Rām*, 4.41.45-46).

The name of Yama's city is given as Saṁyamanī[52] The *MāP*, 3.18ff provides that Lord Śiva, pleased with Yama's penance at Gokarṇa made him a *loka-pāla* his city being Saṁyamanī. Yama is invariably connected with the south direction. His city is in the south. He is also the guardian of this direction. According to *VP*, the city of Yama is in the south. Varuṇa-nagar in the west and Kubera-nagar in the north. The *MP* states that Yama's city is in the south of Meru on the back side of Mānasa.[53] The *BhāgP*, 5.26.2-5 also states that Yama's abode is in the south.

Yama's city lies eightysix thousand leagues (*yojanas*) from the world of man.[54] According to *GP* this distance is greater than this. It states that the dead soul walks 200 *yojanas* everyday for 47 days and nights and then he reaches the abode of Yama (*GP*, 2.5.78).

The area of Yama's city is a thousand *yojanas* in the

VarāhaP two rivers flowing in the city of Yama are beautifully described. One of them is Puṣpodakā (194.12) which abounds in the clusters of lotuses. It can destroy all the sins of the living-beings. The other river is called Vaivasvatī (194.22). The water of this river is clean, fragrant and pleasant to taste. The river has a divine appearance. It flows through the city nurturing it like a mother her sons.

There is another river called Vaitaraṇī flowing in Yama's city, but it is different from the other two since the dead have to cross this blazing river in order to reach Yama. The *AgniP* specially recommends that one who is on the verge of death should make gift of a cow (preferably a black one). This cow would enable him to cross the river Vaitaraṇī in the world of Yama.[55]

According to the *GP*, 2.6.47. There are 12 guards in the city of Yama. They are 12 Śravaṇas, the sons of Brahmā.[56] They declare the good and evil actions of the people to Yama and Citragupta (*GP*, 2.6.47).

The abode of Yama resounds with pleasing music. Sounds of drums, stringed instruments and flutes and the songs of beautiful maidens fill the atmosphere. The air is fragrant with perfumes and people are seen engaged in sports.[57]

According to the description in the *VarāhaP*[58] the city of Yama has three gates. They are made of copper. The southern and western gates are for the entry of the sinners, while the northern gate is meant for deities, sages and other virtuous people. The southern gate is frightening, very hot and difficult to look at. By Yama's command the entry of the wicked, the cruel, the flesh-eaters and sinners is through this (i.e., southern) gate.

The city of Yama is a place of justice. Even the weakest gets justice here for the wrongs done towards him. The weak take revenge for the injustice and atrocities done to them. Here the powerful cannot harrass the weak. Yama's city is called Saṁyamana because it controls the conduct of the people (*Mbh*, 13.102.16). Here nobody can speak untruth.

Yama's Sabhā (The Court of Yama)

The *sabhā* of Yama is said to be luminous like gold and is of thousands of *yojanas* in size. According to the *Mbh*, 13.102.16 it is fashioned by Viśvakarman. The *Mbh*, 13.71 contains the story of Nāciketa. On being cursed by his father to go to Yama, Nāciketa fell down as if thunder-struck. His father's tears bring him to consciousness and he tells what he had seen when he went to Yama. Yama welcomed him as he would an honoured guest (*Mbh*, 13.71.16) Nāciketa saw the *sabhā* of Yama which was shining like gold and was very big in size. Nāciketa says that he found the Vaivasvatī *sabhā*, or the assembly hall of Yama, a very charming place. He also saw the world of the pious where rivers ran milk and the mountains were made of butter.

The *sabhā* of Yama is more fully described in *Mbh*, 2.8. It is made by Viśvakarman and is more than a hundred *yojanas* in extent, golden and sunny, where wishes are granted and there is no cold, hunger, sorrow, old age, etc. All good things to be relished are there. This palace contains royal priests and seers, saints and heroes. Kāla, Mṛtyu and the Pitṛs who die during the southern course of the sun, etc. They are cheered by songs and dance. The fire-god is in the *sabhā* too and all respect Dharmarāja (Yama).[59]

The *VarāhaP* describes the court of Yama in great details.[60] According to it, in the beautiful city of Yama there is a grand and beautiful assembly-hall. It is inlaid with all types of gems and is governed by Yama. This assembly is attended by the pious and the truthful and by those who have conquered anger, desires and all types of allurements. This court decides all matters of good and evil deeds and lays down the code of Dharma (moral law).

In this assembly the scholars, well-versed in the laws of Dharma, judge the actions of the people in the light of the laws laid down by the scriptures. They carry out the task without any fear and without deviating from the righteous path. These scholars think over the matter strictly in accordance to the scriptures and report their decision at the right time.[61]

Manu, Prajāpati, Vyāsa, Atri, Auddāliki, Āpastamba Bṛhaspati, Śukra, Gautama, Śaṅkha, Likhita, Aṅgiras, Bhṛgu, Pulastya, Pulaha and other scholars of Dharma in addition to a large number of celestial and human beings are seen in the Yama-*Sabhā*. Nāciketa saw divine sages, all well-versed in the *Vedas*, seated on the sides of Yama. He also saw many sages and Manus in the court of Yama (*Varāha P*, 195.20.23).

YAMA'S MESSENGERS AND ASSISTANTS

Yama-dūtas

Yama-dūtas are Yama's assistants. Their main task consists of approaching a dying person to take away his soul to the kingdom of Yama. An early reference in the *TB*, 1.5.15 provides that Yama's assistants bring victims forcibly and torment them.

Yama's assistants are of horrid appearance (*Mā*, 3.136). They carry a noose[62] and clubs with which they bind and bash the sinners. Generally the soul of a dying person is taken away by Yama's assistants, but in rare cases this task is carried out by Yama himself as is done in the case of Satyavat (*Mbh*, 296.15, *MP*, 210.16).

According to the *MāP*, 10.59, at the time of a sinner's[63] death *Yama-dūtas*, who are terribly frightening and foul-smelling, arrive near him carrying their noose and rods. The dying man starts trembling at their sight and dies under terrible pain.

The *PP Bhūmi-Khaṇḍa*, 13.54.54 describes the appearance of *Yama-dūtas*. According to it they have a frightening appearance with their crooked faces, fiery eyes and large bellies. Some of them are yellowish, some black and some are reddish-brown in colour. They are very rough and ruthless.[64] Describing their terrible appearance the *PP* (*Kriyā-yoga-sāra*, chap. 6) mentions their deformed faces, fierce teeth and red eyes. They hold the noose and clubs. They are called *mahāvīrāḥ*, (possessing tremendous strength). It is clear from these and other similar accounts that Yama's assistants are visible only to the dying man and not to others who might be present near him.

According to the *GP*, 2.9.12—The servants of Yama hold nooses and rods. They are 16000 in number. Each *pura* of Yama is guarded by one thousand *Yama-dūtas*.

When a man dies the *Yama-dūtas* take away the soul (i.e., the individual soul) to Yama's region and his lifeless body is left behind on the earth. The individual soul is of the measure of the thumb and it resides in the heart of the man.[65] The soul is above pains and pleasures, and it is considered to be obligatory that one is punished for the evil deeds committed by him during his earthly life. The soul, therefore, after the fall of his earthly body takes up a new body in order to experience the torments of the hells. This new body is similar in age and condition to his previous body and it is referred to as *yātanā-deha*.[66] The *Yama-dūtas* quickly bind the body with the terrible-*pāśa*.

Yama-dūtas are very fearsome and violent,[67] they beat the sinners with their rods and drag them towards the south direction.[68] They make him move on the terrible path which leads to Yama's region and is full of torment. They also frighten them by describing the tortures which are in store for them in the different hells.

When the messengers of Yama came to take away Ajāmila, the *Viṣṇu-dūtas* (the messengers of Viṣṇu) immediately stepped into save him from the *yāmya-pāśa*, i.e., the noose of Yama.[69] They tell *Yama-dūtas* not to take Ajāmila by the wrong way,[70] since he has completely expiated all his sins by muttering the Lord's name at the time of his death.

Story of Ajāmila

Ajāmila was a learned brahmin. He possessed the knowledge of the scriptures. But driven by lust he abandoned the righteous path. He left his lawfully wedded wife and started living with a maid-servant. He even raised a family with her. He ignored all his religious duties and plunged himself fully in the worldly pleasures. He doted on his youngest son 'Nārāyaṇa'. When the period of his life on the earth was over, *Yama-dūtas* came to fetch him. Terrified by their frightening form, he called out to his son Nārāyaṇa, who was playing at some distance. On hearing the name of Lord Viṣṇu, the *Viṣṇu-dūtas* immediately rushed in and stopped the messengers of Yama who were taking out the soul of Ajāmila from his heart (6.1.31). A dialogue between, the *Yama-dūtas* and the *Viṣṇu-dūtas* ensued. *Yama-dūtas* said that they intended to take Ajāmila, who had done nothing for expiating his sins, to Yama. There he would get purified through undergoing the prescribed punishment.[71]

The *Viṣṇu-dūtas* argued that by muttering the name of Lord Nārāyaṇa he has expiated all his sins (6.2.13). He was no longer a sinner and hence it was unfair to carry him by the wrong path, i.e., the sinners' path leading to Yama's kingdom. They reiterated that even one syllable of the Lord's name was sufficient to destroy all the sins.

At this juncture the *Yama-dūta* raised doubt that Ajāmila had not uttered the Lord's name, 'Nārāyaṇa' out of his devotion to him nor did he knew the efficiency of the Lord's name. Even the call of 'Nārāyaṇa' was not made for the Lord but for his own son named Nārāyaṇa. Under such circumstances a question arises as to how he could be benefited from the utterance of the Lord's name.

The *Viṣṇu-dūtas* cleared this doubt with the help of a beautiful simile. According to it a man uttering the Lord's name even without knowing its power of purifying the sins, burns away all his sins just as fire though thrown ignorantly by a child on a heap of fuel burns the fuel completely (6.2.18).

Just as a medicinal drug even though taken by chance, without being aware of its effect, is bound to show its remedial effect; the Lord's name, even when muttered by chance without knowing about its highest purifying power shows its efficacy in destroying all the sins.

On hearing these convincing words the *Yama-dūtas* retreated without taking Ajāmila with them. In this way, the *Viṣṇu-dūtas* got him released from the clutches of death and then they too disappeared.

Ajāmila, who had been watching the happenings realised his mistake. He thereon resorted to a pious life. When his mind and intellect was established in *Brahman*, the *Viṣṇu-dūtas* appeared before him. He cast off his body and immediately assumed the angelic form of the *Viṣṇu-dūtas* (*BhāgP*, 6.2.43).

The fate of the pious dead is described in the *BhāgP*, 6.2.44. According to it the pious ascend the heavenly car, made of gold and proceed through heavens to the abode of Viṣṇu.

The authority of *Yama-dūtas* is put aside here in the case of Ajāmila. In the *ViṣṇuP*, 3.7.20 *Yama* advises his servants not to touch the Viṣṇu-worshippers, one of whose characteristics is their devotion to the institution of *varṇāśrama*. By observing the rules of *varṇāśrama* one can attain Viṣṇu, Śiva or other gods. They can also be saved from hells and the power of Yama.

Two Dogs

The two messenger-dogs of Yama mentioned in the *ṚV*, 10.14.11 also appear in the *Purāṇas*. They are called *sārameyau*, i.e., sons of Saramā. It may however be noted that the term *sārameya* stands as a synonym of 'dog' meaning 'born in the clan of Saramā'. A description of these sons of Saramā is found in the *BṛP*, 131.3. They are called *caturakṣau*, i.e., four-eyed (sharp-sighted); *pavanāhārau*, i.e., who consume air; *Yama-priyau*, i.e., dear to Yama; *mahāśreṣṭhau*, i.e., most excellent and *janānugāminau*, i.e., followers of men.

Similarity of these epithets of Yama's dogs with those mentioned in the *ṚV* is worth noticing. In the *ṚV*, 10.14 they are called *sārameyau*, i.e., sons of Saramā; *asutṛpau*, i.e., delighting in taking away lives; *caturakṣaḥ*, i.e., four-eyed, sharp-sighted. A parallel to *asutṛpau* can be seen in *pavanāhārau* which may mean "consumer of the vital breath (*prāṇa*)".

But these dogs are not mentioned as sitting on the path leading to the *Yama-loka* as in the *ṚV*, 10.14.11. Here their task consists of protecting the gods' cows, and also the animals brought for the sacrifice.

It is important to note that dogs are connected with Yama and at *śrāddha* (rituals for the manes) dogs as well as crows are given food.

The *SkandaP*, 2.4.9 states that the two dogs of Yama should be given lamp-offering on the fourteenth day of the dark half of the Kārttika month. One should take a bath and with wet clothes one should give the *dīpa-dāna* (lamp-offering) to the two dogs, the sons of Mṛtyu. The lamp should be placed with the recitation of these lines "O Śyāma and Śabala! two brother-dogs! servants of *Yama*! sons of Mṛtyu! May you be pleased with the offering of this lamp". Thereafter he should again take a bath and perform Yama-*tarpaṇa* by giving libations to the fourteen forms of Yama[72] (*MP*, 102.22; *PP*. 4.124, 13-14, *BvtP*, 104.10).

Birds

In the *Vedas*, pigeons and owls are considered to be the messengers of Yama. In the *MP* they are described as connected with bad omen. Their entry in house is considered to be precursor of ill-fate. The *MP*, 237.6 says that if a pigeon enters the house it foretells the death of the householder. It is important to note that a pigeon's entry in the house is considered a bad portent and the *ṚV*, 10.165 (*devāḥ kapotaḥ*) is recited to remove the ill-effect of a pigeon putting its foot near the fire, i.e., coming well inside the house. *MP*, 237.6 further says that if a crow lands on one's head or the bees 'make honey', i.e., make a beehive, the death of the householder is predicted.[73] Hooting of an owl predicts loss of property and death of the family-head.[74]

The *MP*, 237.13 suggests that on such behaviour of the birds, etc. a *havana* must be performed and five brahmins should recite the hymn *devāḥ kapotaḥ* (*ṚV*, 10.165).[75]

Citragupta

Judging man's good and evil deeds and rewarding him by granting a passage to heaven or sending him to one or more torturous hells comprises the main function of Yama in the Purāṇic literature. Yama knows about all the sins of man. In some *Purāṇas* he has an assistant named Citragupta to help him in his task. In his record-book Citragupta keeps the account of all the good and bad deeds of men. Thus Citragupta, the scribe, is Yama's chief assistant.

A brief description of Citragupta's house is found in the *GP*, 2.23.24-27. According to it the palace of Citragupta stands in the *Yama-loka* near its entrance. This divine palace is of twenty-five *yojanas* in size and enclosed by a strong iron-wall.This palace has one hundred lanes which are decorated with flags. Hundreds of lamps brighten the palace which is filled by sweet sound of music.[76] It is beautifully painted by expert artists. In this palace there is a divine gem-studded throne. Sitting on this throne Citragupta calculates the life-span of all the creatures. He also keeps an account of the their good and evil deeds. While carrying on this task he is not influenced by any factor and gives a proper thought to all good and evil deeds. He notes down a deed, if it is free from the eighteen faults, it is recorded as a good deed by Citragupta. In this way Citragupta daily sits on his throne and writes down as to what action is done by whom (*GP*, 2.23-32).

In the court of Yama also where he pronounces the judgement, Citragupta is his chief assistant. He not only presents the account of man's good and evil deeds he also recommends the fate that a dead man deserves for his actions. The *VarāhaP* contain a dialogue between Yama and Citragupta. Citragupta says "this man attains total emancipation since he died in the battlefield after killing the enemy";[77] "this other man who was killed for the cause of a brahmin, a cow or for his country should be immediately sent to Amarāvatī, the kingdom of Indra" (*Varahā P*, 205.9-11).

Agni Puraṇā 371.12 states that sinners fall into horrible hells that are declared by Citragupta at the order of Yama.

On the second day of the bright half of Kārttika, which is

called *Yama-dvitīyā* people worship Citragupta, his pen and ink-pot. In later Hindu belief the *Yama-dvitīyā* comes to be regarded as a unique festival of brothers and sisters. The brother visits his sister's house. She makes *kumkum*-mark on his forehead and he gives her clothes, ornaments, etc. as gifts. According to the Purāṇic belief Yama and Yamunā (the twin) have become divine symbol of the selfless affection of brothers and sisters. Here another story connected with *Yama-dvitīyā* is worth mentioning. According to *SkandaP*, 2.4.11 Yamī once invited her brother Yama to come to her place along with his *gaṇas* (assistants), and have food there. Yama being busy in his work could not come. Then one day Yamunā persuaded him to come on the second day of bright half of Kārttika. She offered him food in gold-vessels. Yama asked her to choose a boon and Yamunā said — you must come to have food on this day every year. On this day you should release all creatures from the hells and whoever goes to his sister's house and eats there should be prosperous and happy.

Kāla

In the Epics and the *Purāṇas* Kāla and Mṛtyu are mentioned as close associates of Yama. They are conceived as distinct personalities (*Mbh*, 9.45.17), though often identified with each other (cf 2.56.10).

Kāla primarily means 'Time'. Kāla ripens creatures forcibly by turning months and seasons, changes the names of months and seasons with 'the fire of the sun and the fuel of the day and night'. In the *Mbh*, 12.309.90 Kāla is shown as composed of day and night, months and seasons. The seasons are caused by rainfall, hence Kāla (Time) is identified with death. The word *kālyamāna* means 'being killed'. It is to be noted here that the *JB*, 1.246 equates Yama with year (*saṁvatsara*). According to it Yama is time and the seasons are his faces.

The *VarāhaP* describes Kāla as the main attendant of Yama. It says that a dark-complexioned, high-chinned one with upraised hair was seated by his side. He held a massive stick in his left hand, had a deformed face, fierce teeth, and looked always angry and frightful. He is entrusted time and again by the Lord of Dharma (Yama) to administer punishment and he, the eternal Kāla, obeys him diligently (*VarāhaP*, 195.24-25).

Mṛtyu

Mṛtyu is mentioned as an assistant of Yama and he is Yama's constant companion. In the Yama-Rāvaṇa battle (*Rām*, 7.22) Mṛtyu, armed with his *pāśa* and deadly club accompanied Yama. The fierce battle went on for many days. When Yama was wounded by Rāvaṇa (*Rām*, 7.22.22) Mṛtyu sought Yama's permission to kill him. Mṛtyu is mentioned both as a god and a goddess in the *Mbh*. The goddess Mṛtyu was created by Brahmā out of his wrath and was ordered by him to kill the creatures. Unwilling to do such a cruel task, she protested. On being rebuked by Brahmā for her disobedience, she wept. As her tears got collected in her cupped palms, Brahmā transformed those tears into dreadful diseases which would kill people. Thus Mṛtyu was saved from performing the gruesome task of a killer (*Mbh*, 12.250).

According to the *Mbh*, 7.54.17 the goddess Mṛtyu dreaded the amount of sin she would collect for killing the creatures. She practised severe penance. Then Brahmā assured her that any destruction by her would not be considered a sin (*Mbh*, 7.54.44). Terrible strength of goddess Mṛtyu is described in *Mbh*, 12.8-9.

Mṛtyu performed the task of taking away the life. In the *Mbh*, 13.1.50 Mṛtyu confirms the snake's statement that he was ordered by Mṛtyu the god of death, to bite the boy. He consoles the people and says that the god has programmed all events beforehand and the boy's death was not due to a mistake on anybody's part.

According to the *VarāhaP*, 195.31 Naciketā sees Mrtyu in Yama's court. He described him as haughty by nature (*durvinīta*) extremely wrathful (*mahākrodhaḥ*), terrible (*sudāruṇaḥ*) extremely mighty (*mahā-sattvaḥ*) and vigorous (*mahātejaḥ*) free from old age and death, unassailable (*dur-*

dharṣah), and bearing celestial pastes and perfumes on his body.

In the *BhāgP*, 4.8.4. Mṛtyu is said to be born to Adharma (Brahmā's son) and his wife Mṛṣā. In the *PP*, 30 a daughter of Mṛtyu named Sunīthā is mentioned. The cruel king Vena was born to her.

It is important to note that in the *VS*, 35.13 Yama is mentioned along with Antaka and Mṛtyu (although till then Yama was not directly connected with death), who in the *Purāṇas* become close associates of Yama.[78]

Lady Assistant

In the *Varāha P*, a lady is described as seated by the side of Yama in the latter's court. In the *VarāhaP*, 195.27-28 Naciketā gives the description of this lady in the following way:

> There, in Yama's court, I saw a beautiful lady endowed with lustre and honoured by Yama. She was the annihilator of all. All gods, demons sages fear her. All painful diseases come from her. (*Varāha P*, 195.30)

This reminds one of Nirṛti in the Vedic literature. Nirṛti is also described as having malevolent character who brings death, destruction and diseases to the people.[79]

Notes

1. A.D. Pusalkar, *Studies in the Epics and Purāṇas*, Introduction, p. 22.
2. Cf. *ChāUp*, 7.1.2, *itihāsa-purāṇam pañcamam vedānām/*, *itihāsapurāṇah pañcamaḥ vedānāṁ* — *Mbh*. cr. edn. 1.57.74.
   itihāsa-purāṇābhyām vedaṁ samupbṛhaṁyeta/
   vibhetaplpaśrutād vedo mām ayaṁ prahariṣyati/ — *Mbh*, 1.1.204 and 1.1.267-8.
3. M. Winternitz, *A History of Indian Literature*, p. 4.
4. F.E. Pargiter, *An Article on the Purāṇas*, *ERE*, Vol. X, p. 448.
5. *yasmāt purā hi anatīdaṁ purāṇam tena hi smṛtam,*
   niruktam asya yo veda sarva-pāpaih pramucyate/ — *VāyuP*. 1.203.
6. *purātanasya kalpasya purāṇāni vidur budhāḥ* — *MP*, 53.63; *vide*

also S.G. Kantawala, *Purāṇic Etymologies*, (on the vocable *Purāṇa*, *Indological Studies* Jr. of the Department of Sanskrit University of Delhi, Vol. II, No. 1, pp. 13-16.

7. A.D. Pusalkar, *op. cit.*, p. 22.
8. M. Winternitz, *A History of Indian Literature*, Vol. I, p. 518.
9. *ṛcaḥ sāmāni candāṁsi purāṇam yajuṣā saha* — *AV*, 11.7.24.
10. A.D. Pusalkar, *op.cit.*, p. 41.
11. *Ibid.*, p. 40.
12. *sargasca pratisargasca vaṁso manvantarāṇi ca /*
    vaṁsānucaritaṁ ceti purāṇam pañca-lakṣaṇam / /
    This verse, with minor variations is found in many *Purāṇas*, e.g. *ViP*. 3.6.24; *MāP*, 134.13; *AgniP*, 1.14 *BhaviṣyaP*, 2.5 *BrVaiP*, 133.6, *VarāhaP*, 2.4, *MP*, 53.64, etc.
13. *Vide* A.D. Pusalkar, *op.cit.*, p. 23.
14. R.C. Hazra, *Studies in the Purāṇic Records on Hindu rites and customs*, p. 8 ff.
15. *Vide* A.D. Pusalkar, *op.cit.*, p. 25.
16. R.C. Hazra has written two volumes under the title *Studies in Upapurāṇas*.
17. R. Dikshitar, "The Purāṇas : A Study", In *I.H.Q.*, V. 8, p. 766.
18. Mārtaṇḍa and Vivasvat are other names of Sūrya — *Amarakośa*, 1.3.29,30.
19. Yama, raised his leg to strike Chāyā in righteous indignation but controlled himself quickly and did not strike her.
20. i.e., 'her shadow or image', H.H. Wilson, *ViP*, Transl, p. 214.
21. *tadā anyā iyaṁ asau buddhiḥ iti āsīt Yamasūryayoḥ.*
22. According to *MP* he trimmed Sūrya everywhere except the feet, the extent of which he could not discern.
23. *MP*, 11.4.
24. In the later part of the story it is told that she went to her father's house.
25. He might have got this name because of his resemblance to Manu.
26. This reminds one of the epic idea :
    sarveṣāṁ eva śāpānāṁ pratighāto hi vidyate /
    na tu matrābhiśaptānāṁ mokṣaḥ kvacana vidyate / —*Mbh*, 1.33.4.
27. This reminds one of his position in the *Vedas* as the king of the dead.
28. *BVP*, 1.47.18.
29. In the *VāP* and the *LP* versions Sūrya is Vivasvat and Āditya respectively.
30. In the *MP* version Viśvakarman is Tvaṣṭṛ.
31. *ViP, MāP, MP, LP.*
32. According to the *Bṛhaddevatā* Manu was a son of Vivasvat and Savarṇā (Savarṇā is named Chāyā in the *Purāṇas*).
33. With the view of Yama's function as a controller in the *Purāṇas* the name Yama can be derived from $\sqrt{yam}$ = to control.

34. Yama raised his leg to strike Chāyā in righteous indignation but controlled himself quickly and did not hit her. Thus he displayed immense control on himself and also a righteous vision. So his name can justifiably be derived from the root *yam*, to control.

35. Gokarṇa is a place sacred to Śiva on the western coast about 30 miles south of Goa in the Kumta Taluka of North District — *Vide* P.V. Kane, *HDS*, p. 753. The *LP* speaks of two Gokarṇas (1.92.134; 135); *KūrmaP*, II.35.31 mentions Uttara Gokarṇa and the *Varāha P*, 213.7 mentions a southern and a northern Gokarṇa — *Vide* P.V. Kane, *op.cit.*, p. 754.

36. This reminds one of his position in the *Vedas* as the king of the dead.

37. According to lexicography these are synonymns — Cf. *Amarakośa*, 1.3.28-30.

38. *Vide* chapter 2 'Yama's Parentage'.

39. F. Max-Müller, *Lectures on the Science of Language*, p. 620.

40. *Vide* V.S. Agrawala, *Matsya Purāṇa — A Study*, p. 88.

41. Yama also is Sūrya, the regulating principle, and Yamī his sister, is the female power that is in the Sun. The two Aśvins also represent the principles of *prāṇa* and *apāna* or twofold energy as it is becoming manifest on the plane of Matter in the conscious world — *Vide* V.S. Agrawala, *op. cit.*, p. 89.

42. *MP*, 11.2 ff, *ViP*, 3.2.1 ff, *MāP*, chapter 74.

43. Yamunā is called Śamanasvasā in the *Amarkośa*, 1.10.32. Śamana is no other than Yama, the brother of Yamunā (*Yamunābhrātā*) — *Amarakośa*, 1.1.58.

44. Śani is therefore called 'Yamāgraja'.

45. *Vide supra* under 'Parentage' chapter 6.

46. *Vide supra* 'Yama and Yamī' chapter 4.

47. The *ṚV*, 10.10 is called a real ballad with a moral point by Geldner, *Der Rigveda*, Dritter, Teil, *HOS*, 35, 132.

48. *Yamasya dve bhārye, Dhumorṇā Vijayā ca iti Jaṭādharaḥ* — *Śabdakalpadruma*, *Kāṇḍa* 4, p. 21.

49. *BVP*, 1.15.21-22.

50. *Vide* W.J. Wilkins, *Hindu Mythology — Vedic and Purāṇic*, pp. 83-84.

51. *VāyuP*, 63.23, 69-61; 75-56, 82.1.

52. *Mbh*, 7.50.41; 7.95.18; 7.117.10; *BhāgP*, 6.3.3; 10.45.40, *VP*, 5.29-30.

55. *AgniP*, 210.34. See *HDS*, P.V. Kane, Vol. II, pt. II, p. 879.

56. The *GP*, II.7.11.14 provides a story related to the birth of Śravaṇas. According to it Rudra, Viṣṇu and Dharma ruled the earth. They wanted to know the good and evil deeds of men. They consulted the other gods and approached Brahmā. Brahmā created twelve sons out of the *kuśā* grass in his hand. These Śravaṇas inform all the happening in the world to Brahmā. They also know all the endeavour of all living beings which they report to Dharmarāja, i.e.,

Yama, at the time of death (*GP*, II. 7.16).

57. *VarāhaP*, 194.31.
58. *VarāhaP*, 195.5-8.
59. Also *Mbh.* 2.8.34 — *dīrghakālam tapas taptvā nirmito viśvakarmaṇā.*
60. On some points this version of the story differs from the *KaṭhaUp*, version.
61. *VarāhaP*, 195.10-14.
62. *MāP*, 10.60; *ViP*, 3.7.19; 3.7.44; *GP*, 2.9.12; *BhāgP*, 6.1.22.
63. Here, one who acts as a false witness and one who censures the *Vedas* — *MāP*, 10.59.
64. *yamdūtāḥ samāyānti dāruṇāḥ ghoradarśanāḥ,*
    lambodarāḥ vakramukhāḥ krūrāḥ piṅgala-cakṣuṣāḥ/
    kecit piṅgala-sarvāṅgāḥ kṛṣṇāh kecit tu babhravaḥ
    svidyanti pāpino dṛṣtvā kampante ca bhṛśam bhiyā//
    — *PP Bhūmi-Khaṇḍa*, 13.54.54.
65. *Cf. aṅguṣṭha mātra-puruṣaḥ "madhye ātmani tiṣṭhitaḥ* — *ŚvetaUp*, 3.13.
66. **See** *infra* chapter 8.
67. *Rām*, 21.12.
68. *Vide MāP*, 10.59-65.
69. *BhāgP*, 6.1.29-30.
70. The 'wrong way' here is the path meant for the sinners. *Viṣṇu-dūtas* hold that Ajāmila should not be taken on this path. They argue that since all his sins are expiated, he should not be taken as a sinner on the path of hells by the *Yama-dūtas*.
    atha enaṁ mā apanayata kṛtāśeṣāgha-niṣkṛtam/
    yad asau bhagavannāma mriyamāṇo samagṛhīta//
    — *BhāgP*, 6.2.13.
71. According to the Purāṇic belief one can expiate for their sins by undergoing the prescribed punishment for his sins.
72. *Vide* 'Epithets of Yama' chapter 4.
73. *gṛham kapotaḥ praviśet kravyādo mūrdhni līyate/*
    madhu vā makṣikāḥ kuryuḥ mṛtyur gṛhapater bhavet//
    — *MP*, 237.6.
74. *ulūko vāśate yatra nṛpadvāre tathā gṛhe/*
    jñeyo gṛhapater mṛtyur dhananāśaś tathaiva ca// — *MP*, 237.7.
75. *mṛgapakṣivikāreṣu kuryād homam sadakṣiṇam/*
    devāḥ kapotāḥ iti vā japtavyā pañcabhir dvijaiḥ// — *MP*, 237.13.
76. Cf. *ṚV*, 10.135.7.
77. Cf. *hato vā prāpyase svargam/* — *BG*, 2.37.
78. *Yamāya svāhā, Antakāya svāhā, Mṛtyave svāhā/* — *VS*, 39.13.
79. *Vide* chapter 3 "Yama & Nirṛti".

7

Personality and Functions of Yama

Appearance of Yama

THE details of Yama's physical features are found in *Mbh* (3.281.16 ff.), *MP* (210. 5-7 ff), *VarāhaP* (195.18 ff), *PadmaP Kriyā-Khaṇḍa*, 22.74, etc. He is generally described as having a terrifying appearance.

According to the *Mbh*, 3.281.16 Sāvitrī saw him as a dark figure with red eyes, holding noose and looking very fearsome.

The *MP* (210.5-7) also contains a description of Yama's appearance as seen by Sāvitrī when she saw him coming near. She had accompanied her husband Satyavān to the forest on that day, since she was aware of the forecast according to which the day of Satyavān's death had arrived. After some time Satyavān felt headache. He told Sāvitrī about his headache and failing vision. He also expressed a desire to rest his head on her lap and sleep. As Satyavān slept on her lap, Sāvitrī saw 'Dharmarāja'[1] himself coming over there. His colour was like that of a blue lotus. He was wearing yellow clothes. His glittering crown and ear-rings made his dark body look like a dark rain-cloud illumined by the flashes of lightening. He was bedecked with garlands and armlets. Mṛtyu and Kāla followed him (*MP*, 210.2-8).

In the *VarāhaP*, 195.18 Nāciketa sees Yama the great

ascetic (*mahātapāḥ*) wearing many ornaments and a highly lustrous crown presented to him by Brahmā. Due to his dazzling lustre he could be hardly be looked at. Here Yama appears to him as an amalgam of the collective energy of all powerful beings.

In the *BVP* Yama is also called Kāla and is described as black in colour and shining like the summer-sun. Here he is mentioned as wearing red-clothes and having six faces, sixteen hands, six legs and twenty-four eyes. The mention of an unusual number of faces, eyes, hands, etc. indicates his unusual powers and capacities.

As Yama judges the good and the bad deeds of the people and grants punishment according to the sins committed during the life on earth, everybody has to go to Yama after his death. But the appearance of Yama is said to be different for the sinner and the pious.

On seeing a pious soul approaching Yama feels happy and assumes the form of Nārāyaṇa. Thus, a pious soul finds Yama as four-armed, dark in complexion, having eyes like bloomed lotuses, holding the conch, the discus, the club and the lotus. He is seen with Garuḍa, the mount of Nārāyaṇa, and wears the sacred thread made of gold. He also wears a crown, ear-rings and a *vanamālā* (*PP Kriyā-Khaṇḍa*, 22.74). It may be noted that all these assets belong to Nārāyaṇa, i.e., Viṣṇu. Hence this description shows that Yama completely transforms himself into Viṣṇu and assumes his pleasing appearance. When these pious souls reach his palace, Yama, the presiding deity of Dharma, himself welcomes them happily as one would welcome one's friends (*PP*, 23.78).[2]

On the other hand his form is fierce for the sinners. His body takes a huge form of thirty *yojanas*. His eyes look like big lakes and his terrible voice sounds like a thunder at the time of the universal destruction. In the form of breath great winds blow from his nostrils. He looks fearsome with his very big teeth, and his lip pressed by them. His nails are as big as winnowing baskets. He is seen wearing an animal-hide, holding a *daṇḍa* and riding on a ferocious buffalo and thus looking very dreadful.

fig. 7.1 Tricinopoly Painting, 1820 Victoria and Albert Museum, London

The *MP* gives some directions regarding the icon of Yama. According to it the image of Dharmarāja (i.e., Yama) should be made as holding a mace and a noose, riding a huge buffalo. He should be black like soot with eyes blazing like fire.[3]

According to the *ViDhP*, 3.47 the image of Yama should be made dark as a rain-cloud, while the colour of his garments should be like that of hot gold.[4] He should be seated on a buffalo and adorned with all ornaments. On his left lap should be Dhūmorṇā, his consort, whose complexion is like that of a blue lotus. Here Yama is mentioned as having four hands. In his two right hands he holds as rod (*daṇḍa*) and a sword (*khaḍga*) and in the two left hands a flaming trident (*jvālā-triśūla*) and a rosary (*akṣamālā*). On his right side Citragupta stands with a pen and palm-leaf to record the deeds of the mortals. To the left of Yama stands the terrible Kāla who is armed with *pāśa*.[5]

According to other authorities in iconography the image of Yama should be made as follows:

He should be dark in colour resembling a rain cloud having two arms and fiery eyes. His face should be made fearsome with sharp teeth. He should be covered all over with red sandal paste and draped in red garments. He should be adorned with crown and ornaments.

His hands should be shown holding a sword (*khaḍga*) and a club (*kheṭaka*). He can be depicted as seated on a throne or mounted on his buffalo.[6]

At another place Yama is described as holding (in addition to his rod) a pen, a book, and a cock.[7] It may be noted here that a cock was given to Yama by his father Sūrya in order to minimize the effect of Chāyā's curse to him.

All the Purāṇic accounts depict him as a dark and fearsome god. He wears many ornaments, among them is a highly lustrous crown which was presented to him by Brahmā (*VarāhaP*, 195.18)

In spite of his fierceness he possesses a divine lustre which is equated with that of the summer's sun. He makes himself look more fearsome to the sinners.[8] On the other hand he takes the form of Viṣṇu when the pious souls reach near him.[9] He welcomes them there as a friend (*PadmaP*, 23.78). His main weapons are his noose and rod (*daṇḍa*). He is also mentioned as holding a sword and a mace (*MP*, 261.13). His clothes are yellow (*MP*, 261.7) or golden (*ViDh P*, 3.48). Sinners find him fearsome and, wearing hides (*PadmaP Kriyā-Khaṇḍa*, 23.100 ff). A huge and ferocious buffalo is his mount (*MP*, 261.12, 90). In the Purāṇic accounts Yama is invariably described as black in colour. This is significant since all dangerous things are painted black as this colour represents *tamoguṇa*. For example while learning is conceived to be white; no-learning or absence of knowledge is of black colour.[10] Yama assumes the *tāmasī* form for the destruction of people with a view to maintaining the bounds of morality[11] and moral laws.

The *Nāṭya-śāstra* describes various colours as expressing various sentiments. According to it the *bhayānaka rasa* is of black colour.[12] Each sentiment represented by one particular colour is presided over by a deity.

For obtaining *siddhi*, i.e., success and good effect, in a particular *rasa* the deity concerned has to be pleased. Yama is said to be the presiding deity of the *karuṇarasa*, while Viṣṇu is of the *śṛṅgāra*, Pramatha of the *hāsya*, Rudra of the *raudra* and Indra of the *vīra*.[13]

Yama as a Judge

The most majestic aspect of Yama's personality is as Dharma or Dharmarāja. Yama, as Dharma, is a judge of man's good and evil deeds. He sends the pious to higher world while drops the evil-doers into the hells of which he is the lord. Yama is often lauded for his function as an impartial dispenser of justice. One of his epithets is Samavartī which speaks volumes about Yama's equal bearing to all beings. An ideal king is therefore aptly compared with Yama (*Mbh*, 12.68, 25.76, 25.79). No sin done anywhere at any time can escape Yama's notice. An often quoted text says that whereas a king punsihes the open sins and offences, Yama punishes men even for their secret sins hidden in their hearts.[14] Through prayers to gods one wishes to be freed from all the sins he might have done by action, speech or even thought (*manasā, vācā, karmaṇā*), because Yama can know even the sins which are deeply hidden in the heart of a man and not seen by anybody. *Vasiṣṭha Dharma Sūtra*, chapter 20[15] states that Yama punishes those who offend secretly. According to the *BhāgP*, 6.4.48 Yama sees through this mind's eye all the deeds of man and decides their fruit.[16]

This aspect of Yama's personality controls the moral behaviour of people. The fear of Yama's horrid punishments prevents people from leaving the righteous and moral path. Thus he is also 'a moral governor; the god of conscience'.[17]

In this capacity his name 'Yama' derived from the root *yam* to control, is very appropriate.

Yama judges the deeds of man when he reaches his kingdom after death. He grants the pleasure to the virtuous by sending him to heaven and the torments by sending him to hells. The sinner goes to various hells, each of them is prescribed for a particular set of crimes.[18]

Sitting in his magnificent court Yama imparts justice. There he is helped by Citragupta, his scribe, who keeps a record of all the deeds of a man.[19] Citragupta gives this account to Yama when the man reaches Yama's region after death.[20]

Yama as a Warrior

In the *Purāṇas* Yama is primarily the lord of hells. He is also one of the *dikpālas*, i.e., the guardians of the directions. Yama is the guardian of the south direction.[21] Other *dikpālas* are — Indra of the east, Varuṇa of the west, Kubera of the north.[22]

As a guardian of the south direction Yama is seen in the role of a great warrior. When Rāvaṇa attacked him to conquer the south direction, he had to fight a fierce battle with Yama and his close associate Mṛtyu (*Rām*, 7.22 ff). Yama's chief weapon is *kāladaṇḍa* which is described here as divine, bright like fire (7.22.5) and fashioned by Brahmā (7.22.44).

He also took with him his *pāśa* and club (7.22.6). For seven days the battle went on. Rāvaṇa could not be subdued, although he was severely wounded, and fought vigorously. Mṛtyu asked Yama's permission to kill Rāvaṇa. At this Yama, determined to kill Rāvaṇa, lifted his never-failing weapon, the *kāladaṇḍa*. As he was about to kill Rāvaṇa, Brahmā appeared before him and asked Yama not to use the *kāladaṇḍa* on Rāvaṇa. He told Yama that he (Brahmā) had given a boon to Rāvaṇa and this *kāladaṇḍa* was also made by him (Brahmā). Therefore, whether Rāvaṇa was killed by the *kāladaṇḍa* or *kaladanda* failed in killing Rāvaṇa both the situations would make his (Brahmā's) word false.

At this request from Brahmā Yama kept back his *kāladaṇḍa* and unwilling to fight the battle, disappeared (*Rām*, 7.22.50). In the *devāsura* battle Yama fought with demon Kālanābha. He rode a buffalo to help Indra against Kṛṣṇa when he was taking away the *pārijāta* tree, but was discomfitted by Kṛṣṇa (*BhāgP*, 8.10.29).

Yama also took active part in the Tripura war where, he used his *daṇḍa* (*MP*, 135.77) and rode on his fearsome buffalo (*MP*, 133.63). Indra was told to attack the 'ocean of *asura*' which had entered the Tripura-fort, and defeat them with the help of Yama. Kubera took charge of the western entrance (*MP*, 138.25). Yama was defeated by Kālanemi in this battle (*MP*, 177.50).

In the *devāsura* battle described in the *MP*, 148.79.81. Dharmarāja (Yama) advanced forth on his buffalo surrounded by his violent-tempered assistants. Yama's eyes began to blaze as if flames were rising towards the sky at the end of a *kalpa*.

Yama's fight with Grasana is described in detail in the *MP*, 150.1-49. Several weapons, used by Yama are mentioned here e.g., formidable arrows, clubs, a javeline named *prāsa*, etc. With the blow of *prāsa* Grasana fell unconscious. When he came to senses, he threw a heavy club towards Yama. At this Yama hurled the most formidable, all-destroying blazing *daṇḍa*, Yama's *daṇḍa* and the demon's club collided in mid-air and a tumultuous sound was produced. They fought with blows too. After a long fight Yama was exhausted and was subdued by the demon.

Yama and Dharma

The early commentary of Guṇaviṣṇu on *ChāBr* refers to Yama as Dharmarāja.[23] In the Epics and the *Purāṇas* Yama is called 'Dharmarāja.[24] Dharmarāja is also one of the several names of Yama which are enumerated in the *Amarakośa* and *Śabdaratnāvalī*.[25] Although Vedavyāsa has used the term 'Dharmarāja' and 'Yama' as synonyms of Dharmadeva in the *Mbh* whereas Yama is extensively called Dharmarāja in the *Mbh*.[26] Thus it is clear that the term Dharmarāja is used for both, i.e., Dharmadeva as well as Yama. This has, perhaps, led to a certain amount of confusion in some *Purāṇas* where Yama and Dharma are taken to be two names of a single deity. But a study of the stories around each of them clears the confusion and establishes that they are two separate gods.

Dharma is one of the twelve Prajāpatis created by Brahmā. They are—Dharma, Dakṣa, Marici, Atri, Pulastya, Kratu, Vasiṣṭha, Gautama, Bhṛgu, Angiras and Manu.[27] In the *Mbh* Dharma along with Yama is counted among the twenty-one Prajāpatis.[28]

First of all, the parentage of Yama and Dharma confirms that they are two separate deities. Dharma is a son of Brahmā. He came out in the human form from Brahmā's right breast.[29] He married thirteen daughters of Dakṣa. On the other hand Yama is a son of Sūrya and Saṁjñā. Yama is the sixth descendant of Viṣṇu. From Mahāviṣṇu were descended, in the following order Brahmā-Marici-Kāśyapa-Sūrya-Yama.

Dharma is also the name of a deity who presides over righteousness and religious life. He is said to be the father of Yudhiṣṭhira[30] who is also called Dharmarāja[31] as well as Dharmaputra. It was Dharma who tested the sincerity of and righteousness of Yudhiṣṭhira (*Mbh*, 3.296.5; 3.298.24) and king Hariścandra. He was especially pleased with Hariścandra due to his qualities of tolerance, self-control and truthfulness (*MāP*, 8.46). Dharma tells him that he was knowing about the calamities which would befall on Hariścandra. He had assumed, with his special power, the form of a *cāṇḍāla* (*MāP*, 8.56). Dharma tested the righteousness of Yudhiṣṭhira when the Pāṇḍavas were staying in the *Dvaita-vana*. Dharma, as the Yakṣa of the lake asked Sahadeva, Nakula, Arjuna and Bhīma, who had come there one by one, to answer his questions before drinking water. They arrogantly refused to do so and ignoring his word they drank water. Consequently all of them fell dead one after another. After some time Yudhiṣṭhira came there looking for his brothers. He too was asked by the Yakṣa to answer his queries before drinking water. Yudhiṣṭhira agreed to do so. He pleased the Yakṣa by answering all his questions to his utmost satisfaction. The Yakṣa discloses his identity that he was none other than Dharma himself who had come there to test Yudhiṣṭhira. Pleased by his answers the Yakṣa told Yudhiṣṭhira that he could bring one of his brothers to life and asked him to make the choice. Yudhiṣṭhira chose Nakula to be granted the gift of life, with a view that since one of Kunti's son (he himself) was alive, may, at least, one of Mādri's sons also live. This gesture further pleased the Yakṣa who granted life to all his brothers.

There is another instance, at the time of Yudhiṣṭhira's ascent to heaven through Himālayas, when Dharma tested his righteousness. While Draupadi and Nakula, Sahadeva, Arjuna and Bhīma fell dead on the way one by one, a dog faithfully followed Yudhiṣṭhira. Indra welcomed Yudhiṣṭhira in heaven but he would not allow a dog to enter heaven. Here Yudhiṣṭhira refused to enter heaven unless the dog who had followed him all the way was also granted entry. Indra insisted that the dog should be left behind but Yudhiṣṭhira was firm on his stand. At this the dog transformed himself into Dharma, the deity of righteousness. Extremely pleased with Yudhiṣṭhira he said, "There is no one equal to you even in the heaven who has refused ascending on Indra's chariot for the sake of a dog" (*Mbh*, 17.2.1 ff).

Though Yama is also called 'Dharmarāja' it does not conclude that Yama and Dharma are identical. Yama is conceived as an imparter of justice. He weighs the evil and good deeds of man after his death and awards punishment according to the sins committed by him. Because of this special function of his, he is called Dharmarāja. On the other hand Dharmadeva is righteousness personified. Thus it is clear that in spite of both of them being called 'Dharmarāja' Yama and Dharma are two separate deities. The title Dharmarāja needs to be interpreted differently in connection with Yama and Dharma. Yama is called Dharmarāja because he imparts justice by granting the fruit of good and evil deeds of men, and in this capacity he is Dharmarāja. While Dharma (i.e., Dharmadeva) is the presiding deity of Dharma, or the righteousness personified.

Although Yama and Dharma are separate deities a tendency to identify them with each other is seen in the story connected with Vidura.

Sage Māṇḍavya was punished severely by Dharma for a sin he committed in his childhood. The sage could not tolerate this injustice because a child's action does not amount to a punishable sin. He cursed the 'unjust imparter of justice' that he would be born to a śūdra woman. Here it is seen that Yama who judges others actions and punishes them was also, at least once, punished for his fault. Due to Māṇḍavya's curse Dharma was born as Vidura, the son of Kṛṣṇa-dvaipāyana and the maid-servant of Ambikā, a wife of Vicitravīrya.[32] According to *Mbh*, 1.57.77-81 Dharma was born in śūdra order as Vidura due to the curse of Aṇimāṇḍavya. According to the *BhāgP*, 3.5.20 and *BrahmāP*, 2.27.25 also Yama was born, as Vidura to a maid-servant.

Aṇimāṇḍavya (or Māṇḍavya) cursed the god who awarded him the punishment. This god, here called Dharma, could be none other than Yama since it is Yama who performed the task of judging and punishing the people. Thus, it is not difficult to deduce that the god whom sage Māṇḍavya cursed to be born to a śūdra, was Yama, though he is called Dharma here. The *Mbh* knows Yama as Dharma in 1.108.8 where the sage goes to the abode of Dharma and cursed him to be reborn as Vidura. This scene is repeated in the *Mbh*, 1.63.93 but without a complete identification.

Dharmarāja and Yama are mentioned as identical in the

MP, chapter 226. According to the *BrahmaP*, 94.16-32 Yama is another name of Dharma. The *BrVaiP* contains a eulogy of Yama by Sāvitrī.[33] According to it sun got a portion of Dharma as his son and this was Yama. This clears the confusion and explains convincingly why Yama is called Dharma. Yama was a portion of Dharma, whom Sūrya got as his son after pleasing Dharma with his devotion.

In the *Skanda Purāṇa* Yama himself reveals his identity as Dharma. He says, "I am Yama for the evil-doers and Dharma for those who win hearts (with their noble deeds)" (*SkandaP*, 3.24). Yama practised severe austerities. Indra was troubled and sent an *apsarā* named Vardhanī. There is a dialogue between Yama and Vardhanī. Here Yama says that he is Yama for sinners and Dharma for the pious. He also disclosed to her that his penance was to gain a good name in every *kalpa* and *mahākalpa*. Vardhanī returned to Indra and reported that Yama is practising penance for the purpose of gaining fame hence there was no reason for Indra to worry. After one hundred years of hard penance Śiva appeared before him and fulfilled the wishes of gaining good name in all the three worlds and make Dharmāraṇya holier than Kailāsa by promising that "a portion of mine shall always stay here". In the *Mbh*, 3.319 Sāvitrī follows Yama who is taking away the soul of her husband Satyavān. Even after being granted three self-chosen boons and repeatedly being asked to return back, she keeps following Yama. Sāvitrī eulogises to please Yama and thereby gets back Satyavān's life. In the *Mbh*, 3.319 she says to Yama. "You are the son of Vivasvat, therefore, you are called Vaivasvata. You are also called Dharmarāja because you please people with your quality of the controller and Dharma".[34]

V.S. Agrawala comments that Yama is the lord of death as the principle of Matter, and of immortality as Dharma. In this later aspect he is *deva* drinking *soma* with the host of *devas* sitting on the summit of the cosmic-tree (*ṚV*, 10.135.1). Each newborn life-principle is a Yāmāyana Kumāra, and is a link in the endless chain of the preceding fore-fathers (*purāṇam anuvenati*).[35]

Yama and Other Gods

The personality of the Vedic Yama has undergone a tremendous change in the Purāṇic mythology. In the *ṚV* he is the overlord of a special region where all the dead go and rejoice. There are earnest prayers too which express a strong desire to become immortal in the region where Yama rules. In the Vedic literature Yama stands like any other major god of the pantheon. With his growing connection with death and hells Yama has now become a feared-god, though many *Purāṇas* emphasise that Yama shows his dreadful appearance only to the sinners, and that he is extremely gentle and benevolent towards the pious.

DHARMA, KĀLA AND ANTAKA

With his new personality Yama's relation with other gods has undergone a change. In the Epics and the *Purāṇas* Yama became a killer-god, as well as the upholder of the ethical laws, the judge of man's actions and a punisher. The multiple aspects of his personality came to be personified as different deities.

One of Yama's name is Kāla. In this aspect he represents the time which is moving and progressing and, therefore, with its march it makes everything grow older and older. Antaka declares the end of a life, while Mṛtyu brings death and carries the dead to the other world.

Another aspect of Yama's character, of which only glimpses are seen in the Vedic literature, is that of a punisher and an upholder of the ethical laws. In the *Purāṇas* it becomes his most prominent function. Here he is all in all of the faculty of judging man's actions and punishing him in the various torturous hells of which he is the supreme lord. Here Yama as Dharmarāja, with his code of justice, ensures a fair play in all this.[36]

Mrtyu is stated to be a chief assistant of Yama.[37] He remains present in the court of Yama when Yama listens about man's good or evil actions and announces rewards or punishment for him. Mṛtyu also accompanies Yama to the battles. In the Yama-Rāvaṇa battle when Rāvaṇa was not discomfitted even after seven days, Mṛtyu asked for Yama's permission to kill Rāvaṇa.

YAMA AND ŚIVA

According to the *MP*, 10.20.21 the overlordship of the yonder world as well as the position of a moral judge was granted to Yama by Śiva.

Being a son of Sūrya Yama is a solar god. His brother Manu came to be regarded as the progenitor as well as the guardian of mankind. His position is complimentary to that of Yama who is the lord of the dead, but Yama's solar connection gradually became dim and he became increasingly related to the lunar (Śiva, Agni, Soma) group of the gods.[38]

Yama's connections with Śiva are important. He became closely connected with Śiva, the god of destruction and the other two gods of the triad are Brahmā, the creator and Viṣṇu, the sustainer. Yama was made the king of the departed by Śiva (*Mbh*, 12.122), whose mount (the bull) is also called Dharma (*Mbh*, 12.91.13), an appellate of Yama in this context, then Yama as the lord of the Fathers became an integral part of Śiva-complex.[39] Furthermore, Yama is frequently called Kāla and it is only as Kāla he imbibes the attributes of Śiva-complex more and more that he becomes the true representative of Kāla or Time, for Śiva is Mahākāla. The three eyes of Śiva represent the three division of time, i.e., past, present and future. The crescent moon in Śiva's matted hair portrays the measuring of time by years, while his *ḍamru* has a shape like that of a time-measuring sand-glass.[40]

Yama as the god of the lunar associations controls the path of the Fathers through moon and of the repeated births (*pitṛyāṇa*). The other path is the *devayāna*. By this path the solar god Viṣṇu leads the righteous to liberation through the sun.

In the *Purāṇas* too Yama is the lord of a special region. Although his overlordship is restricted to the hells only, he is the established king of the next world. He performs his duty by sending his *dūtas* to bring the souls of the people whose life span was over. On certain such occasions Yama's authority is set aside by other gods. In the story of Ajāmila,[41] the *Yama-dūtas* arrive to take him away but they are stopped by the *Viṣṇu-dūtas*. They tell *Yama-dūtas* that although that man had committed many sins, but since he had pronounced the Lord's name at the hour of death he should not be taken away by them.

At another place Yama is found to have been defeated by Kṛṣṇa. According to the *BhāgP*, 8.10.29[42] Indra, with Yama and others as his accomplices fought with Kṛṣṇa when he tried to take away the Pārijāta tree from Indra's garden. Here Yama was defeated by Kṛṣṇa in the battle.

Yama was also there with other gods in the *devāsura* battle, especially the Tripura-battle. Thus, Yama, who was the lord of a special region, assisted other gods in their endeavour.

Epithets of Yama

In most places Yama is referred to as 'Dharmarāja' (*MP*, 102.22; 107.27; 135.76; 136.5; *BrVaiP*, *Prakṛti Khaṇḍa*, 26.1, *BvtP*, 104.10; *PP*, 4.124.13-14; *VarP*, 191.7). He is also called Dharma. Dharmajña and Dharmaśila (*GP*, 2.3.22). When Hariścandra sees Yama disguised as a *cāṇḍāla*, the latter is called Dharma (*MāP*, 8.80).[43]

In the Epics and *Purāṇas* Yama is invariably called a controller. In the *Mbh*, 6.34.29 Lord Kṛṣṇa called himself 'as Yama among the controllers'.[44] In the *Mbh*, 3.296.66 states that Yama is the controller of all the creatures.[45] Yama controls the actions of people by awarding them reward or punishment in accordance to their deeds.[46] Obviously the vocable *yama* here is derived from the $\sqrt{yam}$, to control.

In the *Purāṇas* Yama is a god who controls the dead as well as the living creatures (through fear and by the ethical code) and also as a god who punishes the souls in the hells. Yama, who was the king of the dead in the *Vedas*, gradually moves towards a Kāla-Dharma pattern of divinity and was relegated to the sphere where Śiva was a central deity to whom Yama became an associate.[47]

Yama controls people under his discipline and hence he is called 'Yama', i.e., the restrainer.[48] The fear of Yama's punishments stops people from going astray from the righteous path. Fourteen names of Yama are mentioned in the *Purāṇas*.

On the fourteenth-day of the bright-half of Kārttika the water-offerings are made of Yama. Here the fourteen names of Yama are given as — Yama, Dharmarāja, Mṛtyu (death), Antaka (ender), Vaivasvata (son of Vivasvat), Kāla (time, as the consumer) and Sarvabhūtakṣaya (destroyer of all creatures). Auḍumbara, Dadhna, Nīla (dark), Parameṣṭhin Vṛkodara, Citra and Citragupta (*MP*, 102.22; *PP*, 4.124.13-15, *BvtP*, 104.10). All these names are taken as those of *pitṛs* by the *purāṇakāra*. It is said here that water with sesamum should be offered thrice to each of the fourteen Yamas. By doing so a man gets immediately freed from all sins done by him during the whole year.

In the *Mbh* Yama is called *samavartin* (*Mbh*, 12.207.35 cf 122.27). The origin of this name is not explained here. Kṛṣṇamitra, commenting on the *Amarakośa*, 1.1.58; where *samavartī* is listed among fourteen names of Yama, explains this epithet as *samaṁ mitre ripau ca*. The epithet highlights Yama's quality of a fair judge and punisher. He is neither lenient to his friend nor biased against his foe. As an impartial judge he punishes only on the basis of the crime done.

According the *VarāhaP*, 196.8. ff when Nāciketa reaches Yama's palace, he was received there with honour. He recited an eulogy to please Yama. In this prayer Yama is given several names and epithets. They are:

> *Dhātā* (producer), *Vidhātā* (creator), *Pitṛpati* (lord of the Fathers), *Catuṣpāda* (four-footed). It is to be noted here that Yama is also called Dharma and Dharma is conceived to be four-footed[49] *Kālajña* (knower of time), *Kṛtjña* (knower of action), *Satyavādī* (truthful),

Dṛḍhavrataḥ (having firm resolve).

Daṇḍapāṇi — holding a rod in his hand, Virūpākṣa—having fearsome eyes, Pāśahasta — holding a noose, Durādharṣa — hard to be subdued, Havya-kavyavāhaḥ — carrier of oblations, Pāpahantā—destroyer of the sins, Mahā-tapāḥ — great ascetic, Mṛtyu — death. Earlier in this episode he is called 'Dharmarāj' and 'Pretarāj'.

The *Amarakośa*, 1.1.58 provides the following list of Yama's fourteen names:

Dharmarāj, Pitṛpatī, Samavartī, Paretarāt, Kṛtānta, Yamunābhrātā, Śamana, Yamarāt, Yama, Kāla, Daṇḍadhara, Śrāddhadeva, Vaivasvata, Antaka.

Another list of Yama's fourteen names/epithets which occurs in the *Śabda-ratnāvalī*[50] is as follows:

Dharma, Dharmarāt, Jīvitesh, Dharmarāj, Auḍumbara, Daṇḍadhara, Kīnāśa, Dadhna, Mahiṣavāhana, Śīrṇapāda,[51] Bhīmaśāsana, Kanka, Hari.

In the *BrVaiP Prakṛti Khaṇḍa*, 261.8 Sāvitrī prays to Yama by reciting a Yamāṣṭaka, i.e., an eulogy consisting of eight verses, sung in laudation of Yama. Here eight names of Yama are given as follows:

Dharmarāja, Śamana, Kṛtānta, Daṇḍadhara, Kāla, Yama, Puṇyamitra (i.e., a friend of the pious) and Brahmavaṁśa (born in the lineage of Brahmā).

The names and epithets of Yama can be broadly classified in the following way:

Epithets bases on relations — Vaivasvata (son of Vivasvat, Ravitanaya, Sūryātmaja, Yamunā-bhrātā.

Epithets based on his physical features — Śīrṇapāda, Daṇḍapāṇi, Pāśahasta, Mahiṣavāhana.

Epithets based on his position — Dharmarāj, Pitṛpati, Daṇḍadharaḥ (a judge), Yamarāt, Paretarāt, Śrāddhadeva, Kṛtānta.

Epithets based on his function — Antaka, Kāla, Śamana, Samavartī (*Mbh*, 12.207.35; cf. 122.27), Puṇyamitra (*BrVaiP Prakṛti Khaṇḍa* 26.7), Dharma, Śubhakarman (*Mbh*, 8.45.31), Bhīmaśāsana, Mṛtyu, Kāla.

J. Gonda has pointed out that the same word may be, in a particular context an epithet, but in another passage a proper name, apposition or a purely attributive adjective.[52] He observes that an adjective used as an epithet is not always distinctive. Sometimes it mainly serves to express appreciation.

Notes

1. Dharmaraja is Yama.
2. *tataḥ svayaṁ Dharmarājastān sarvān manujottamān/ paramāṁ prītiṁ āsādya mitravat ca arcayet dvij!* — *PP*, 23.78.
3. *MP*, 261.12-13.
4. *taptacāmīkaraḥ* — *ViDhP*.
5. *ViDhP*, 3. 47.
6. *Vide Pratimā-lakṣaṇāni* cf. Gopinath Rao T.A., *Elements of Hindu Iconography*, p. 256.
7. *lekhanī pustakaṁ dhatte kukkuṭaṁ daṇḍameva ca/ mahāmahiṣam ārūḍho Yamaḥ kṛṣṇāṅga īritaḥ//* *Roop-maṇḍana* quoted by Gopinath Rao, *Elements of Hindu Iconography*, p. 258.
8. *PadmaP, Kriyā Khaṇḍa*, 22.100 ff.
9. *PadmaP, Kriyā Khaṇḍa*, 23.74.
10. *vidyā śuklā vinirdiṣṭā, kṛṣṇaṁ ajñānaṁ ucyate/* — *ViDhP*, 3.47.5.
11. *Vide* U.N. Dhal, *Colour concept of a deity*, *Viśveśvarānanda Indological Journal*, June-December, 1983, p. 231.
12. *Nāṭya-Śāstra*, 4.42-45.
13. *Ibid.*, 4.44-45.

14. *iha pracchanna pāpānāṁ śāstā vaivasvato Yamaḥ/ — Mbh*, 1.68.31. *GP*, 2.34.8.
15. Chapter 20 *Vasiṣṭha DS, SBE* 14.102. 33.230.
16. *manasaiva pure devaḥ pūrvarūpaṁ vipaśyati/*
    anumīmāṁsate' pūrvam manasā bhagvān ajaḥ// — Bhāg P, 64.48.
17. Nārāyaṇa Ayangar, *Ancient Hindu Mythology*, p. 205.
18. *Vide* under 'Yama's court', chapter 6 and 'Hells', chapter 8.
19. *Vide* 'Citragupta' chapter 6.
20. For other details *vide* "Yama-sabhā" in chapter 6.
21. *Rām*, 3.44.41.
22. Rāvaṇa defeated all *dikpālas* after a fierce battle with each of them *Rām*, 7.15-29.
23. *Yame dharmarāje, Chā Br*, 2.2.1.
24. *Mbh*, 71.17; 28
    pitṛṇām dharmarājam taṁ Yamaṁ rājye' bhyaṣecayat — ViṣṇuP, 1.22; 2.7; 19.35.
    VāyuP, 84.80; 106.44; 108.5; 113.38
    BrahmaP, 2.29.65; 3.13.67; 59.79.
25. *Vide Śabdakalpadruma*, Vol. IV, p. 18.
26. *Dharmarāja prhṛṣṭātmā Sāvitrīm idamabravīt/ — Mbh*, 3.261.
    evaṁ tasyai varaṁ datvā Dharmarājaḥ pratāpavān/ — Mbh, 3.263.
27. *BhāgP*, 3.6.7; 4.5.17.
28. *Mbh*, 12.11.14.
    Vide Vettam Mani, *Purāṇic Encyclopaedia*, p. 599.
29. *Mbh*, 1.60.30.
30. *Dharmād Yudhiṣṭhiro jajñe/* — 1.57.97
31. *Dharmasya aṁśaṁ tu rājānam viddhi rājan Yudhiṣṭhiraṁ/ — Mbh*, 1.61.84.
32. This story occurs in *Mbh*, 1.63; 108.8; *BhāgP*, 6.6; *ViP*, 3.2; *MP*, 11.56; *PP*, 5.6; *VāyuP*, 84.
    Yama-sādana is called Dharmasādana. This suggests that Yama and Dharma are considered to be identical.
33. *tapasā dharmamārādhya puṣkare bhāskaraḥ purā/*
    dharmāṁśam yam sutam prāpa Dharmarājam namāmyaham//
    — BVaiP, Prakṛti Khaṇḍa, 26.
34. *śamena dharmeṇa ca ranjitāḥ prajāḥ tatas tavaheśvara dharmarājata/ — Mbh*, 3.319.
35. V.S. Agrawala, *Matsya Purāṇa — A Study*, p. 109.
36. *Vide* S. Bhattacharji, *Indian Theogony*, p. 60.
37. *Vide* under "Yama's assistants", chapter 6.
38. Cf. S. Bhattacharji, *op. cit.*, p. 104.
39. *Vide* S. Bhattacharji, *op. cit.*, p. 53.
40. *Vide* E. Moore, *Indian Pantheon*, p. 35.
41. *BhāgP*, 6.1.20-6.3.

42. Also *ViP*, 5.30.
43. *Dharma cāṇḍāla rūpadhṛk/* — *MāP*, 8.80.
44. *Yamaḥ saṁyamatām aham/* — *MāP*, 6.24.29.
45. *prajāsaṁyamano Yamaḥ/* — *Mbh.*, 3.296.66.
46. *karmaṇānurupena Yasmāt yamayase prajāḥ/*
    tasmāt vai procyate deva Yamaḥ ityeva nāmataḥ// — *MP*, 212.2.
47. *Vide* S. Bhattacharji, *Indian Theogony*, p. 108.
48. *prajās tvayemā niyamena saṁyatā, niyamya caitā nayase na kāmyayā/*
    ato yamatvaṁ tava deva viśrutam nibodha cemāṁ giraṁ īritām mayā — Sāvitrī to Yama — *Mbh*, 3.312.
49. *catuṣpāt sakalo dharmaḥ/* — *MS*, 1.81.
    cf. *vṛṣo hi bhagvān Dharmaḥ/* — *MS*, 1.86. According to Medhātithi the four feet represent the four priests.
50. Referred to in the *Śabdakalpadruma*, pt. IV, p. 18.
51. *Vide* Chāyā's curse to Yama see Chapter IV.
52. J. Gonda, *Epithets in the Ṛgveda*.

8

Eschatology, Metempsychosis and Worship of the Manes

In the Epics and the *Purāṇas* much thought was given to man's life after death. It was now believed that good and evil deeds of men incurred merit and sins respectively which ultimately designed his post-mortem existence. The pious enjoyed a life in heaven, while the sinners, in accordance with the nature of their evil-deeds were tortured in various hells. With the development of the *Karma-vipāka* theory, elaborate account of heaven and hell are seen the *Mbh* and the *Purāṇas*. They provide graphic pictures of the rich pleasures of heaven and, in greater details, the horrifying tortures of the various hells. Yama's personality as a judge and a punisher also gains dimensions and he becomes the lord of hells, i.e., the regions where the evil-doers are punished. He is now an awe-inspiring god who frightens men into piety.

The description of the hell also has a didactic and deterrant purpose as they make people adopt the accepted code of behaviour and morality by infusing in their minds the fear of the torturous hells.

It is interesting to note that the manner in which the pious and the evil-doers are taken to the yonder world is enough to suggest that people start getting the reward for their deeds even before reaching the court of Yama. The passage of the pious and the sinners to the region of Yama is described as follows.

Path of the Pious

Generally Yama sends his assistants to fetch the souls of the people at the time of their death. Since the sight of the *Yama-dūtas* (i.e., Yama's assistants) is inauspicious, Yama does not employ them for bringing a pious soul. He himself comes to take away the souls of the noble and meritorious people, as in the case of Satyavat (*Mbh*, 3.281.15).[1] In the *MP* version of this story Yama says "Satyavat has earned a lot of religious merit by serving his parents and therefore, I myself have come to take him".[2]

In the contrast with *Yama-dūtas* who drag the sinners on the horrible path to *Yamaloka* beating and frightening them all the way,[3] the *dūtas* of heaven are said to take the pious souls very comfortably to the heaven. The *GP*, II.5.19 states that the behaviour of the *Yama-dūtas* towards the pious souls is like that of loving friends. Thus there are certain people who do not have to go to Yama's kingdom.[4] They go directly to heaven. According to the *Mbh*, 9.50.20 the habitants of Kurukṣetra go directly to heaven.

According to *Mbh*, 9.50.20 a person can go to *Brahman* without going to Yama. It says that people unnecessarily tremble on hearing the name of Yama. One, who has controlled himself, is not remembered by Yama.[5] Similar views are expressed in the *Yama śarmillopākhyāna* in the *AgniP*.[6] The ten types of 'Yamas' or controls enumerated here are —

> Kindness, forbearance, truth, non-violence, control, simplicity, meditation, lovingness, sweetness and contentment.

According to the *VarāhaP* certain people do not have to go to hell. They include the keeper of the sacred fire, the giver of land, sesamum, cow, gold and land; the master of the *Vedas*, one who respects the twice-born and the sacrificer and one who studies the *Vedas* daily.[7]

The *BhāgP*, 6.2.44 mentions that the pious ascend the

heavenly car made of gold and proceed through heavens to the abode of Viṣṇu.

The *PP* records that the people who have done noble deeds enjoy pleasures in this life and after death they become *Khecaras* and *Vidyādharas* and go to heaven.[8]

A man is said to be saved from going to hells, if he is freed from his sins by someone offering him the fruit of his own good deeds or by the Lord's (Hari's) grace. Śūkari states that if she were not freed from the sins through the queen Sudevā's merits, she would have to bear the sufferings of the hells.[9]

Fate of the Pious

As a reward for their meritorious deeds the pious at their death are taken to *Brahma-loka* in the shining aerial cars drawn by swans and peacocks, tinkling with bells; adorned with flags, studded with various jewels and resounding with the songs of the nymphs.[10]

They enjoy the pleasures till the end of a *kalpa*.[11] The different paths and different vehicles are also mentioned in *PP*.[12]

The *GP* states that when Yama sees a pious soul coming to him, he moves from his place and announces that there he surpasses his region and goes to the *Brahma-loka*.[13] This shows the *Yamaloka* is not meant for the pious souls.

In the *NrP* (chapter 13) at the end of the Yama-Yamī dialogue it is stated that whoever reads the dialogue, his ancestors feel satiated and they no longer stay in the abode of Yama.[14] This version of the dialogue highlights the strong moral character and firmness of Yama, who did not let himself be allured to do a deplorable and condemned act. One who reads this dialogue also shares this firmness of mind and thereby he not only pleases his ancestors, but also frees them from their sins. This entitles them to be saved from a stay in the kingdom of Yama.

According to the *BrP*, 22.5.6.7 a generous donor goes to

heaven where he enjoys the pleasures in the company of the nymphs in the heavenly garden named *Nandanavana*.

From these references it is clear that according to the Purāṇic belief the pious led a happy life on earth and after their death they went to heaven directly without going to the region of Yama. In brief, heavenly regions and the pleasures thereof are for the pious and they do not have to visit the torturous *Yamaloka*.

By performing various meritorious deeds man secures a place for himself in the various celestial regions or *lokas* as the reward of his merits. The *PP* has named several *lokas*, e.g., *Śivaloka, Indraloka, Sarasvatīloka, Brahmaloka, Gaurīloka*, etc. At places the *PP* has graded them in order of supremacy as *Indraloka, Brahmaloka, Śivaloka* and above all in the *Viṣṇuloka*.[15]

Onward Journey of the Sinner

As the time of a person's death arrives, Yama or his assistants come to fetch him away. The dead man has to leave his body, but he gets a special body[16] which is termed as *yātanā-deha*. The *AgniP* mentions the dead man acquiring a body in order to suffer the torments of the hells;[17] he has to undergo the punishments for the sins committed during his life-time (*MāP*, 10.62). This body is similar to the age and condition of his earthly body. At Yama's command his servants take away the *yātanā-deha* of the dead man and drop it into the different hells. The *yātanā-deha*, as the word implies, means the body which is meant for undergoing the sufferings after death.[18] It is subjected to many death-like tortures in hells, but it does not perish thereby and get freed from further tortures. It is not destroyed even on being burnt or cut into pieces in the hells like *Raurava, Mahāraurava* and *Asipatravana*. It regains it complete form after each punishment and thus makes the man experience the pain and torture till the period of the punishment awarded to him is over.

Yama sends his servants to bring the people whose time on earth is over. But as their appearance is inauspicious, he does not employ them to bring the noble and the pious souls.

In such cases he honours the pious man by himself appearing before him to take his soul away. The *Mbh*, 3.281.15 tells that Yama himself came to fetch Satyavān.[19] In the *MatsyaP* version of this story, Yama discloses the reason to Sāvitrī, that on account of his serving his elders, Satyavān had earned enormous religious merit and therefore he himself had come to take him.[20]

The *BhāgP* states that a person who is engrossed in worldly pleasures, who is deeply attached to his own self, his wife, son, house, cattle and wealth, often adopts immoral ways. At the time of his death two frightful messengers of Yama arrive. He is so terrified at the mere sight of them that he voids stool and urine. The *Yama-dūtas* give him the special body for undergoing the sufferings of the punishment in the hells; they put a noose around his neck and drag him on a long way just as a king's men take the convicts.[21] His heart is riven by their intimidations and threats and he trembles in every limb. Hounds are let loose to feed on him. His mind is full of remorse and sorrow, as he recalls his sins. Tormented by hunger and thirst, scorched by sun and the forest-fire he is also lashed on the back. In this manner he is taken to Yama's kingdom. On the way there is no water or shelter. With great difficulty he moves on this path which is plunged in darkness. Stumbling and falling at every step due to exhaustion he is led on this path to Yama's region.[22]

The *yātanā-deha* has to travel ninety-nine thousand *yojanas* to reach Yama. This distance he covers in two or three *muhūrtas* but they seem very long and unbearable to him. He is further tormented in various ways, e.g., by burning of his body, by having to consume his own flesh cut either by others or by himself, having his entrails torn out by the dogs and vultures of Yama's kingdom. He is plunged in water; or buried in a pit. Thus he has to bear numerous sufferings.[23]

According to the *MP a preta*, i.e., one who has died recently, hovers about in the sky in the form of air for a period of sixty thousand and eighty terrible years and then at the time of their fall the *pretas* are devoured by terrible *rākṣasas* (*MP*, 39.7-8). It also says that those who are not conscious of their duty during their life on earth and whose actions are not meritorious, go to the horrible hells. The *PP* says that the sinners after death follow the path of Yama (*PP Pātāla-khaṇḍa*, 97.10.23). The messengers of Yama bind the sinner with the *kālapāśa* and bring him to the hells, where he is beaten up by the servants of Yama (*PP Pātāla-khaṇḍa*, 48.7-8).[24] They bind his body with ropes and drag it on the path to *Yama-loka* which is full of thorns, insects, serpents, hot sands and wild animals.[25] This path is terrible, difficult to tread on and full of torments due to excessive heat, cold and darkness.

The *GP* states that the path to Yama's kingdom is eighty-six *yojanas*.[26] This path which connects the earth with Yama's kingdom is full of sufferings. *Yama-dūtas* bind the sinners with the *pāśa* and they also beat them on the way.[27] They frighten the sinners by describing the horrible hells they are heading to and forcibly drag them on the path (*GP*, 2.5.28). There is neither food nor water, no place to rest and no shadows of trees on this path which is full of thorns.[28] These sufferings are meant for the sinners only. The noble and pious are taken very comfortably to *svarga* (i.e., heaven) by the messengers of heaven (*svarga-dūta*). Yama treats the pious souls in a friendly manner, while the sinners suffer intolerable tortures and are threatened by Yama with his rod when they reach him. The *preta* (i.e., one who has recently died) walks two hundred *yojanas* daily and reaches Yama's region in forty-seven days and nights (*GP*, 2.5.78).

At the time of death *Yama-dūtas* take away the *aṅguṣṭha mātra-puruṣaḥ* from the body of the dead[29] (*GP*, 2.5.22). This spatial dimension finds a reference in the *Upaniṣads*. The *aṅguṣṭha-mātra-puruṣaḥ* is conceived to be the individual soul.[30] The soul (*puruṣa*), which is of the measure of a thumb and dwells in the middle of the body, is the lord of the past, the future (and the present times).[31]

Fate of the Sinner

A new body of the dead is formed in nine days time.[32] This body partakes whatever is offered to the dead man, as the part of the *śrāddha*-rites on the tenth, eleventh and the twelfth day after the death. On the thirteenth day the dead is taken on the path of *Yama-purī*. Thus on the thirteenth day the dead now possesses a special body and leaves his house. Bound by the noose he is now taken to the region of Dharmarāja, i.e., Yama. He reaches there after twelve months, since he has to first cross eleven regions which takes a period of eleven months.[33] These regions are —

(1) Yāmya-pura
(2) Sauri-pura (here he stays for two months)
(3) Gandharva-pura
(4) Saitāgama-pura
(5) Krūra-pura
(6) Citra-nagar
(7) Pura
(8) Duḥkhada-pura
(9) Nānākranda-pura
(10) Tapta-pura
(11) Raudra-sthāna
(12) Śita-pura

From there he proceeds to the land of 'Dharmarāja', which is inhabited by divine *gandharvas* and nymphs and it is forty-four *yojanas* in size.

The *Purāṇas* thus bring out the differential treatment meted out to the pious and the sinner. The object is too obvious to be missed. These horrors are supposed to act as deterrents to prevent people from doing such acts which were considered sinful. Thus the concept of hell has a didactic purpose.

Rebirth

The concept of rebirth was well established in the time of the *Purāṇas*. As the doctrines of *karma* and *punarjanma* were formulated, the Vedic idea of heaven and hell also came to be modified. Unlike the early Vedic thought that the heaven or hell are granted for once and for ever whence the man had no return, the Purāṇic thought entertains the belief that man's stay in heaven/hell is for a limited time. Duration of this period varied from person to person according to his *karma*.

Now the pious did not go to heaven and become immortal there, nor do the sinners fall in the dark pit and disappear.[34] Now heaven and hell are places for reward or punishment where the soul has to stay for the required period depending upon his merits and sins. Thus it was now believed that the pleasures of heaven and the torments of hell came to an end after which the soul takes up another earthly form, i.e., it is reborn on the earth as an animal, a tree or a human being.[35] Thus it was believed that a man has to pass through several births and deaths. The amount of good or evil deeds done during his life on the earth not only sent him to heaven or hell, but also contributed in deciding his successive birth and also his fate therein.

In the *MāP*, 10.17 Sumati, a young brahmin reveals to his father that he remembered the period of past ten thousand years and his numerous lives during that period. In this long chain of births he was born as a brāhmaṇa, a kṣatriya a vaiśya, a śūdra and also as several insects, animals and birds.[36] In his different births he was born as a rich man as well as a poor man, a master as a servant (*MāP*, 10.24).

RETURN FROM HEAVEN/HELL

It is believed that after exhausting most of his *karmas* by staying in heaven and hell, a man is again born on the earth. He returns to earth, when some of his *karmas* are still unexhausted. The *MP*, 39.2 states that after enjoying the fruit of his meritorious deeds, a man falls down on earth[37] or goes to lower regions. With most of his religious merit exhausted, the status of this man is now similar to that of a penniless fellow. As a penniless man is abandoned by his companions and relatives, a man whose religious merit is exhausted, is deserted by gods in the heaven.[38]

REBIRTH OF THE PIOUS

The *MāP* (15.1-42) provides the details of the different births the sinners get on account of their particular sins. It further states that the pious retain their noble character, when they are reborn on the earth. Thus, after his death the pious enjoys the pleasures of heaven till his merits last and with a little of his religious merit still with him he is born as a man with noble qualities. The *BrahmaP*, 225.6-7 states that when all their religious merit is exhausted, the pious have to leave heaven and be born on the earth, and they are born in rich and noble families.

According to the *PP Sṛṣṭi Khaṇḍa*, 15.243-244 the meritorious people, after enjoying the deserved pleasures in heaven, are reborn on the earth. Similar ideas are contained in the *PP*, *Uttara Khaṇḍa*, 36.37. The *PP Ādi Khaṇḍa*, 42.12, 44.11 state that the pious attain the leadership of the Jambu-dvīpa. The *PP* (*Sṛṣṭi Khaṇḍa*, 15.199-232) also tells that virtuous people are born on earth as kings and princes, rich, and handsome people and as glorious devotees. To Kālidāsa, the city of Ujjayinī is nothing less that a bright portion of heaven borne down to earth by the heaven-dwellers. They had to descend on the earth, when the stock of their religious-merit was nearly exhausted and they, with their remaining merits, had brought to earth this portion of the heaven (*Meghadūtam*, 1.31).[39]

REBIRTH OF SINNER

A sinner also, after having undergone the punishment in the hell is born on earth with some of his sins still unconsumed. Due to his remaining sins he is afflicted by diseases and suffers in many ways.[40] His actions in this birth again take him to hell after his death. This process of births and deaths goes on till he has taken punishment for all his deeds (*PP Bhūmi Khaṇḍa*, 52.30-31).

According to the *MāP*, 10.20 the sinners are born as insects and other lowly creatures and animals. After hundreds of such births he gets a human body again. The stages of his transmigration are worm → insects → fish → birds → animals → human being.[41] Thus the sinners gradually migrate through the several inferior births until he is once more born as a man.

The *VarāhaP* (198.57-60) provides that when the period

of his punishment is over, the deceased becomes fixed objects. From the state of fixed objects he takes birth as animals, insects, birds, kine, etc. whereafter he regains a human body.

Thus the present life of a man is indicative of his past deeds, while his present deeds present an idea of his future life. The *BhāgP*, 6.1.47[42] states that just as the present time is an index of the characteristic of the other periods that precedes and succeeds it, similarly the present life (of human beings) indicates the righteous and sinful actions committed in the past and likely to be committed in the future existence as well.

According to the *BhāgP* people experience pleasures or sufferings in this world in accordance with their meritorious or evil deeds. Wise men say that heaven and hell are here on the earth itself, for one may see creatures on the earth suffering from torments of hells (*BhāgP*, 3.30.29). Thus in accordance with his good or evil deed the earth is the extended heaven and hell for man. This theory can reasonably explain the miserable plight of even the innocent people on earth. When Sītā was abandoned by Rāma, she could not think of any fault of her which could have brought to her such a sorrowful fate. She believed that it must be the result of the sins committed by her in the previous lives.[43]

So long a man continues to do *karma*, he has to be reborn on the earth. In each new life he collects a new stock of *karma* and as the result again goes to heaven and hell and from there returns to the earth. This forms a circle of births and deaths. Even performing one's duty gives special fruit, if done with a desire for its fruit. If they are performed without such desire, they bring total release (*ViP*, 6.7.36-38 cf. *BG*, 3.19). Thus *niṣkāma-karma* is conductive to release. Performance of one's duties without the attachment to their fruit wears off merits and demerits and leads to liberation.

The three ways to the total liberation are *karmayoga*, *bhaktiyoga* and *jñānayoga*.[44] The *karmayoga* consists of dedicating all actions to God with mind firmly fixed in Him : Performance of actions is like prayers to God. One is bound by the fruit of his actions, if they are not surrendered to God. Complete renunciation of righteous and evil deeds leads to *mokṣa* (*VāyuP*, 17.7).

Hells

Though the Vedic seers did not give much though to the life after death, much lesser to the sufferings therein, the germs of the doctrine of *karma-vipāka*, i.e., fruction of action can be seen there. According to them a man is obliged to bear the fruit of his good or evil deeds. The *ṚV* mentions a special region for the pious deed (*sukṛtām lokaṁ*) as well as a dark abyss for the sinners.[45] It also refers to a man attaining higher or lower regions on the basis of his good or evil deeds. The Brāhmaṇic texts contain the doctrine of reward and punishment after death for the acts done by a man during his life on earth. The *ŚB*, 11.2.7.33 mentions that in the yonder world the good and bad deeds of man are weighed on a balance. He gets the reward, if his good deeds outweigh and is punished if the evil deeds outweigh. The doctrine of rebirth was not formulated in the early Vedic thought.

The concept of *karma-vipāka* is found to be well established in the *Purāṇas*.[46] A man is believed to be compulsorily rewarded or punished for his good or bad actions respectively. The *PP* (*Bhūmi Khaṇḍa*, 81.47) states that as a calf goes to its mother only, though she may be standing in the midst of thousands of cows, similarly the fruit of good or bad action invariably goes to its doer only. The punishment came in the form of a life full of sorrows and deprivation on earth or a torturous life in one or more hells. The *BhāgP*, 3.30.39 states that according to the wise men the heaven and hell are to be found here on earth, for one may see creatures suffering the torments of hells even on the earth.

A man is freed from the sins committed by him in two ways: (1) by making atonement during his life on earth, (2) by bearing the punishment awarded to him after his death.

In the *BhāgP*, 6.1.68 *Yama-dūtas* pronounce that since that sinner had not done anything to expiate his sins, he could be purified only by undergoing the prescribed punishment. The *BhāgP*, states various means of making atonement for one's sins, e.g., asceticism (*tapas*), absolute continence (*brahmacarya*), control of mind (*sāma*), restrain of senses (*dāma*), giving gifts (*tyāga*), purity (*śauca*) and truth (*satya*) etc. (*BhāgP*, 6.1.13; 11.5.9; 6.2.11).

Atonement

If a man, after committing a sin, realises his mistake and makes atonement for it, he is freed from the sin. There are several instances where a sin is made away by performing atonement. By killing the demon Vṛtra Indra had incurred the sin of brahminicide. For this he sought expiation by leaving the heavenly throne to live in seclusion in the *Mānasa* lake for one thousand years. After the expiry of this period he also performed one thousand horse-sacrifices (*BhāgP*, 6.13.15; 18.21). Yudhiṣṭhira performed three horse-sacrifices to atone for the sin incurred by him due to the slaughter of his cousins in the Great War.[47]

In the absense of expiation, the punishment becomes necessary. This is the only other way of getting retrieve from one's sins. The man, after his death is punished with a stay in the torturous hells. The period of his stay and the type of hell are in accordance with the sin committed. After undergoing the punishment he gets freed from the sin.

Life in heaven is meant for joy and happiness on the basis of *dharma* observed here. There are hells where punishments are inflicted upon the dead on the basis of *adharma* committed by him when he was alive. The *BhāgP*, 6.1.40ab states that performance of actions prescribed by *Veda* is *dharma* and *adharma* is its reverse.[48] Hells are the result of violation of proper mode of conduct.[49]

The *ViP*, 2.6 gives a philosophical garb to the concept of heaven and hell. It says that heaven is that which delights the mind and hell is that which gives it pain, hence vice is hell and virtue is heaven.

After death the sinners are taken to Yama by his assistants.

Their fate is decided in the court (*sabhā*) of Yama. The *VarāhaP*, chapter 205.9-10 contains a dialogue between Yama and Citragupta in which the latter recommends the fate that the dead deserves for his acts.

The *PP* mentions that the sinners go to various hells, namely, *Raurava*, etc. at the command of Yama[50] The *AgniP*, 371.12 states that a sinner falls into horrible hells that are declared by Citragupta at the order of Yama.[51] Several hells are described in the *Purāṇas*. The types of tortures in these hells are also described in detail.[52]

Location of the Hells

According to *ViP*, 2.6 the hells are situated beneath the earth and beneath the waters. In the *BhāgP* the hells are said to be situated in the abode of Yama. They are within the three worlds, in the south, below the earth and above the waters. Manes live there and Vaivasvata Yama is the king (*BhāgP*, 5.26.5-6; 26). According to the *VāP* the hells are situated in the Puṣkara island which is the last and the farthest of the seven islands which encircle the Jumbu-dvīpa. The Puṣkara island is fearsome and full of tortures.

According to the *VāP*[53] the earth is fifty crore *yojanas* in size and it floats on water like a boat. Brahmā has established the Sumera Mountain; Prajāpati named many islands (*VāP*, 11.31) and places and made Jambu-dvīpa in its centre.[54] This *dvīpa* is encircled by seven oceans and six islands. The six islands are (1) Plakṣa-dvīpa, (2) Śālmali-dvīpa, (3) Kuśa-dvīpa, (4) Krauñca-dvīpa, (5) Śāka-dvīpa, (6) Puṣkara-dvīpa.

The seven oceans which separates them are:

(1) *Kṣāra-samudra* (salt-water ocean)

(2) *Ikṣurasa-samudra* (sugarcane-juice ocean)

(3) *Surā-samudra* (wine ocean)

(4) *Ghṛta-samudra* (*ghī* ocean)

(5) *Dadhi-samudra* (curds ocean)

(6) *Kṣīra-samudra* (milk ocean)

(7) *Svāhūda-samudra* (sweet-water ocean)

Jambu-dvīpa is one lakh *yojanas* in size, and these seven oceans and six islands encircle the Jambu-dvīpa alternately. Each island/ocean is conceived to be double the size of the previous island/ocean. Hells are said to situated in the Puṣkara-dvīpa.

Number of Hells

According to Śaṅkarācārya the *Vedānta Sūtra*, 3.1.15 refers to the seven types of hells, namely Raurava, etc. The *MāP*, 10.81 and the *ViP*, 1.6.41 also describe seven hells. The *ViP* 2.6 mentions twenty-eight hells. The *BhāgP*, 5.26.6 also states that there are twenty-eight hells. There names, however, differ from those given in the *ViP*.

Some works enumerate twenty-one hells, e.g. *ManuS*, 4.88-90, *ViDhP*, 43.2-22, *AgniP*, 371.20-22.

The *BrahmaP*, 214.14-17; 51.203; 215.83 speaks of twenty-two hells and provides horrowing description of the torments of the hells. Elsewhere the *BrP* (chapter 22) names twenty-five hells.

However, the *BrahmaP* (215.82-83), *ViDhP* (quoted by P.V. Kane in *HDS* Vol. IV, p. 164) and the *GaruḍaP* (*Preta Khaṇḍa*, 3.3) declare that there are thousands, and lakhs and crores of hells.

HELLS IN MĀRKAṆḌEYA PURĀṆA

Each hell is a place of punishment for a particular set of crimes. Most of them have there own methods of inflicting tortures. The *MāP* (chapter 10; 14; 15) deals with the *karma-vipāka* in great details and mentions several places and modes of tortures. The hells, distinctly named and described in *MāP*, 10.81; 12.4-48 are seven in number. They are:

(1) *Raurava* (2) *Mahāraurava*

(3) *Tamas* (4) *Nikṛntana*

(5) *Apratiṣṭha* (6) *Asipatravana*

(7) *Tapta-kumbha*

Another hell named *Kālasūtra* is mentioned in *MāP*, 14.89.

Raurava

It is two thousand *yojanas* in size. Heaps of coals constantly burn there making it extremely hot. The sinner is scorched in this heat, as he is made to walk on the hot surface. Being burnt by the flames he runs about here and there. Only after he was walked one thousand *yojanas* a sinner is freed from this hell. But this is not the end of his sufferings, for he is now sent to other hells. After finishing his period of punishment in the other hells too he is born as a bird and also as worm insect, fly, mosquito, cow, horse, elephant, tree, creeper and many lowly births (*MāP*, 10.84-89).

A person who gives false witness, speaks untruth, kills his father or a brahmin, or a cow, one who kidnaps a woman, one who has illicit relationship with the wife or daughter of one's preceptor falls in the Raurava hell (*MāP*, 10.81-82).

Mahāraurava

As the name denotes it is extremely terrible. It is twelve square *yojanas* in size.

Eating prohibited things, cheating a friend, breaking the faith of the master, abandoning his own wife and having lust for other women, destroyer of a path, a pond or a garden — these are the sins which take a man to be burnt in this hell.

The *Mahāraurava* hell is extremely hot due to its copper surface which is constantly heated by fire. The sinners are kept here with their heads and feet bound. They move by rolling and are preyed upon by crows, herons, wolves, owls, scorpians and vultures, etc. (*MāP*, 12.3-9) . They have to stay there for thousands of years (*MāP*, 12.11).

Tamas

This hell is bitterly cold and dark. People suffer due to hunger and thirst. Afflicted with cold the sinners run about in total darkness and seek refuge in clasping each other. The wind laden with snow particles pierces their bones. The hungry sinners feed on marrow and blood dropping therefrom.

The killer of a brother, a child, a cow and the destroyer of water and food falls in this hell. He has to remain there till all his sins are washed away (a man consumes his sins by undergoing the punishment) (*MāP*, 12.13-18ab).

Nikṛntana

In this hell the sinner is mounted on an incesssantly revolving (potter's) wheel and is cut by the strings of 'Fate' which are borne on the finger's of Yama's servants. The bodies of the sinners are cut again and again, because the parts of their bodies join together everytime they are cut. In this manner they suffer the pain of being cut again and again for thousands of years till their sins are consumed. A man of bad character, one who is disobedient to his preceptor and one who does not respect a person as his *guru* even when one was taught something by him — these sinners are destined to fall in this hell (*MāP*, 12.18d-24).

Apratiṣṭha

There are jars, wheels and ropes in this hell, which cause intolerable pain to the sinners for a thousand years. The sinners are bound to the jars and well-rope like a jar in water. Men whirl around continuously spitting out blood. One who creates obstructions to a brahmin engaged in his work is thrown into this hell (*MāP*, 12.25-30).

Asipatravana

This hell is of one thousand *yojanas* in size. This is a forest of sword-leaves. It also has a blazing fire. Winds blow and hurl the sinners on the sword-leaves of the forest. In this way they are cut into pieces again and again. Terrifying dogs, with their large teeth and as fierce as tigers, tear away the limbs from the bodies of these wailing sinners (*MāP*, 12-39). One who poses obstacles for a celibate, an observer of a vow or an ascetic is thrown into this hell (*MāP*, 12-31).

Taptakumbha

This hell contains hot-pitchers. These pitchers are filled with oil and ferrous-powder and they are constantly heated. In these pitchers the *Yama-dūtas* lower the sinners with their heads downwards. There are vultures who pull them out and drop again in the pitchers. Vigorously stirred up by Yama's servants the sinners are churned in the pool of oil. (*MāP*, 12.43-44).

One who violates the sanctity of *Dharmaśāstras* and holy places, one who does evil to a friend and one who abandones his innocent wife is thrown into this hell.

Kālasūtra

One more hell is mentioned in the *MāP*, 14.89. In this hell the sinners are cut into pieces.

Apart from these hells *MāP*, 13,14 also describe in great detail the fruit of different sins committed by a man. Due to his sins a man has to suffer various types of tortures like that of swallowing burning coals, being flung down from high mountains or being eaten up by worms.

HELLS IN VIṢṆU PURĀṆA

The *ViP* (2.6) enumerates twenty-eight hells. They are (1) *Raurava*, (2) *Śūkara*, (3) *Rodha*, (4) *Tāla*, (5) *Viśāsana*, (6) *Mahājvālā*, (7) *Taptakumbha*, (8) *Lavaṇa*, (9) *Vimohana*, (10) *Rudhirāndha*, (11) *Vaitaraṇī*, (12) *Kṛmīśa*, (13) *Kṛmibhojana*, (14) *Asipatravana*, (15) *Kṛṣṇa*, (16) *Lālābhakṣa*, (17) *Dāruṇa*, (18) *Pūyavāha*, (19) *Pāpa*, (20) *Vahnijvālā*, (21) *Adhośiras*, (22) *Saṁdaṁśa*, (23) *Kālasūtra*, (24) *Tamas*, (25) *Avīci*, (26) *Śvabhojana*, (27) *Apratiṣṭha* and (28) another *Avici*.[55]

These hells and many other places of torture are the provinces of Yama's kingdom. They are terrible with the instruments of torture and the blazing fire therein. Sinners are hurled into these hells where they are tortured with burning sand, fire and weapons. Some are cut with saws, some roasted in forges, some chopped with axes and some buried in the ground, some are mounted on the stakes, thrown to wild animals in order to be devoured by them, gnawed by vultures, torn by tigers and fried in oil.[56] Different hells and the types of sinners punished therein are mentioned as follows:

(1) *Raurava* (dreadful) — for bearing false witness.

(2) *Rodha* (obstruction) — for causing abortion plandering a town, killing a cow and for strangling a man.

(3) *Śūkara* (swine) — for murdering a brahmin, stealing gold, drinking wine. A person assisting in these is also punished in this hell.

(4) *Tāla* — for murdering a vaiśya or śūdra; adultery with the preceptor's wife.

(5) *Tapta-kumbha* (the hell with heated pitchers) — for incest with sister, for killing an ambassador.

(6) *Tapta-loka* — for selling one's wife, a gaoler, a horse dealer, and one who deserts his adherents fall into this.

(7) *Mahājvālā* (of great flame) — for committing incest with daughter-in-law or daughter.

(8) *Lavaṇa* (i.e., salt hell) — for being disrespectful to one's spiritual guide, for abusing the betters, for selling the *Vedas*.[57]

(9) *Vimohana* — for stealing.

(10) *Kṛmibhakṣa* — one who scorns his father, brahmins and the gods and also one who spoils the precious gems.

(11) *Kṛmiśa* (hell of worms) — for practising magic-rites with an intention to harm others.

(12) *Lālābhakṣa* — for eating meals before offering it to the gods, to the manes and to the guest.

(13) *Vedhaka* — this hell is for the maker of arrows,

lances, swords and other weapons, where the sinners are pierced).

(14) *Viśāsana* — one who offers in sacrifices improper objects and one who is observer of stars (for the prediction of events.[58]

(15) *Adhomukha* (head-inverted) — he who takes unlawful gifts goes to this hell.

(16) *Pūyavāha* — who eats by himself the sweets mixed with rice, and a brahmin who sells lac, flesh, liquor, sesamum, or salt, or one who commits violence falls into this hell. Those who rear cats, cocks, goats, dogs, hogs or birds, also fall in this hell.

(17) *Rudhirāndha* — public performers, fishermen, a poisoner, an informer and one who lives by his wife's prostitution are punished in the *Rudhirāndha* hell.

(18) *Vaitaraṇī* — a treacherous friend, one who destroys a bee hive is condemned to this hell.

(19) *Kṛṣṇa* — one who trespasses on others land, is impure and who deceives others is punished in this dark hell.

(20) *Asipatravana* — he who wantonly cuts down trees goes to this hell.

(21) *Vahnijvālā* — this is the hell of fiery flame. One who tenders sheep and hunts deer go to this hell.

(22) *Saṁdaṁśa* (the hell of pincers) — one who violates his vow is punished in this hell.

(23) *Svabhojana* — the religious student who sleep in the day and those who are instructed in sacred literature by their children go to this hell where the feed upon dogs (or eaten by dogs!).

The *ViP*, describes 28 hells in all.

HELLS IN VĀMANA PURĀṆA

According to the *VāmanaP* there are twenty-one hells

(*VāmanaP*, 11.50). The names of these hells are given as follows:

(1) *Raurava*: It is two thousand *yojanas* in size and is full of burning coal.

(2) *Mahāraurava* : It is double the size of *Raurava* hell. Its floor is of hot copper. One who steals gold, commits brahminicide or adultery with the preceptor's wife, grabs others' cows and land, one who kills a cow, a woman or a child; a brahmin who sells cow, *Soma* or the *Vedas* (teaches *Vedas* for money) one who stays impure, one who does not perform his *nitya* (daily) and *naimittika* (occasional duties) and one who offers false witness all these fall in the *Mahāraurava* (i.e., extremely terrible) hell (*VāmanaP*, 12.38-40).

Such a sinner has to spend ten thousand years in each of these hells *Raurava, Tāmisra, Andhatamas, Asipatravana, Ghaṭīyantra* and then *Taptakumba.*

The other hells are,

(3) *Tāmisra*

(4) *Andhatāmisra* — this is double the size of *Tāmisra*

(5) *Kālasūtra*

(6) *Apratiṣṭha*

(7) *Ghaṭīyantra*

(8) *Asipatravana* — it is seventy-two thousand *yojanas*

(9) *Taptakumbha*

(10) *Kūṭaśālmalī*

(11) *Karapatra*

(12) *Śvānabhojana*

(13) *Saṁdaṁśa*

(14) *Lohapiṇḍa*

(15) *Karambhasikatā*

(16) A terrible, salty river

(17) *Kṛmibhojana*

(18) *Vaitaraṇī*

(19) *Soṇitpūyabhojana*

(20) *Cakraka* — this is sharp like blades

Another hell is mentioned in *VāmanaP*, 12.37, this is *Vṛkabhakṣa* hell.

HELLS IN BHĀGAVATA PURĀṆA

According to the *BhāgP*, 5.26.7 there are twenty-eight types of hells. They are situated between the three worlds in the south direction, below the earth and above the water. Manes live there. Vaivasvata Yama, the lord of the Fathers, rules there. He is helped by his assistants who never transgress their lord's command. Yama inflicts punishments according to the crime.

The twenty-eight hells mentioned in the *BhāgP*, are — *Tāmisra, Andhatāmisra, Raurava, Mahāraurava, Kumbhīpāka, Kālasūtra, Asipatravana, Śūkaramukha, Andhakūpa, Kṛmibhojana, Saṁdaṁśa, Taptasūrmi, Vajrakanṭakaśālmali, Vaitaraṇī, Pūyoda, Prāṇarodha, Viśasana, Lālābhakṣa, Sārameyādana, Avīci* and *Ayaḥpāna, Kṣārakardama, Rakṣogaṇabhojana, Daṇḍaśūka, Śūlaprota, Avaṭanirodhana, Paryāvartana* and *Śūcimukha* (5.26.7-36).

Tāmisra

A person who seizes others' property, progeny or woman is sent to this hell. Another hell called *Saṁdaṁśa* is for a person who steals or grabs the gold or jewellery of a brahmin or of any other person.

Andhatāmisra

This is a place of absolute darkness. A man who deceives someone and molests other's wife is sent to suffer in this hell. Another hell *Taptasūrmi* is enjoined for a person practising illicit relations. For such grave sins (*MS*, 11.54). Manu prescribes an expiatory rite. "The seducer of the preceptor's wife shall sleep on hot iron bed admitting his guilt or shall embrace the hot (iron) image of the lady. Death verily is his purifier (*MS*, 11.103).

Raurava

Raurava is for a person who is always engrossed in selfish motives, and who troubles others for himself or his family. These victims become *Rurus* (fierce animals) and torment him.

Mahāraurava

Mahāraurava is styled on the same lines. The *Khumbhīpāka* is the hell for a person who kills animals for eating them. In this hell Yama's assistants throw the sinners into the boiling oil.

The *Kālasūtra* is the hell for a person who insults his parents, brahmins and the sacred texts. A man who, unless in utter difficulty, adopts the religion of the 'non-believers of the *Vedas*' is destined to go to the *Asipatravana*. *Śūkaramukha* is the hell for a man who uses his authority for punishing innocent person and who awards corporal punishment to a brahmin. The *Andhakūpa* is for those who kill insects.

Kṛmibhojana

The hell *Kṛmibhojana* is for a person who does not perform any of the five great sacrifices, nor gives anything to others. Various kinds of worms trouble the sinners here.

Vajrakanṭakaśālmalī

In *Vajrakanṭakaśālmalī* the sinner is pierced by thorns. A man is dropped in this hell for dealing badly with others.

Vaitaraṇī

Vaitarṇī is a river-hell. It is full of blood, hair, bones, etc. The hot water of this stinking river moves swiftly carrying bones and hair, etc. If a king or his official breaks any code of morals he is thrown in this river.

Pūyoda

Pūyoda is the hell for a person who does not follow the rules of purity. *Prāṇarodha* is enjoined for persons who though belonging to a higher *varṇa* tame dogs and donkeys and who kill the animals that are not ordained to be killed.

Viśāsana

Viśāsana is for those who kill animals in mock sacrifices.

Sarameyādana

Sarameyādana is the hell for the theives, or kings and his officials who burn people's houses, grab their property and poison others. Yama's attendants become dogs and bite the sinner in this hell.

Avicimān

Aviciman is for there who lie as witness. When a brahmin (man or woman) takes wine, and a kṣatriya or vaiśya drinks *Soma*, he is destined to go to *Ayaḥpāna Yama-dūtas* thrust red hot iron in the mouths of the sinners.

A low-caste man who thinks himself to be of a higher caste and does not respect the people of the higher caste goes to the *Kṣārakardama* hell. Those who sacrifice a human being in the human sacrifice are sent to the hell called *Rakṣogaṇabhojana*. One who deceives others goes to the *Śūlaprota*. Those who trouble others go to *Daṇḍaśūka*. Those who imprison others in dark places (caves, etc.) go to *Avaṭanirodhana* hell. He is imprisoned here in the smoke of the poisonous hell-fires.

One who does not treat his guests properly goes to the *Paryāvartana* hell. Here he is bitten by sharp-beaked birds. *Śūcimukha* is for those who do not trust anybody and think themselves to be very wealthy. Here, Yama's men sew all the limbs of the sinners.

After describing these various hells the *BhāgP*, 6.26.37 says that there are hundreds and thousands of hells in the region of Yama. Various types of hell for various sins are described here. The possibility of new types of sins under new circumstances cannot be ruled out and therefore *BhāgP* adds that there are many more hells, though they are not specially mentioned.[59] Sinners exhaust their sins by undergoing the punishment after which he is born again. Thus a stay in hell purifies man and he does not carry the load of his sins to his next birth.

Apart from the two paths, one leading to heaven and the other to hell, there is another path for human being and that is the path to *mokṣa*, i.e., the total liberation (IInd *Skandha*). Thus the *mokṣa* is considered to be the highest fate of man from where he does not return to earth and he gets totally liberated from the cycle of births and deaths.

HELLS IN GARUḌA PURĀṆA

The *GP* describes the torturous journey of the sinners as they are taken to the kingdom of Yama. The *GP*, 2.57 gives the list of the names of the hells as follows:

1. *Raurava*
2. *Śūkara*
3. *Voḍha*
4. *Tāla*
5. *Viśāsana*
6. *Mahājvālā*
7. *Taptakumbha*
8. *Lavaṇa*
9. *Viṁdhita*
10. *Rudhir*

14. *Asipatravana*
15. *Kṛṣṇa*
16. *Nānābhakṣa*
17. *Pūyavāha*
18. *Pāpa*
19. *Vahnijvālā*
20. *Saṁdaṁśa*
21. *Kṛṣṇasūtra*
22. *Tama*
23. *Avīci*

11. *Vaitaraṇī*
12. *Kṛmīśa*
13. *Kṛmibhojana*

24. *Śvabhojana*
25. *Apratiṣṭha*
26. *Ūṣṇavīci*

HELLS IN VARĀHA PURĀṆA

The *VarāhaP* (198.1-2) mentions eight hells. They are (1) *Tapta*, (2) *Mahātapta*, (3) *Kālasūtraka*, (4) *Andhakāra*, (5) *Andhakarpara*, (6) *Raurava* and *Mahāraurava*. Here the sinners are burnt, severed, pricked, torn and tortured in many ways (*VarāhaP*, 198.19). It also mentions *Asipatravana* and *Śṛṅgāṭakavana* and *Kūṭaśālmali*. The sinners have to cross a river Karambhavālukā which is of hundred *yojanas* in size and very dreadful.

Vaitaraṇī, very big in size and full of fierce creatures, and *Yama nadī*, a river full of hot pus are other two rivers mentioned in the *VarāhaP* (198.26-28) where the sinners are trortured.

It is to be noted here that some hells, e.g., *Raurava*, *Tapta-kumbha*, (or *Kumbhi-pāka*), *Asipatravana*, *Kṛṣṇasūtra* (or *Kālasūtra*) and *Apratiṣṭha*, etc. are mentioned in most of the *Purāṇas*.

Worship of the Manes

It is traditionally believed that the death is not the ultimate end of one's existence. After the completion of the funeral rites the deceased joins the rank of the Fathers. The Fathers, even though they are far removed from the world of the living, take keen interest in the welfare and happiness of their descendants on earth. They are remembered and invited with due honour to the *śrāddhas* which are performed to please them. They are also invited on the happy occasions to shower on their descendants their blessings and also share their joy. It is obvious that they are still considered a part of the family and respected as the family-elders. It is expected that the Fathers would be pleased with the offerings made to them and would grant prosperity and happiness. An element of fear can also be seen here, since it is believed that the discontented Fathers can also cause harm.

The word Fathers (*pitaraḥ*) is used in two senses viz.

(1) A man's three immediate ancestors.

(2) The early and ancient ancestors of the human race that were supposed to inhabit a separate world (*loka*) by themselves.[60]

Classification of Fathers

The Fathers are divided in many categories, some of them are (1) Agniṣvātta, (2) Barhiṣad, (3) Haviṣmat, (4) Somapā, (5) Uṣmapā, (6) Ājyapā (*MP*, 102.20-21).

Agniṣvātta and Barhiṣad are *pitṛs* of Ṛgvedic antiquity.[61]

Ancestor Worship

The love, gratitude and respect to the deceased members of this family prompt people to remember and present solemn offerings to them. *Śrāddha* or the rites to the manes is a form of ancestor-worship. On the occasion of a *śrāddha* the ancestors are invoked and conceived as actually present.

At the time of some approaching festivity like a marriage; or on the occasion of the birth of a son it is natural to express gratitude and to assume that the Fathers also share the joy of those happy occasions.

The vocable *śrāddha* is derived from *śrat* + √*dhā*. i.e., truth, reality and *dhā* to hold, therefore, it signifies the belief in truth. One who performs *śrāddha* does so with utmost faith in it, with the conviction of these rites being true.

The importance of the *śrāddha* is highly stressed. The *Manu S.*, 3.203 says the rites to the Fathers are even of more importance than those to the gods.[62]

Śrāddha-rituals are performed by a man for his deceased father, grandfather and great-grandfather. Offerings which are comprised of rice-balls, and water mixed with sesamum, are offered to the Fathers. The efficacy of the *śrāddha* depends upon, among other things, on the proper oblations. A verse quoted by Nārāyaṇa the commentator of *AGS*, 1.96 mentioned the following ten substances as fit for the (*haviṣ*) offering, viz. milk, curds, gruel (*yavāgu*), clarified butter (*sarpis*), cooked rice, (*odana*) and husked rice (*taṇḍula*), flesh, sesamum oil and water.[63] There is, however, "general prohibition against offering of flesh as a fire oblation in the *homa* (fire-rite) at a *śrāddha*".[64]

Madhu (honey) and sesamum seed are specially recommended for *śrāddha*. A simplified form of the sacrifice to the Fathers is making libations with water for them (*pitṛ-tarpaṇa*).

Classification of Śrāddhas

The *śrāddhas* have been classified variously. One classification divides them as (1) *Nitya*, (2) *Namittika* and *Kāmyu*. The *Nitya śrāddha* is performed on a certain or fixed occasion viz. everyday or on every *amāvasyā*, etc. In these *śrāddhas* no oblation ot invocation or the Vaiśvadeva-worship is necessary. It is done thrice daily — once before the daily meal, once after the noon rite and once at night again. The *śrāddha* is done in the form of feeding a qualified brahmin everyday for one year at least (*Āpastamba*, 2.18.6-19), as this would give permanent satisfaction to the Fathers.

The food prepared for the *śrāddha* may, after being offered to a brahmin as a representative of the Fathers, be given to the ascetics and acolytes. The *Āpastamba Smṛti* (2.18.6-19) cited for the daily *śrāddha* directs that it should be performed in a pure place, outside the village using new vessels for preparing and serving the food. After the rites these vessels are given to the brahmins who are fed in them.

NAIMITTIKA ŚRĀDDHAS

These *śrāddhas* are performed on occasions which are not fixed, such as on the birth of a son.

KĀMYA ŚRADDHAS

These *śrāddhas* performed with the desire to get some reward are called *Kāmya śrāddhas* e.g. a *śrāddha* perofmred on Kṛttikā or Rohiṇī by one who desires heaven or progeny.[65] In the true spirit of Dharma, a *Kāmya śrāddha* is an inferior act. As said earlier the *śrāddhas* are performed with *śraddhā* (faith) in order to gratify the Fathers and in the *Kāmya śrāddha* only follow the ritual, not the spirit of the *śrāddha*.[66]

PĀRVAṆA ŚRĀDDHAS

They are performed on the *parvans* hence this designation.[67] Some of the *Pārvaṇa śrāddhas* are:

1. *Anvāhārya*: It is always performed on the *amāvasyā*.
2. *Sādhāraṇa*: This can be performed even by one who is not invested with the sacred thread (*MP*, 17.63).[68]

EKODDIṢṬA ŚRĀDDHAS

The *śrāddha* done for a person who has recently died is performed only for one individual in contrast with other *śrāddhas* which are performed for all Fathers in general, and therefore, it is called *Ekoddiṣṭa*. In this *śrāddha* gods are not invoked (as in *nitya-śrāddhas*) and the movements are from right to left and with the sacred thread kept on the right shoulder. In this *śrāddha* the dead is not addressed or referred to as *Pitṛ* since he does not unite with the *Pitṛs* until the *sapiṇḍīkaraṇa* is done. The first *Ekoddiṣṭa* is done on the eleventh day after the death of the person for whom it is done. The brahmin is invited and offerings of food and flowers are made. He is also given clothes, umbrella and shoes, etc. (*Viṣṇusmṛti*, 20.1-11). The *ekoddiṣṭa śrāddha* is performed every month (on the date of death) for one year, after which the *sapiṇḍīkaraṇa* is performed.

SAPIṆḌĪKARAṆA

This *śrāddha* is performed for the peace of the deceased and to unite him with Fathers in their world. Apart from getting an honourable title of *Pitṛ* the *sapiṇḍīkaraṇa* guarantees the supply of the *śrāddha* benefit to the deceased, even if his direct descendants fail to perform further *śrāddhas*. He gets the offerings made to all the manes is general.

This ritual is ideally done after one year when all *ekoddiṣṭa* (sixteen in all) have been performed, but *sapiṇḍīkaraṇa*-rites on the twelfth day after death are also sanctioned by *Viṣṇusmṛti* (21.12-21).

Vṛddhi śrāddha, performed at the time of an auspicious occasion like marriage, etc. cannot take place in the family, if the *sapiṇḍīkaraṇa* rites are due.

The ritual of *sapiṇḍīkaraṇa* is symbolic. Four vessels of *arghya* are kept, one for the recently dead and one each for his three immediate ancestors, i.e., father, grandfather and great-grandfather. Similarly balls of rice are offered to the deceased and his three ancestors. With the recitation of the *mantras* the *arghya* meant for the deceased is sprinkled over the other three vessels. Similarly the rice ball offered to the deceased is divided in three parts and offered to the three ancestors. The father and the grandfather of the dead are invoked to unite with the deceasd. By the *sapiṇḍīkaraṇa* rites the third ancestor of the dead gets released.[69]

VṚDDHIŚRĀDDHA

As the ancestors are also believed to be a part of the family, it is natural that they too are remembered on the occasion of happiness and an auspicious ceremony in the family. The *śrāddhas* being a means of inviting and pleasing the Fathers, they are preformed on such occasions too and they are called *Vṛddhi śrāddhas* or *Ābhyudayikas*. They are also designated *Nāndiśrāddhas*. The *ViP*, 3.13.56 states that on the occasion of the wedding of a son or daughter, moving into a new house, birth of a son, the naming ceremony or the *cūḍākarma*, etc. the householder should worship the *nāndimukha* ancestors. Thus no important event should pass without performance of the *nāndiśrāddha* as the preliminary rites.

The *Vṛddhiśrāddha* is different from the usual rites to the

Manes. Firstly the sacred thread is worn in a normal way, i.e., as in the rites to the gods and not placed on the right shoulder, movements are from right to left and not from left to right as in other *śrāddhas*. The *piṇḍas* or balls are not made of cooked rice nor the offereings made with *svadhā*.

It may be observed that, with the doctrine of *karma-vipāka* and rebirth in mind, a doubt is expressed regarding the utility of the *śrāddhas*. It is found difficult to believe that the offering made to the ancestors could reach them. A similar doubt is raised in the *MP*, 19.2 that how could the food eaten by the brahmin at a *śrāddha* feast could be enjoyed by the Fathers who might have been reborn. The following verses (*MP*, 3-9) provide the answer. It is said here that the father, grandfather and great-grandfather are identified with Vasus, Rudras and Ādityas respectively. It also says that the name and the *gotra* of the Fathers mentioned at the time of *śrāddha*, the *mantras* uttered and the faith in these rites carry to the Fathers the offerings made to them. If the ancestor has become a god (by his good deeds) the food offered reaches him in the form of nectar, if he has become a *daitya* it reaches him in the form of various enjoyments, if he has become a beast, the offering become grass for it and if he has become snake, the offerings wait on him as wind (it is believed that the serpents subsist on wind). Thus even in the case of rebirth the offerings made to the Fathers gratify them.

Notes

1. *ayaṁ hi dharmasaṁyukto rūpavān guṇasāgaraḥ/*
   nārho mat puruṣair netum ato'smi svayamāgataḥ/
   tataḥ Satyavataḥ kāyāt pāśabaddham vaśaṁ gatam aṅguṣṭha mātra puruṣam niścakarṣa Yamo balāt — *Mbh*, 3.281.15-16.
2. *guru śuśruṣād bhadre tathā Satyavato mahat/*
   puṇyam samarjitaṁ yena nayāmi enaṁ aham svayaṁ/ — *MP*, 210.16.
3. See *infra* "Onward journey of the Sinners".
4. *GP*, II.5.17.
5. *Yamo Yama iti śrutvā vṛthā hi udvijate naraḥ/*
   ātmā ca yamito yena na tasyeva Yamaḥ smṛtaḥ/ — *Mbh*, 9.50.20.
6. *ānṛśaṁsyam kṣamā satyamahiṁśā yama mārjavan/*

dhyānam prasādo mādhuryaṁ saṁtoṣaśca yamāḥ daśa//—*AgniP* referred to in *Śabdakalpadruma*, Pt. IV, p. 18

7. *VarāhaP*, 207.19-28.
8. *PP, Sṛṣṭi Khaṇḍa*, 18.457-460 cf *Bhūmi Khaṇḍa*, 13.24-25; 31-32.
9. *PP Bhūmi Khaṇḍa*, 73 ff.

   PP also states that the performance of various meritorious deeds enables one to secure a place in various celestial regions or *lokas*. The *PP* has named several *lokas* as *Śivaloka, Indraloka, Viṣṇuloka, Sarasvatīloka, Brahmaloka* and *Gaurīloka* and many others. At places the *PP* has graded them in order of supremacy as *Indraloka, Brahmaloka, Śivaloka* and above all the *Viṣṇuloka* (*PP Bhūmi Khaṇḍa*, 83.26.47; 71.22.23; 79.28).
10. *PP. Sṛṣṭi Khaṇḍa*, 15.240-242 cf. *Bhūmi Khaṇḍa*, 14.38-43; 71.23-24.
11. *PP Sṛṣṭi Khaṇḍa*, 15.245.
12. *PP Uttara Khaṇḍa*, 226.11; 18.33; 38.39.
13. *prāptam sukṛtinaṁ dṛṣṭvā sthānāc calati sūryajaḥ/*
    eṣa me maṇḍalaṁ bhitvā brahmalokaṁ hi gacchati//—*GP*, II.9.9.
14. *santuṣṭāḥ pitaraḥ tasya na viśanti yamālayaṁ/*—*NrP*, 13.39.
15. *PP Bhūmi Khaṇḍa*, 71.22.23; 79.28; 83.26.46; For *Viṣṇuloka PP*, 83.47-67.
16. *BhāgP*, 3.30.19-20, *AgniP.*, 20.3.4-5, also *MāP*, 10.62.
17. *anyat śarīramādhatte yātanīyaṁ sva karmabhiḥ/*
    bhukte'tha pāpakṛt duḥkhaṁ sukhaṁ dharmāya saṁgataḥ//
    Yamājñaptaih kinkarais tu pātyate narakeṣu ca/—*AgniP*, 202.4-5. Also *BhāgP*, 3.30.19.
18. *śarīraṁ yātanārthīyaṁ*—*ManuS*, 12.16.
19. The text is quoted in fn 1.
20. *MatsyaP*, 210.16.
21. *BhāgP*, 3.30.19-20.
22. According to *GP* this distance is eighty-six thousand *yojanas*, *GP*, 2.5.3.
23. He, the *Puruṣa* of the measure of a thumb, is always residing in the heart of the man, *vide* E. Roer, *The Twelve Upaniṣads*, Vol. 1, p. 289, Transl. of *ŚvetaUp*, 3.13.
24. For the description of the tortures when the assistants of Yama come to take the sinners *vide PP Bhūmi Khaṇḍa*, 52.15.28.
25. *PP Bhūmi Khaṇḍa*, 15.18.24; 71 similar ideas in *Bhūmi Khaṇḍa*, 15.18.29.
26. *GP*, 2.5.3.
27. *GP*, 2.23.24.
28. *GP*, 2.23.58.
29. Yama took away the *aṅguṣṭha-mātra-puruṣaḥ* from Satyavat at the time of the latter's death.
30. *KaṭhaUp*, 4.12; 4.13; 6.17.

31. *ŚvetUp*, 3.13.
32. *GP*, 2.5.66.
33. *kramena gacchate sa pretaḥ puraṁ vaivasavataṁ subhaṁ/* — *GP*, 2.5.79.
34. See under 'Heaven & Hell', chapter 5.
35. According to Śaṅkarācārya the *Vedānta-Sūtra*, 3.1.13 makes it clear that after enjoying the fruit of one's actions in the abode of Yama (i.e., *saṁyamana*) evil-doers ascend to this mortal world. Śaṅkarācārya in his *Bhāṣya* refers to *KaṭhaUp* 11.6 & *ṚV*, 10.14.1 in support.
36. *MāP*, 10.22.
37. Cf. *BG*, 9.21b — *kṣiṇe puṇye martyalokom viśanti.*
38. *Mbh*, 3.261.28-29; 33.
39. "*Śeṣaiḥ puṇyaiḥ hṛtamiva divaḥ kāntimat khaṇḍamekam*"/ — *Meghadūtam* 1.31.
40. *PP Pātāla Khaṇḍa*, 48.6-9.
41. H.H. Wilson, Transl. *ViP*, p. 172-73.
42. *vartamānā'nyayoḥ kālo guṇābhijñāpako yathā/ evamjanmānyayoḥ etad dharmādharma-nidarśanam//*—*BhāgP*., 6.1.47.
43. Kālidāsa's *Raghuvaṁśaṁ*, 14.62.
44. *Vide* J. Sinha, *A History of Indian Philosophy*, Vol. 1, p. 135.
45. See 'Heaven & Hell' in chapter 5.
46. *MāP*, Chapter 14.
47. *BhāgP*, 1.12-32ab; 34 *vide* 1.8.48-51.
48. *vedapraṇihito dharmaḥ adharmaḥ tad viparyayaḥ/* — *Bhāg P*, 6.1.40ab.
49. *narakam karmaṇān lopāt phalamāhur maharṣayaḥ/* —*BrP*, 233.26.
50. *PP Kriyā Khaṇḍa*, 22.16.
51. *AgniP*, 371.12.
52. *MārP*, chapter 12.14.
    VāyuP, 101.
    BrahmāṇḍaP, 4.2 *ViP*, II, 6; VI.5.
    MP, 39, *BhāgP*, III.30; *VāmanaP*, 11.51 ff.
    VarāhaP, 196, 206; *GP*, *Uttara Khaṇḍa*
    BrP, 214-218.
53. *VāP*, 11.33.39.
54. There are two types of concepts about the geography of the earth are (1) *sapta-dvīpā vasundharā*, (2) *catur-dvīpā vasundharā.*
55. Some of these names are same as these given in the *ManuS*, 5.58-90.
56. *ViP*, VI. 5.
57. i.e., who teach *Veda* for hire — H.H. Wilson, Transl. *ViP*, p. 171.
58. *Vide* H.H. Wilson, Transl. *ViP*, 171.

59. *Vide* S.S. Dange, *Mytho-Social Study of the Bhāgvata Purāṇa*, p. 133.
60. P.V. Kane, *HDS*, Vol. IV, pp. 340 ff.
61. *ṚV*, 10.15.4.11, also *vide* P.V. Kane, *HDS*, Vol. IV, pp. 343 ff.
62. *devakāryād dvijātīnām pitṛkāryam viśiṣyate* — *ManuS*, 3.203.
63. K.V.R Aiyangar, *Introduction to Kṛtyakalpataru of Bhaṭṭa Lakṣmīdhara, Śrāddha-kāṇḍa*, G.O.S., No. CX, Baroda, p. 110.
64. P.V. Kane, *HDS*, II, p. 681.
65. P.V. Kane, *op.cit.*, Vol. IV, p. 369.
66. *Vide* K.V.R. Aiyangar, *op. cit.*, p. 13.
67. S.G. Kantawala, *The Cult of manes as depicted in the Matsya-Purāṇa*, *J.O.I.* (Baroda), Vol. VI, p. 22.
68. *Vide* S.G. Kantawala, *op.cit.*, p. 29 fn 80.
69. *Vide* K.V.R. Aiyangar, *op.cit*, pp. 40-41.

9

Yama : The Preacher and Law-Giver

Yama : The Preacher

A FACET of Yama's personality as a preacher which is reflected in the *KaṭhaUp*, is also seen in the *Mbh* and the *Purāṇas*. There are several instances in the *Mbh* as well as in the *Purāṇas*, where Yama is seen preaching some kind of higher knowledge and philosophy to others. Some of these passages where Yama is depicted as a preacher project him as a great moral teacher. In others he is sometimes seen describing the merits of charity, while in some others he is telling about the supremacy of Viṣṇu (*BhāgP*, 6.3.12-24) or Śiva (*Mbh*, 13.71.178-179). In the *Mbh* also he plays the part of a great moral teacher. The *Mbh*, 12.127.4-11 contains a dialogue between Yama and the sage Gautama. On being asked by Gautama Yama tells him the way to get released from the debt which one owes to one's parents. He also tells Gautama the way to attain the divine regions which are hard to be obtained. This story is narrated to Yudhiṣṭhira by Bhīṣma who, as desired by Yudhiṣṭhira, was instructing him about *Dharma*. According to this story the sage Gautama performed penance for sixty thousand years in his *āśrama* on the Pāriyātra mountain. Once a *lokapāla* happened to come to

Gautama's *āśrama* and see the sage performing severe austerities. Brahmarṣi Gautama, by the power of his penance, discerned that he was none other than the god Yama. With folded hands he approached 'Yamadeva' who welcomed the sage and said "I am Dharmarāja. What good shall I do for you?" On being asked like this Gautama took it as an opportunity and asked Yama to tell him the way for getting freed from the debt towards his parents. He also wanted to know how one can attain heaven, i.e., the regions of the pious and Yama replied to these queries.

In the *KaṭhaUp*, Yama reveals to the earnest seeker, i.e., Naciketas, the secret knowledge relating to the nature of the Supreme Self and death.[1] A version of this story is also found in the *Mbh*, 13.71-74. In the *Mbh* story, the young boy Nāciketa is told by his father to bring the gift-objects from the river-bank. Those gift-objects were, in the meantime, swept away in the river. Nāciketa went to the river and not finding any gift-objects there, reported to his father that he did not see any items at the river-bank. The father, was extremely angry on hearing that the boy could not 'see' the items which he told him to fetch. He cursed Nāciketa, "See Yama (*Yamaṁ paśya*)." Nāciketa immediately fell down as dead. The father realised his mistake and his anger gave way to deep remorse and anguish.

All night the father wept over his son, who was at last, revived by his tears. Greatly pleased on seeing his son alive Uddālaki asked the boy about his night-long trance. Nāciketa related that he had actually gone to Yama's region. Yama greated him in his court (Vaivasvatī *sabhā*). There Nāciketa, at his own wish, was shown by Yama the regions of the pious, i.e., those who have given proper gifts to the brahmins.

In both the versions (the *KaṭhaUp*, version and the *Mbh* version) Yama is depicted as a preacher. In the *KaṭhaUp* he is seen eleborating the nature of the Supreme Self and eschatological doctrines whereas in the *Mbh*, he is louding the merits of giving gifts to the brahmins, but the character of Yama as Dharma is present in both legends. Though "the mysteries are different but in both the instances Yama is the all knowing preceptor revealing mystic truths to the eager enquirer'.[2] Yama also tells Nāciketa about the intricate topic of *āyu kṣaya, Mbh,* 13.104.72-76.

Yama also taught the merits of charity to the brahmin named Śarmin (*Mbh,* 13.69). *Yama-dūtas* had brought him to *Yamaloka* by mistake. On seeing Śarmin coming near him, Yama rose up from his throne and greeted him. At Śarmin's request Yama also told him about the merits of charity.

In the *MP*, 49.68 it is mentioned that Yama, pleased with Janamejaya, imparted to him the highest knowledge about redemption.[3] In the *BrVaiP*, 2.23ff contain the story of Satyavān and Sāvitrī. Here too Yama granted self-chosen boons to Sāvitrī and additionally he gave a discourse on *karma, karma-vipāka,* heaven, hell and the total emancipation. (*BrVaiP*, 2.20; 2.27-34).

In the Ajāmila-episode in th *BhāgP*, 6.1.20ff Yama is seen praising Lord Viṣṇu with utmost humility. He relates of his *dūtas* the glory of Lord Viṣṇu and commanded them not to go near a worshipper of Viṣṇu. According to the *Mbh*, 13.71.178-179 the *Śiva-sahasranāma* was taught to Yama by Lord Nārāyaṇa and he instructed Nāciketa in chanting this eulogy of Śiva. Thus, Yama is seen accepting the supremacy of Viṣṇu and Śiva.

The *BhāgP*, 7.2.36-56 contains a story about Yama preaching the relatives of a dead king about the immortality of soul and the futility of crying for the dead.

The story goes like this : Lord Hari, assuming the form of a boar, killed Hiraṇyākṣa, the brother of Hiraṇyakaśipu. Hiraṇyakaśipu, filled with grief and anger told the *dānavas* to destroy everything which was related with the worship of Viṣṇu. Then he tried to console his mother and other relatives grieving over Hiraṇyākṣa's death saying that the soul is immortal. Hiraṇyakaśipu tells them about an ancient legend which contains a conversation between Yama and the relatives of a dead king. In the Uśinara city a king named Suyajña was killed in a battle. His queens were deeply grieved. They wailed and grasped their dead husband, and were not prepared to allow the funeral-rites to begin.

As the sun set in the sky, Yama approached them in the form of a boy and told them the impropriety of weeping for a man who has (at his death) returned to the unmanifest state from which he has come (originally).[4] He also said that the Lord at his own will creates, protects and destroys the universe. Bodies of all species come into existence and perish at a particular time according to the *karma*. But the soul, though it inhabits the *Prakṛti* (the corporeal body), is not affected by the attributes of *prakṛti* (body) and he is different from it. This corporeal body of the *puruṣa* is different from the soul, just as the house is different from the dweller. Like bubbles made of water, pots made of earth, this body which is formed out of the elements of time also undergoes modification and perishes. Just as fire which remains latent in a piece of wood, is different from it, or the vital breath existing in the body remains different from it, or the sky pervading all things does not stick to anything, similarly the soul is distinct from body. It is foolish to cry over the dead. He can neither see you, hear you nor give a reply. The principle which is the master and controller of senses is the *ātman*, and it is distinct from the body and the life-breath (*mukhya-prāṇa*). The *ātman* takes up a body consisting of the five elements (*bhūtas*), sense and mind, and regards himself as one with them. But with the power of his wisdom and knowledge he casts them off at will.

He also gives an example of a Kuliṅga bird who was grieving for his mate caught in a net. As it kept sorrowing over this situation, it was totally unaware of the fowler who was aiming at it and was pierced by the fowler's arrow. Yama tells the queens that like Kuliṅga they do not see their own destruction. Even if they wailed for a hundred years, they could not get their husband back (so they should think about their own lives that lie ahead).

In this way Yama in the form of child admonished all the relatives of Suyajña and made them realise that everything was transient and unreal.

Yama-gītā

There are also some dialogues between Yama and (mostly)

his messengers in which Yama is seen as a preacher. These dialogues (i.e., *ViP*, 3.7, *AgniP*, chapter 382 etc.) are called *Yamagītās*.

The term *gītā* as a literary form may be traced to *gāthā* or *gītā* mentioned in earlier literature. They are connected with some important event and a discourse of an authority on the relevant topic. It may conveniently be inferred that in olden days, it may have been a popular custom to commemorate events of importance illustrating royal valour (or wisdom) by means of popular songs knowns as *gāthā* or *gītā*.[5]

The *AgniP* devotes the chapter 382 to *Yamagītā*, which was, as its name denotes, told by Yama, the god of death, to Nāciketa.[6] The story of Naciketas and his dialogue with Yama can be traced back to the *KaṭhaUp*. When Naciketas reached Yama's abode, he had to wait for three nights before he could see Yama since Yama was away. When Yama returned, he thought that it was a great offence that a brahmin was kept waiting. As a compensation he asked Naciketas to choose three boons. After being granted two self-chosen boons Naciketas, as the third boon, wanted to know whether man existed after death or death was the end of a man's existence. On finding in Naciketas a true seeker of knowledge, Yama revealed to him the secret of man's existence after death and also about the final emanicipation, which can be achieved by realising the identity of the individual soul with the Supreme Self (*Brahman*).

The *Yamagītā* (*AgniP*, 382) begins with referring to the doctrine of the various teachers about the spiritual upliftment. Yama said that due to his utter foolishness man, without realising that his own existence is momentary, wishes for worldly pleasures and possessions.[7] The doctrines of other teachers are also mentioned here. Kapila stressed that self-realisation was much greater and more beneficial than the gratification of one's senses. The holy sage Pañcaśikha (382.4) declares that the feeling of equality towards all and keeping oneself free from desires was highly beneficial to man.[8] According to Gaṅgāviṣṇu (382.5) true knowledge is the correct perspective of the miseries of birth, youth and old age, and it is the highest good in life. In the opinion on Janaka (382.6) guarding himself the threefold evil (i.e., *Ādhyātmika, Ādhidaivika* and *Ādhibhautika*) is the best thing for a man. According to Jaigīṣavya (382.8) performing one's duty, as laid down by the *Vedas* is highly beneficial for man. According to Sanaka (382.10) the knowledge gained after abandoning all desires leads one to *Brahman*.

The Viṣṇu cult supplies the basis for the philosophy of the *Agni Purāṇa*. In the 382.12 Viṣṇu is called *Brahman* (*brahmaṇā viṣṇu saṁjñena*).[9] Reaching Viṣṇu is the most desired goal of the man (*nāsti viṣṇu samam dhyeyaḥ* — 382.14).

Whosoever remembers Viṣṇu at the time of his death gains oneness with the Lord (382.16). A man can reach to Viṣṇu by performing holy deeds, taking dips in water at holy places, by meditation, fasts, worships and listening to holy discourses.

The physical body is compared to a chariot of which the intellect is the charioteer, the mind is the reins, the senses are the horses, Self or *ātman* is the occupant. This imagery is traceable to the *KaṭhaUp*.

The man, who does not realise this knowledge, never attains the region of Viṣṇu amd falls in the cycle of births and deaths. The man, who gain this knowledge, reaches Viṣṇu and therefore, is not born again (23, 24). He, who know that his intellect is the charioteer which controls the reins (mind), crosses the path and reaches the highest abode of Viṣṇu. The objects of senses are higher than the senses, the mind is higher than the objects, the intellect is higher than the mind, and the *mahat* is higher than the intellect (26, 27), the unmanifested self is greater than *mahat*, and *puruṣa* is greater than the unmanifested self. Nothing is higher than the *puruṣa* (the Supreme Self). The hidden Supreme Self is not realised by all. Only those with sharp intellect and sharp vision can attain the knowledge of the Supreme Self (28, 29).

By knowledge, worship and yogic poses, by meditation, *samādhi* and realisation of the fact that 'I am *Brahman*' (*ahaṁ brahmāsmi*), a *jīvātman* becomes liberated and gets merged in *Brahman*. This is beautifully expressed with the allegory of an empty earthen pot. When the pot is broken, the sky inside the pot becomes one with the sky outside it; in the same manner when the body of an enlightened man falls (at his death), his soul becomes one with the Supreme Self. The highest goal of the *jīva* or individual soul is to realise that he is *Brahman*, and this is possible only through knowledge.

The *Yamagītā* in the *ViṣṇuP*, 3.7 consists of a dialogue between Maitreya and Parāśara. Maitreya asks Parāśara that by performing what pure actions people are freed from subjection to Yama. At this Parāśara asks him to listen what Bhīṣma had said to Nakula this connection. Bhīṣma relates to Nakula a dialogue between Yama and one of his assistants:

> Beholding his *dūta*, with a noose in his hand, approach, Yama said in his ears : Never bring anyone here who has obtained the shelter of the slayer of Madhu, i.e., Lord Kṛṣṇa, for I am the lord of all spirits but not of the spirits of those who are devoted to Viṣṇu. I was appointed by Brahmā, honoured by immortals to judge the good and evil conduct to mankind. Hari is my Lord, and I am not independent, for he can mete out punishment to me. Though gold (in reality) is one substance, it appears in many forms like bracelets, ear-rings, etc., so Hari, though he is one, appears many gods, animals and men.

Yama asks his *dūtas* to avoid a man who is freed from his sins due to his devotion of Viṣṇu, self-control and moral discipline. Yama's speech is followed by a long eulogy of Viṣṇu.

In the above-mentioned passage Yama is also seen instructing the non-dual entity of the Supreme Self and also its presence in all beings, i.e., gods, men and animals. The non-duality of *Brahman* is also beautifully expressed with the help of an allegory. Yama says that although gold is one substance, but it appears diversified as bracelets, ear-rings and tiaras, in the same way Hari, although he is one appears many as gods, men and animals.

There is a striking similarity of this expression with that found in the *ChāUp*, 6.1.5. Here Āruṇi in the process of instructing his son Śvetaketu about the oneness of the soul, explains the point by similar allegories. The *ChāUp*, 6.1.5 states "as on knowledge of a single lump of gold one knows that all articles of gold indicated by different words are mere variations of form of the same substance; in the same way the Supreme Being is manifested in various ways. Thus in this passage Yama is described as an instructor of non-dualism. Here he appears very near to his Vedic personality of a preacher of philosophy who imparted the secret knowledge to Naciketas."[10]

There are several other instances where Yama is seen explaining to his *dūta* about who could not be taken to his region (*ViP*, 2.66; 3.7.5, 13.20). It is also said that Yama, *Yama-dūtas*, *Yama-pāśa* (Yama's noose) *Yama-daṇḍa* (Yama's club) and *Yama-yātanā* (the torments inflicted by Yama) can bring no harm to a man whose heart is totally devoted to Lord Kṛṣṇa. Different versions of story of Naciketā are found in the *TB*, 3.11.81; *KaṭhaUp*, (*vide* chapter V) *Mbh*, 13.71 and *VarāhaP*, chapter 193-213.

According to the *TB*, 3.11.8 version Vājaśravas performed a sacrifice in which everything the sacrificer possesses are to be gifted away. Young Naciketas thought that since he too was his father's 'property' he should also be given away as a gift. And he asked his father, 'whom would you give me to?' When he asked this question again and again the father was angry. He retorted, 'I give you to Yama'. As Naciketas stood surprised, a divine voice spoke to him and told him to go to Yama when he is away, and stay there without eating for three days. When asked by Yama as to what did he eat during that time, he should tell him that by fasting there for three days he had eaten all his people, his animals and his *sukṛt*. Naciketas did as he was told to when he reached Yama. Yama told him to select three boons.[11]

In *VarāhaP* (chapters 193-212) the story is similar in contents to the *KaṭhaUp*, version.[12] Nāciketa goes to Yama's place. Yama welcomes him and then sends him back to the earth. Uddālaka who was happy beyond words, collected all the hermits and Yama replied their questions regarding his visit to the *Yamaloka*.

Discussion

The different versions are quite similar in their contents and this shows that the basic story is the same, i.e., Father performing the sacrifice — getting angry and cursing his son to go to 'death'. But a comparative study of these versions reveals that this story is used, at different places to serve a different purpose. In the *KaṭhaUp* Naciketas displays a tremendous maturity of thought. His concern for his father who was incurring sins by giving useless cows as gifts, prompts him to ask his father to give him to someone, since by doing so his father would earn some merit. The father could not understand what the son wanted him to realise (that these cows would not bring him any merit and that a giver of such cows would be sent to dark hells). Naciketas' firmness of resolve is revealed at the time of his encounter with Yama. At last Yama finds in him a true seeker of knowledge which is a cherished desire of every preacher. Yama could not help saying — "May we have more enquirers like you, Naciketas!"

In the *Mbh* and the *Puraṇas*, Nāciketa is depicted as holding those higher qualities. He is nonetheless an obedient son who was cursed by his father to 'see Yama'. The *Mbh* records the cause of the father's anger that the boy could not find *smidhā*, *darbha*, flowers, etc. at the river bank. *VarāhaP* does not mention the cause of his anger.

It is significant to note that all these versions of the Nāciketa-story are connected with the cows. It was at the sight of useless cows being given as gifts which make Naciketas ponder over the futility of such gifts. In the *Mbh* the greatness of *godāna* (gift of cows) is related to Naciketā by Yama himself. He tells Naciketā that the pleasure of heaven, like river with flowing milk, *ghī*, etc. are enjoyed by those who have offered cows as gifts (*Mbh*, 13.71.29). The remaining chapter is about Yama telling Nāciketa about the greatness of *godāna* (gift of cows).

Thus, except in the *AgniP* version of the Nāciketa story Yama is no more a preacher of metaphysical philosophy. In the *Mbh* he is only telling about the pleasures one would go for gifting away good cows at good time to a worthy receiver. In the *VarāhaP* (193.212) also he tells Nāciketa about different regions for the pious and the sinners.

This story of Naciketā which basically has a ritual purpose in the Brāhmaṇas, evolved into a medium for instructing the knowledge of the Supreme Self and the individual Self (*KaṭhaUp*). In the *Mbh* it stresses the greatness of *godāna*. In the *Purāṇas* the main purpose of the story is to relate the fruit of various actions (*karmaphala*). No sign of Naciketā's previous personality is seen either in the *Mbh* or the *Varāha Purāṇa*.

Yama : The Law-giver

In the Upaniṣadic, Epic and Purāṇic literature Yama appears as a preacher of moral and metaphysical philosophy. In the *Dharma-śāstra* literature also he is the author of *Yama-smṛti*.[15] *Yājñavalkya-smṛti* (1.4-5) mentions Yama as one of the twenty law-givers.

The *Smṛtis* or the *Dharma-śāstras* are the law-books of the ancient India. They deal with a variety of topics relating to the social order and code of conduct based on the *varṇāśrama* system, duties and rights of the ruler and the ruled. They throw light on the customs, religious and social rules and code of conduct. They also serve as guidelines for various ritual practises. Thus all the laws — civil and religious which govern and regulate the life and conduct are styled as *Smṛti*. They are the "earliest Indian work on law, treating fully its religious but only partially and briefly its secular aspect".[14]

There are twenty main *Smṛtis* and their authors are Manu, Atri, Viṣṇu, Hārita, Yājnavalkya, Uśanas, Āṅgiras, Yama, Āpastamba, Saṁvarta, Kātyāyana, Bṛhaspati, Parāśara, Vyāsa, Śaṅkha, Likhita, Dakṣa, Gautama, Śātātapa and Vasiṣṭha.[15]

Yama-smṛti

In the Jivānanda collection (Part I, pp. 560-68) there is a *Smṛti* of Yama in seventy-eight verses dealing with the topics of *prāyaścitta* and purification (*śuddhi*). Here Yama is cited in third person (verse 65). Some of its verses are identical with those of another *Dharmaśāstra-kāra* named Manu (e.g. verses 26, 28 are the same as the *MS*, 11.178; 3.19).

In the Ānandāśrama collection there is a *Yama-smṛti* containing ninety-nine verses. They also deal with *Prāyaścitta*, *śrāddha* and purification. Though the topics mentioned in this *Smṛti* are same as those in the Calcutta text, but the verses are not identical. A few verses are found in both the collections, e.g., the verses about the seven lowest castes (*antyaja*).[16] This *Smṛti* contains the verse saying that after marriage a woman enters into the *gotra* of her husband (verse 78).

The Ānandāśrama collection also has a *Smṛti* of *Bṛhad-Yama* (pp. 99-107). It contains 182 verses which are divided in five chapters.

It deals with the *prāyaścitta* for the various offences, the purification rites which are considered necessary in certain situations/events and the *śrāddha*, etc. In this *Smṛti* Yama is often quoted by his name and at several places it is identical with the Jivānanda text, e.g. the III. 1-3 of the *Bṛhad-Yama* are identical with the verses 15-17 of *Yama-smṛti* in the Jivānanda collection.

The numerous MSS of the *Yama-smṛti* contain either one or the other of the above three texts or different texts bearing on the same topic.[17] Over three hundred stanzas of Yama on all topics of *Dharma-śāstra* are quoted by Viśvarūpa (a commentator of the *YājS*), Vijñāneśvara (the author of the *Mitākṣarā* commentary on the *YajS*) and Aparārka.[18] Some other works also quote Yama, e.g., the *Kṛtyakalpataru* of Lakṣmīdhara Bhaṭṭa, etc. This establishes that they had an extensive work of Yama before them. Aparārka quotes five verses of Yama referring to the twenty-five *tattvas*, mentioned in the *Sāṁkhya* philosophy, and regarding Puruṣottama as the 26th *tattva*.

In the *mokṣa-khaṇḍa* of the *Kṛtyakalpataru* (pp. 101, 102) Lakṣmīdhara quotes five verses of Yama.

As noted earlier the main subject of the *Yama-smṛti* is expiation. It tells about the penance for drinking spirituous liquor, for one who returns from the order of hermits, penance, for taking the forbidden food, for a brahmin who in spite of being a mendicant wishes to become a householder again. Apart from these, it also tells about the right age for the marriage, a girl, conditions for performing the religious rites. It tells about the persons who are to be shunned at a *śrāddha*. What gratifies the Fathers is also said here. According to the verse 37, one who purchases articles at fair price and sells them at a higher price is called Vardhūśika. He is censured by the *Brahmavādins* (i.e., knowers of the *Vedas*).

Aparārka (p. 596) quotes Yama's verse which requires a king to look into the disputes very carefully and impartially[19] Yama lays down that a brahmin was never to be awarded corporeal punishment, but that a brahmin, if found guilty of a crime, should be imprisoned and made to work. Vasiṣṭha *Dharma-sūtra*, 18.13-15 and 19.48 cite the stanzas of Yama. Yama prescribes punishment for those who wrongfully take the water of a lake, or disturb the course of water (Aparārka, p. 822). Yama observes that the *Vedas* or the *Śāstras* do not permit the order of *sanyāsa* for women, and that their real *dharma* is to bear children of someone of their own caste (*Smṛti-candrikā*, p. 254).[20]

From this brief account of the contents of the *Yama-smṛti* it may be said that Yama's character as a moral and ethical preacher/philosopher is not obliterated entirely.

Notes

1. *Vide* chapter 5.
2. S. Bhattacharji, *Indian Theogony*, p. 59.
3. *yamaḥ tuṣṭaḥ tatas tasmai, muktijñānam dadau param/* —*MP*, 49.68.
4. Cf. *avyāktadini bhūtāni vyakta madhyāni bhārata!/ avyaktanidhanāni eva tatra kā paride·;anā//* —*BG*, 2.28.

5. *Vide* S.D. Gyani, *Agni Purāṇa, A Study*, p. 225.
6. In the *KaṭhaUp*, the name is Naciketas whereas in the *Mbh* the name is Nāciketa.
7. *AgniP*, 382.3.
8. Incidently it may be noted that Kapila and Pañcaśikha are well-known *Sāṁkhya*-teachers.
9. Also, *sa Viṣṇu paramo brahma yato nā' vartate punaḥ//* — *Agni P*, 382.20.
10. *Vide* chapter 5.
11. Cf. *KathaUp* version, *vide* chapter 5 *Mbh* version, ***see*** *supra*.
12. *Vide* S.G. Kantawala, *Some Remarks on the Naciketas legend, Ludwik Sternbach Felicitation Volume*, pp. 293 ff.
13. The term *smṛti* initially denoted the vast Vedic literature which included the six *Vedāṅgas*, *Dharma-sūtras*, Epics, *Purāṇas*, etc., but gradually came to be used in a narrower sense, i.e., the *Dharmaśāstra*. (*śrutis tu vedo vijñeyo, dharma-śāstram tu vai smṛtiḥ/* — *MS*, 2.10). In the *ṚV* the word *dharma* is used as an adjective or noun and it means upholder or supporter. In most of the Ṛgvedic passages it means religious ordinances or rites and in rare cases 'fixed principle and rules of conduct' (*vide* P.V. Kane, *HDS*, Vol. 1, pt. 1. pp. 1-4).

    Cf *Śruti smṛtiḥ sadācāraḥ*
    svasya ca priyam ātmanaḥ
    samyak samkalpajaḥ kāmo
    dharma mūlam idaṁ smṛtam — *YājS*, 1.7
14. A.A. Macdonell, *A History of Sanskrit Literature*, p. 27.
15. *YājS*, 1.4-5.
16. *rajakuś carmakāraśca naṭo buruḍa eva ca/*
    kaivartameda bhillāśca saptaite antyajāḥ smṛtāḥ//
    — Jivānanda collection verse 54, Ānandāśrama collection verse 33.
17. P.V. Kane, *HDS*, Vol. I, Pt. I. p. 232.
18. *Vide* P.V. Kane, *op.cit.*, p. 233.
19. *rājā mantrisahāyastu dvayor vivadamānayoḥ/*
    samyak karyāṇi avekṣeta rāgadveṣa-vivarjitaḥ// — Aparārka, p. 596.
20. *śtriyāḥ śrutau vā śāstre vā pravrajyā na vidhīyate/*
    prajāḥ hi tasyāḥ svo dharmaḥ savarṇād iti dhāraṇā// — *Smṛti-candrikā*, p. 254.

10

Epilogue

THE character of Yama is unique in the whole Vedic mythology. In spite of his being a major god very few hymns are addressed to him and there is a conspicuous absence of legends connected with him which could throw light on the real character of this god.

On the basis of the number of hymns addressed to them and the occurrence of their names in the *ṚV* the Vedic gods are classified in five categories.[1] In such statistical classification Yama cannot be regarded a major god in the *ṚV*. Only three hymns (*ṚV*, X.10,14,135) are addressed to him and his name occurs about fifty times in the *ṚV*, mostly in the *Maṇḍala* X, a few times in the *Maṇḍala* I and in a few scattered places in other *Maṇḍalas* (e.g. 7.33.9; 7.76.4, 9.113.8). Yama is the ruler of the region of the dead (*yamarājñaḥ*[2]) (*ṚV*, 10.16.9). He is, therefore, also mentioned in the hymns connected with the dead and the funeral rites (*ṚV*, 10.15, 18, *AV* 18th *Kāṇḍa*). Yama is mentioned as a path-finder. He himself passed through death and discovered a path for all the dead to follow for reaching a special abode meant for them.

There is a considerable amount of inconsistency, discrepancy and vagueness in the picture of Yama as derived from the *ṚV* references. The most striking fact is that he is not explicitly called a god, but only a king (*ṚV*, 9.113.8, 10.14.1, 4, 7, 11). Although he is not expressly called a god, there are a number of clear references which leave little room for any doubt regarding Yama's divine character. He is the son of Vivasvat and is often referred to by the patronymic 'Vaivasvata', i.e., 'son of Vivasvat'. Apart from his divine birth, the divinity of Yama is also ascertained by his enumeration among other gods (*ṚV*, 1.164.46, 7.46.4, 10.135.1). He is also mentioned with individual gods like Varuṇa (*ṚV*, 10.14.7) and Bṛhaspati (*ṚV*, 10.13.4, 14.3). As a conductor of the dead Agni is also closely related with Yama. Agni is also called a dear friend of Yama (*ṚV*, 10.21.5).[3] The *ṚV*, 10.51.1 and 3 tell that a god (who, it can be implied, is Yama) found out the hidden Agni. When Agni's three elder brothers, were killed while performing their task as the oblation-bearers of the gods, Agni was terrified. He concealed himself in waters and eventually all oblations to the gods were stopped. It was Yama who spotted Agni in his hiding place. Agni was given assurances by the gods who requested him to resume the task of their oblation-bearer, Yama is also mentioned with other deities like Agni, Mātariśvan as the different manifestation of the Supreme-Being (*ṚV*, 1.164.46). According to this *ṛc* the Supreme-Being (*Brahman*) is only one, but scholars describe 'It' differently like Agni, Yama, Mātariśvan, etc. Here Yama is counted among the major Vedic gods. Glimpses of his sovereignty can also be seen in the *Vedas*. Yama's relation with Varuṇa, the supreme sovereign in the Vedic pantheon, reveals the former's equally high position. He too like Varuṇa punishes the evil-doers. Defaulters pray to be spared from the *paḍbīśa* of Yama.

Though Yama is not called a god in the *Vedas*, it is equally important to note that he is not called a man either. Further more what contributes to the complexity of his character is that he is mentioned as 'first to die',[4] and it is suggested that he himself passed through death and discovered a path to a settlement where all the dead had a right to live in.

Thus this is the unique case of a divine being who is not called a god in spite of his divine birth; an immoral being who had died, and in spite of his death he is never referred to as a 'mortal'.

Though Yama is mentioned among gods he is constantly

called a *rājan* which highlights his overlordship of the *pitṛloka*. This has led to an assumption that he was not a god, but a mortal king who, due to his virtues, was exalted to the position of a god.[5] But Yama cannot be regarded a human being since his personality and functions are far from human. There are clear references which suggest Yama's superhuman character. His act of self-immolation for the sake of creation is too cosmic or divine for a human being. These paradoxical features of Yama's personality, i.e., 'cosmic' or 'divine' on one hand and 'human' on the other are tactfully represented in the *ṚV*, 10.13.4.[6] The *ṚV*, 10.13.4 states that Yama chose to immolate himself in the primeval sacrfice which was arranged for starting a (human) progeny.[7]

From the study of the obscure, vague and broken account, provided by the Ṛgvedic references different features of Yama's character can be put together as follows:

> Yama, the son of Vivasvat, was initially a god and so he too was immortal like other gods. For the cause of progeny he chose to surrender his immortality. He sacrificed his own body as the final offering in the primeval sacrifice, and hence he is remembered as the 'first to die'. After his self-immolation Yama regained his divine status and became the lord of a heavenly region where all the dead get assembled and enjoy in the company of their king Yama.

Father of Humanity

The *ṚV*, 10.13.4 states that Yama chose to immolate himself in the primeval sacrifice which was arranged for the sake of progeny. It is not stated as to how Yama's self-sacrifice helped in starting a progeny, however, the sacrifice of Yama in the primeval sacrifice appears as an earlier version of the sacrifice of *Puruṣa* mentioned in the *Puruṣa-sūkta* (*ṚV*, 10.90) and in this light Yama is a prototype of *Puruṣa*. The creation of the universe out of a primeval sacrifice can be seen in the *ṚV*, 10.90. Here the cosmic-man *Puruṣa* created out of himself *Virāj* and from there the creation started. An earlier vague version of the primeval sacrifice mentioned in the *ṚV*, 10.13.4 finds a detailed expression in the *ṚV*, 10.90. This hymn (10.90) tells how the creation of the universe started out of the body of a cosmic-man. Thus Yama/*Puruṣa* is considered the creator of the universe as well as the parent of humanity. It may be noted that Yamī does not play any role in the creation of mankind and the Yama-Yamī dialogue (*ṚV*, 10.10) has a ritual purpose as shown earlier. As the ritual was lost and the dialogue remained, it has led to a conception that Yama and Yamī are the progenitors of the human race.[8] The *ManuS* also provides that the cosmic-man divided himself into two parts, one male and the other female, and the creation started with them.[9]

Yama and Godhood

In the *Vedas* there is nothing to suggest that initially Yama was not a god and he gained godhood after defeating the gods. The *TS* (2.4.2) account of a struggle in which Yama defeated the gods only tells that Yama gained more power by defeating the other gods.

It is possible that Yama's gaining the overlordship of the earth is suggested here. Thus it can be said that a god who was already the lord of the yonder world and the king of the Fathers defeated other gods and gained the overlordship of the earth too. The *TS* (2.1.4) records this strife in which Yama is stated to have achieved superiority over goḍs. Yama's victory troubled the gods considerably and they reflected 'Yama has become here the we are' and it is possible that Yama's attaining the overlordship is suggested here. *TS*, 5.2.3[10] and *ŚB*, 7.1.1.3 state that Yama is the lord of the whole earth and therefore his permission must be taken before preparing the fire-altar for a sacrifice.

It is important to note that as a king of the dead Yama comes to be indirectly connected with death. But in the *ṚV* he is not a feared god whose company people would like to avoid. On the contrary there are prayers where the worshipper expresses his earnest wish to live for ever in the kingdom of

Yama (*RV*, 9.113.8). This suggests that region of Yama was believed to be a place for the happiest post-mortem existence. In this capacity, Yama's kingdom is similar to the Purāṇic concept of *Vaikuṇṭha*, the abode of Viṣṇu and a place of total emancipation.

Identity of Yama

Yama, as the god of the dead, himself had to pass through death. In other mythologies also the lord of the other world died and came to life again. Osiris died and rose up again as the king of the departed. Pluto was also swallowed and later disgorged by kronas. It seems that "Transmigration and metempsychosis demanded that the god who was the guardian of the dead should himself pass through death".[11] As a son of Vivasvat Yama is a solar god. It is to be noted that the Sun is also called Yama.[12] The Sun creates days and nights and the rotation of days and nights creates time. With the passage of time man approaches death. In this way Yama is connected with 'time' through the Sun. In an account,[13] connected with Ādityas, i.e., sons of Aditi, it is said that Aditi gave birth to eight sons. She went up with seven and left the eighth (*mṛtaṇḍa*) on earth.

This may suggest that the seven immortal Ādityas ascended and Mārtaṇḍa was left behind. Mārtaṇḍa represents a chain of existence with birth → death → birth cycle. Since the stages of egg → broken-egg → bird also represent death and rebirth. This connects Mārtaṇḍa closely with Yama who after his self-immolation become immortal in the yonder wold.

Yama is connected with one or two other natural phenomena. Yāska and Sāyaṇa give a common explanation that Yama is lightning. According to *Nir*, 12.9 Yama is lightning and Yamī the sound of thunder.

A number of scholars believe that Yama represented a phenomenon of nature. According to Hillebrandt[14] Yama represents night (death) while Vivasvat represents day (life). Bergaigne thinks he is a form of Agni particularly the lightning.[15] According to Max Müller Yama is the setting sun and as such the leader of the Fathers.[16]

Hillebrandt believes that the two characteristics of Yama's personality that he is Vivasvat's son, and that he died, can be explained only on an assumption that Yama was originally the moon-god. But the difficulty in accepting Hillebrandt's hypothesis is that though moon comes back after its each periodical death (dissappearance at no moon-day) Yama does not undergo repeated deaths and births. Thus Yama does not represent the moon.

Yama is also considered to be an ordinary human being because he died. He was an ordinary king who due to his powers and virtues was later exalted to the position of a god. But as R.N. Dandekar observes "The part played by Yama with reference to the creation of universe and to procreation of the human race and also his special connection with sacrifice is not adequately explained on the assumption that Yama was just a human being" and "that he as a matter of fact possesses in the *Vedas* a peculiar character of a god man".[17] The Vedic mythology has been reacting to various changes in the cultural history of the Vedic age. The personality of Yama too has undergone tremendous changes. The various changes contributing to the evolution[18] of Yama-mythology, as observed by R.N. Dandekar, are as follows.[19]

The first stage of Yama's personality is that of a sacrificer who immolated himself in the sacrificial fire. The name Yama is very expressive and reveals the true character of the god. As observed earlier the word Yama means (1) A twin and (2) a hermophrodite. The X.13.4 states that Yama gave up his own dear body. According to R.N. Dandekar this is the first stage of Yama-mythology where a bisexual being sacrificed himself for the cause of creation. *Puruṣa* of the *Puruṣa-sūkta* is only a priestly modification of the original mythological conception of Yama. Mythologically as well as linguistically Yama of the *Veda* is similar toYmir of Edda, a primeval hermophrodite who sacrificed himself for creation.

In the second stage the original function of Yama as the creator of universe is considerably restricted. Yama and his twin sister Yamī procreate a human race.

In the third stage Yama became the ruler of the dead. The idea of the origin of the humanity from an incest was repulsive to the mind of the Vedic seers. In this stage Yamī quietly disappears and both the previous stages were combined and modified in the *Puruṣa-sūkta* where the creation of universe is said to have originated from the different organs and limbs of *Puruṣa*. In the fourth stage the Yama-myth interacts with the Manu-myth as they were co-existing for some time. The Vedic seers found in Manu a suitable alternative to avoid the offensive incest.

In the fifth stage Manu takes over the function of Yama. But Yama's self-immolation in the sacrifice is still remembered. It is this aspect of Yama's personality which is continued and Yama was considered the first mortal (*AV*, 18.3.13) whose self-immolation is preserved in the *ṚV*, 10.13.4.

Upholder of Morality

In the *Vedas* Yama is depicted as punishing the offenders with his *padbīśa*. In the capacity of a punisher he is even considered as a duplicate of Varuṇa.[20]

Yama also displays a high degree of moral sense and self-control in the famous Yama-Yamī hymn (*ṚV*, 10.10), where he does not succumb to Yamī's passionate and immoral request. The *NP* chapter 13 contains a version of the Ṛgvedic Yama-Yamī hymn. Yama observes here, that the high-placed people of the society should be most careful about their moral conduct because common people consider them as their ideals and try to follow their foot-steps. In the closing verses of the *NP* version Yama is louded for morality. It is also said here that by refusing to do an immoral act Yama gained godhood.[21]

The *ṚV*, 10.10.2b is repeated in the *ṚV*, 10.12.6b and the *ṚV*, 10.12.6 can be rendered as follows:

> By doing this condemned act (i.e., the incest) Yama would have earned a bad name (*durmantu*) because he would have treated

> his blood-relative (*salakṣmā*) as a non-relative (*viṣurūpā*), i.e., his sister as his wife. But Yama saved himself from the ill-fame by not indulging in this forbidden act.[22]

It is probable that this verse originally formed the last verse of the Yama-Yamī hymn (and it was later misplaced). In that case it also provides the conclusion of Yama-Yamī legend in the absence of which many scholars hold the view that this hymn was left incomplete because the suggested incest and the human progeny having originated out of it was highly objectionable to the morality of that age. But as the concluding lines of the hymn, this verse sums up the story by telling that Yama did not do the condemned act (i.e., incest).

In an article Shruti Pradhan gives a sociological interpretation of the *ṚV*, 10.10.[23] She refutes the views of a number of the western scholars who think that the twin Yama and Yamī represent the pair of day and night (F. Max Müller), or that they refer to the origin of the human race (Roth, Bloomfield, Geldner, Oldenberg). In her opinion all these views are out-dated. According to her it is questionable that behind this drama there is a ritual (Ulrisch Schneider).

She observes that the explanations given by Yama to his sister, stressing the unnaturalness of incestuous relations, are the poet's rationalisations of a folk memory of the practice of incest.[24]

However, attention may be drawn to an important fact here is that in the hymn special stress is laid on Yama-Yamī being twins (*ṚV*, 10.10.4 and 5) and so it is not about incest between a brother and his sister but a twin-brother and his twin-sister. As the incest of a twin-brother and his twin sister cannot be a wide spread social practice (due to the rarity of such twins) which was required to be rationalised.

The birth of a twin, on the other hand is considered as inauspicious, and it can be assumed that the birth of a twin of both sexes is even more inauspicious, hence the necessity of the ritual. *KātyāyanaŚS*, 25.4.35 tells about the purification rites to be performed in the event of birth of twins to one's wife or to one's cow (*vide* P.V. Kane, *HDS*, V, II, p. 139).

Yama's Region

Yama's abode is a place where all the dead find a resting place. They are described as rejoicing in the company of their king Yama and other gods. The worshipper wants to become immortal in the kingdom of Yama (*RV*, 9.113.8).[25]

In the post-Ṛgvedic literature a gradual change in the concept of Yama's abode can be noticed. There are some references where it is wished that one should not go to the realm of Yama.[26] Thus departure to Yama's region is not something to wish for.

This change in attitude can be attributed to the development of Yama's personality incorporating sinister dimensions. Yama was previously a gatherer of the people, who reach his kingdom after death, because all the dead get collected in Yama's region. It was the place he found for all the dead to live in. But gradually Yama, whose jurisdiction was beyond death, came to be identified with death itself. The element of fear cannot be missed in such lines, 'May you not go to Yama's place'.[26]

In the *Purāṇas*, the kingdom of Yama is regarded as a place for punishment since hells are said to be situated in the kingdom of Yama and there he sits as the magnificent judge of man's deeds.

Thus the region of Yama, which was the goal of all the dead and was conceived to be a place of enjoyment, where they lived under the loving care of Yama[27] has now become a most dreadful place with its gruesome methods of torturing the sinners. In the *ṚV* Yama's region is the abode of the blessed souls and Yama is not connected with *naraka*, i.e., hell. In the *AV*, 12.4.36 the *Nārakam lokaṁ* is mentioned as a region which is different from the blissful *Yamaloka* where men get all their wishes fulfilled. It is no longer the abode of the blessed dead, but of the sinners who are tormented in the numerous hells which are mentioned as situated in the *Yamaloka*.

Yama the Judge

In the *ṚV* Yama is closely connected with Varuṇa, the

supreme sovereign and upholder of the cosmic as well as the moral order. Varuṇa punishes those who break the law (*ṛta*). It is this function of Varuṇa that Yama smoothly takes over and himself becomes, in the later literature, the judge of man's all good and evil deeds. Sūrya, the all-seeing eye of Varuṇa reports all the deeds of man. Like Varuṇa, Yama is also an all-knower. He even know the hidden sins of man.[28]

Tracing the evolution of Yama-mythology from the *ṚV* down to the Epics and Purāṇic age it is noticed that Yama was not originally the god of death but it is in this capacity that his stature grows in the post-Vedic literature. At this stage the Rudra-mythology has significantly reacted on Yama-mythology, because Rudra is a particularly fierce god (*ṚV*, 2.33.9, 11; 10.126.5), who used death-bringing missiles (*ṚV*, 2.33.10), and also is called a cruel god[29] (*TS*, 76.1.7.8 also cf. *MS*, 3.8.1).

In the *Purāṇas* Yama is the regent of the hells. Some aspects of his personality grew into independent gods such as Mṛtyu, Kāla and Antaka. His form is terrible to a sinner but for a pious soul who approaches him he take up the benign form of Viṣṇu and welcomes him. This reminds one of Yama's benevolent form where he on seeing a dead soul reach his kingdom announces that "by reaching here this (the dead) has become mine, he would henceforth get a portion from the offerings made to me" (*AV*, 18.2.37).

Yama the Punisher

It is in the Epics and the *Purāṇas* that Yama's status as a punisher grows. He controls the humanity by granting the appropriate results of their acts. The *BhāgP*, 6.1.48 states that Lord Yama, through his inner vision, sees all the actions of people and decides the fruit to be awarded to them. The fear of Yama's punishment keeps people on the right tracts (*BrahmaP*, 125.23).

Most of the *Purāṇas* give graphic pictures of the hells and the punishments meted out there. Thus Yama who was the lord of a heavenly region, lord of the whole expanse of the earth, upholder of morality who punished the defaulter with his *padbīśa* has now become the lord of hells. His most august position as a judge, however, is not lost sight of. As a judge of man's good and bad deeds he exercises a control over the living beings also. He thus became a god who controls the dead as well as the living (through the fear of hells). The sovereign of the whole earth is now reduced to the position of one of the *dikpālas* and now he is the guardian of the south direction. The benevolent aspect of his character is not forgotten. To the pious he is extremely benign. He does not sent his fearsome *dūtas* to fetch a pious soul. As it was revealed to Sāvitrī by Yama, he himself goes to bring a pious soul. When the pious souls reach Yama's region they find him in a very pleasant form, because for the pious Yama takes up the form of Viṣṇu.

Yama's Counterparts in Other Mythologies

There is remarkable similarity in the characters of Vedic Yama and his Iranian counterpart Yima. The Vedic Yama is the son of Vivasvat and he is mentioned as the first of the dead. He found out a new path and a settlement for the dead. He is the king of this region, he is called the gatherer of people (*saṁgamanaṁ janānāṁ*) since all the dead get collected in his kingdom. His region is a place of happiness and the dead live there blissfully.

Avestan god Yima is son of Vivanghat, who is the Iranian counterpart of Vivasvat. He is also a king and founder of a civilization, the best mortal gather around him in a marvellous palace in 'Airyanam Vaego', which is same as the Yamasādana, the abode of Yama.[30]

According to a myth this world would end due to dreadful winter (Farg. XIX 28ff). This winter will be succeeded by spring. All the blessed souls living in Yima's region will come down and inhabitate the earth. Yima was told by Ahura Mazda to become a preacher and bearer of his (Ahura Mazda's) laws.

It may be recalled that Yama figures prominently as a preacher in the *KaṭhaUp*, where he imparts the secret knowledge to Naciketas. Yama is also one of the

Dharmaśāstra-kāras, i.e., the law-givers.

Yima declined to become a preacher since, he told, he was not taught to be a preacher. At this Ahura Mazda told him to look, to nourish, to rule and to watch over his world which Yima promises to do. Ahura Mazda also gave him a golden ring and a poniard. Darmesteter comments that these are symbols and instruments of sovereignty. Yima took good care of the men, flock and herd, and their number grew. The earth became over-crowded. Ahura Mazda drew Yima's attention to this and Yima stepped toward the south direction, pressed his golden ring on the earth and bored it with the poniard. He requested earth to stretch out so that there can be a place for everyone. Thrice Yima stretched out earth in his manner. (*Vendidad*, Farg. II.7).

Yima also saved his people (the dead) from fatal winters, Ahura Mazda foretold about the deadly winter and asked Yima to make a big vara (literally, an enclosure) and keep the best seeds of all the things, two of every kind.

Yima made a beautiful 'Vara'. There Ahura made special arrangement for light and the 'Vara' remained brightened all the time. One year was equal to one day for the residents of the 'Vara' (*Vendidad*, 2.40, *Yasta*, 19.28). Heat and cold could not torment the people in his 'Vara'. According to the Iranian tradition the 'Vara' would open again after the universal destruction when people would open the Vara and a new creation would start.

In the *R̥V* no 'Vara' of Yama is mentioned. But Manu is said to be the progenitor of the mankind and therefore man is called *manuj*, *mānava*, etc. According to a famous deluge story the water of the ocean covered the whole earth. At that moment a huge fish came and according to his instruction Manu with the seeds of all vegetation and the seven great sages (the *saparṣis*) ascended the boat. The fish drew this boat to a high altitude and when the waters receded Manu started the creation again.

It is significant to note here that though linguistically Yama's name is nearer to Yima but functionally Manu (Yama's brother) and Yima are closer. Yama does not make any 'Vara' but he is surely mentioned as a lord of the region of the dead.

Dogs

Parallel figures of Yama's two dogs can also be seen in the Avesta.[31] Yama's two dogs are described as black and copper-coloured. They guard the path which leads to the region of Yama. These dogs are considered to be the two messengers of Yama. They move among people and spot a person whose life is over. Yama's dogs are described with many epithets. They are called *caturakṣau*, i.e., four-eyed or having sharp eyesight, *asutṛpau* (delighting in takings the *asu* (life) of the people). They are also called *pathiṣadi*, Thus they sit on the path leading to Yama's region and ensure that no unworthy person should enter the region of Yama. Yama's dogs appear to be Indo-European and counterparts of these dogs are seen in the Avestan, the Greek as well as the Egyptian mythologies.

In the Avestā also two dogs are mentioned. They guard the Kinvad, bridge (the bridge of paradise). In the *Vendidad*, X.III.9 the killing of dogs is forbidden because if a dog is killed no soul will come to help the dead on his way to paradise nor will the dogs who guard the Kinvad bridge will come to help him despite his cries of terror and woe (*Vendidad*, XIII.9). In this way, it is believed that, the dogs should be kept satisfied so that they can come to help man in other world, where no one else can come to help them. The look of a dog is also believed to drive away the evil demons. *Vendidad*, III.14-22 state that the dogs come to help the soul when a man dies, as soon as the soul has parted from the body, the evil corpse demon (Druz-Nasu) falls upon the dead. The demon is expelled from the dead by the look of the dog a four-eyed dog. In practice, a dog with a spot over each eye is brought near the dead and is made to look at the dead, whereupon the demon leaves the dead and flees back to hell (*Vendidad*, 8-14-22) *Vendidad*, 8.16 mentions that the death-fiend is driven away by the look of a yellow four-eyed dog (i.e., a dog with two spot above the eyes) or white dog with yellow ears drives away the fiend to his region.

The identity of the four-eyed dog in the Iranian mythology has parallels in Kerberos of the Greek mythology and the two four-eyed dogs Śyāma and Śabala of the Vedic mythology.

In the Greek mythology the entrance of the realm of Hades, the lord of the lower world, is guarded by the dog of Hades. It is the dreaded Kerberos, a monster with three heads and a serpent's tail. He fawns on those who entered, but shows his horrible teeth to those who tried to pass by.[32]

Hades or Pluto

Hades, the brother of Zeus, is the god of the lower world, the region of the dead. He is the monarch of the dark realm inhabited by the dead. This region is considered to be under the earth's surface. It is believed that the vegetation grow steadily upwards due to some divine force below. In addition to that most precious metals are obtained by digging out the most dark region under the world. Therefore, in conceiving a god who should be supreme lord of this dark region, it was necessary to attribute a double character to him. First as the source of all treasures of the earth, and as the monarch of the dark realm of the dead. Whoever entered the realm of Hades was not permitted to return. The fierce dog Kerburos guards the gate of Hades' realm. Hades is not only the ruler of the souls of the departed, but was also believed to exercise the function of the judge of mankind after death. In this capacity also he is Yama's parallel.

In the Egyptian mythology Osiris is the lord of the other world. At the time of the judgement of the disembodied souls, it is believed that Anubis leads the dead man in the court of Osiris. There the heart of the dead is weighed against a feather. Forty-two officers attend the trial and ask question about man's various deeds. These forty-two officers are called Assessors of the Dead, and they are similar to the bench of judges in a court.[33] They are supposed to represent forty-two crimes from which a virtuous man was expected to be free. Each of them examined if the deceased was guilty of the peculiar evil which it was his province to avenge.[34]

After weighing of the heart, Thoth delivers his judgement.

fig: 10.1 An illustration from the Book of the Dead of Hunefer (*c.* 1300 BC) showing the judgement of the soul — the dead man being led by Anubis, the weighing of this heart & Thoth delivering his judgement. Above are shown some of the 42 judges.

In the course of enquiry the dead man speaks the following words — "I have begun no evil against any man, I have ill-treated no beast . . . . nor have I blasphemed against God".

A parallel to Indian Citragupta can be seen in Thoth. He keeps the record for the Great Judge Osiris, and reads it out to him at the time of the judgement. Thoth is also considered the original law-giver who sets forth laws which governed the movement of the heavenly bodies — he also became the god of wisdom and eventually the judge of the dead. He pronounces the verdict when the souls were weighed against the feather of the truth at the weighing of the heart before Osiris.[35]

It is to be noted here that the functions ofYama as the lord of hells as well as the judge of the dead are represented by two different gods. Thus Osiris is the lord of the nether world and Thoth is the judge.

The jackal-faced Anubis, takes the soul to the seat of judgement in the Court of Osiris.

In the Tibetan mythology Yama Gsin-rje (i.e., Yama) is the god of the dead and he also bears the title of the king of the law (in Tibetan *chos-kyi-rgyal-po*).[36]

In the Japanese mythology Yama's parallel can be seen in Emma O (*Yama rājā*). He writes the sins of men in a book. In his work Emma O is helped by a female head (*miru-me*) endowed with the capacity of seeing the most secret faults.[37] There is also a male assistant who with the gift of smelling at the secret of all misdeeds. Emma pronounces his judgement and hands over the condemned to demons, who torment him by administering the penalties proportioned with the degree of the guilt.[38]

Yama-Nakṣatrāṇi

In the Indian astronomy, Yama is said to be connected with certain constellations. These constellation are called '*Yama-nakṣatrāṇi.*[39] The total number of constellations is given as twenty-seven and there names are as follows:

Kṛttikā, Rohiṇī, Mṛgaśīrṣa, Ārdrā, Punarvasu,

> Tiṣya, Āśreṣā, Maghā, Purvā-Phālgunī, Uttarā-Phālgunī, Hasta, Citrā, Svāti, Viśākhā, Anūrādhā, Jyeṣṭha, Mūla, Pūrvāṣādhā, Uttarāṣāḍhā, Śroṇa, Śraviṣṭha, Śatabhiṣaj, Pūrvā Proṣṭhapadā, Uttarā Proṣṭhapadā, Revatī, Aṣvayuj, Apabharaṇī.[40]

Each of these *nakṣatras* has a presiding deity.[41] Some divergence is seen regarding the name of *nakṣatras* and their presiding deities.

Out of the twenty-seven *nakṣatras*, the first fourteen, i.e., from Kṛttikā up to and including Viśākhā are called *deva-nakṣatras*. Rest of them, i.e., from Anūrādhā to Apabharaṇī are called *Yama-nakṣatras*.[42] *TBr*, 1.5.2.8-9 give the etymology of the names of the constellations enumerated as *Yama-nakṣatras*.

Sāyaṇa comments that these are called Yama's constellation because they, like Yama, caused the death of the *asuras*.[43] They are deemed as *adhamanakṣatras* and no religious rites/ceremony should be performed under Yama-*nakṣatras*. All religious rites whether *laukika*, Vedic or *kāmya* should be done only under *deva-nakṣatras*.

Apart from a whole set of constellation named as *Yama-nakṣatras* the last one, *Apabharaṇī*, also known as *Bharaṇī* is presided over by Yama. The gender of this *nakṣatra* is feminine and the number is plural. Its various names are:

Apabharaṇī — *TS*, 4.4.10.1-3; *TBr*, I.5

Bharaṇī — *TB*, III.1.4.5

Bharaṇyaḥ — *AV*, 19.7-5

Apabharaṇīḥ — *KāthakaS*, 39.13

Bharaṇīḥ — *MS*, II.13.20.[44]

Notes

1. *Vide* A.A. Macdonell, *Vedic Mythology*, p. 15.
2. *yamarājñah Yamo rājā yeṣāṁ* — Sāyaṇa on the *ṚV*, 10.16.9.

3. *priyo Yamasya kāmyo* (ṚV, 10.21.5) *ekaṁ sat viprā bahudhā vadanti*— ṚV, 1.164.46.
4. *yo mamāra prathamam/* — *AV*, 18.3.13.
5. E.W. Hopkins, *The Religion of India*, pp. 127 ff.
6. R.N. Dandekar, *VMT*, pp. 130-31.
7. This point is further discussed under 'Identity of Yama' in this chapter.
8. R.N. Dandekar, *op. cit.*, p. 134.
9. *dvidhā kṛtvā'tmano dehaṁ ardhena puruṣo'bhavat/*
ardhena nārī tasyām . . . asṛjat prabhuḥ — *ManuS*, 1.32.
tasmāt virāḍ ajāyata virājo adhi pūruṣaḥ — ṚV, 10.90.5.
10. *yāvatī vai pṛthivī tasyā Yama ādhipatyam pariyāya/* —*TS*, 5.2.3.
11. S. Bhattacharji, *Indian Theogony*, p. 100.
12. *yamo ya eṣa tapati eṣa hi idaṁ sarvaṁ yamayati/* — *ŚB*, 14.1.3.4.
13. ṚV, 10.72.8-9.
14. A. Hillebrandt, *op. cit.*, p. 361.
15. A. Bergaigne, *La Religion Vedique*, I. 89.
16. F. Max Müller, *Lecture on the Science of Language*, II. 634.7.
17. R.N. Dandekar, *VMT*, p. 128.
18. On evolutionary mythology, *vide* R.N. Dandekar, "Some aspects of Vedic mythology : Evolutionary mythology", In *University of Ceylone Review*, Vol. 12.
19. *Vide* R.N. Dandekar, *VMT*, pp. 132 ff.
20. Asko Parpola, "The Sky-Garment", In *Studia Orientalia*, Vol. 57 pp. 64-65.
21. Negative analysis of this statement suggests that here it is believed that Yama was not originally a god.
22. This translation is based on Sāyaṇa's commentary on the ṚV, 10.12.6, found in the palm-leaf MS, referred to in *Ṛgveda-Vaidika Saṁśodhana Maṇḍala*, Poona, Pt. III, Introduction, p. 1.
23. Shruti Pradhan, "The Yama-Yamī sūkta; new perspective", *ABORI*, Vol. LXXI, pt. I-IV, 1990, p. 109-38.
24. Shruti Pradhan, *op. cit*, p. 124.

    The writer quotes Andrew Lytle, "Myth is a fiction regarding a society that is dead but the memories the habits, manners and moral of which are slow to die. The memories of the practises of his ancestors remain very much in a man's mind and he rationalises them by attributing them to gods; Shruti Pradhan, *op.cit.*, p. 123.
25. *yatra rājā Vaivasvato, yatrāvarodhanaṁ divaḥ/*
. . . . . *tatra māṁ amṛtaṁ kṛdhī/* — ṚV, 9.113.8.
26. *Yamasya sādanaṁ mā gāḥ/*
27. When a dead soul reaches Yama he announces that by reaching there the dead has become Yama's own and the he will get a portion from the oblation offered to him (Yama) — *AV*, 18.2.37.
28. *iha pracchanna pāpānām śāstā Vaivasvato Yamaḥ/* — *Mbh*, 1.68.31; *GP*, 2.34.8.

29. *Rudro vai krūro devānām* — *TS*, 6.1.7.8.
30. *Vendidad*, Fargard II.21.
31. J. Darmesteter, *The Zend-Avesta*, Transl. Part-I, *SBE*, Vol. IV, Introduction pp. xxv ff.
32. *Vide* A. Murray, *A Manual of Mythology*, p. 58.
33. Cf. *Scholars and ṣages in Yama's court*, *vide* chapter 6.
34. Murray Alexander, *Manual of Mythology*, pp. 347-48.
35. *Vide* E.O. James, *Myths and rituals in the Ancient Near East*, p. 216.
36. J. Hackin, *Asiatic Mythology*, p. 169.
37. Cf. Yama can see even the hidden sins of man — *vide* chapter 7.
38. J. Hackin, *op. cit.*, p. 416 ff.
39. *TBr*, 1.522 and Sāyaṇa's Commentary on it.
40. *TB*, I.5, However, *TB*, III.1 differ from *TB*, I.5 where the number is twenty-eight. It mentions an additional *nakṣatra abhijit* after *aṣāḍhā*.
41. P.V. Kane gives a list of the Vedic names of the *nakṣatras*, there modern names, the Vedic deity presiding over them and their names as given in *TS*, 1.5, *TBr*, III.1.4.5, *TB*, 1.5, *AV*, 19.7.2-5, *Kathakas*, 39.13, *MS*, II.13.2—P. V. Kane, *HDS*, Vol. V. Pt. I, p. 501-04.
42. *Anūrādhā prathamaṁ Apabharaṇīḥ uttamaṁ Yama-nakṣatrāṇi*, — *TDr*, 1.5.27.
43. *Tāni etāni anurādhādīni yamvad asurāṇāṁ maraṇahetutvād yama-nakṣatrāṇi.*

    Sāyaṇa on *TBr*, 1.5.2.9. *devanakṣatrāḥ dakṣinena pariyanti Yamanakṣatrāni . . . uttareṇa pariyanti iti/* — *TBr*, 1.5.2.7.
44. *Vide* P.V. Kane, *HDS*, Vol. V, Pt. I, p. 504.

Bibliography

A. Original Sources

Agnipurāṇa, Anandashram Sanskrit Series, No. 41, Poona.

Aitareyabrāhmaṇa, ed. by Sudhakara Malaviya, Tana Printing Works, Vanarasi, 1963.

Āpastamba Śrautasūtra, Oriental Institute, Baroda.

Āśvalāyana Śrautasūtra, Anandashrama Series.

Atharvaveda Saṁhitā, Svādhyāya-maṇḍala, Pardi.

Avesta, ed. by J. Darmesteter, *Sacred Books of East Series*, Vols. IV & XXIII.

Bhāgavata Purāṇa, Geeta Press, Saṁvat 2018.

Bṛhadāraṇyakopaniṣad, Īśādidaśopaniṣadaḥ, Motilal Banarsidass, Banaras, 1964.

Bhaviṣya Purāṇa, Gita Press, Gorakhpur.

Brahma Vaivarta Purāṇa, ASP, Poona, 1935.

Chāndogya Brāhmaṇa, Sanskrit College Research Series, 1957.

Chāndogya Upaniṣad.

Dharma Śāstra Saṁgrah, ed. by M.N. Dutta, Munsiram Manoharlal, Delhi.

Garuḍa Purāṇa, with Hindi Commentary by Pt. Shriram Sharma, Saṁskṛti Saṁsthana, Bareli, 1981.

Īśādidaśopaniṣadaḥ, Motilal Banarsidass, Delhi, 1964.

Jaiminīya Brāhmaṇa, ed. by Dr. Raghuvira Sarasvati Vihara Series, Vol. 31, Nagpur, 1954.

Kātyāyana Śrauta Sūtra, ed. by V. Sharma, Banaras, Samvat 1987.

Katha Upaniṣad Īśādidasopniṣadaḥ, Motilal Banarsiḍass.

Kṛtyakalpataru by Laksmidhara Bhatta, *GOS*, Vol. CX, Oriental Institute, Baroda.

Mahābhārata, Critical Text, Poona.

Matsya-Purāṇa, Venkatesvar Press, Bombay, 1923.

Manu Smṛti, Published by J.R. Gharpure, Bombay, 1920.

Maitrāyaṇi Saṁhitā, Svādhyāya Maṇḍala.

Mārkaṇḍeya Purāṇa, ASP, Poona.

Nāṭya Śāstra of Bharata.

Nirukta, ed. by L. Sarup, University of Punjab, 1927.

Nighaṇṭu, ed. by L. Sarup, University of Punjab, 1927.

Padma-Purāṇa, Anandashram Press, Poona, 1893-94.

Rāmāyaṇa, cr. ed. Oriental Institute, Baroda.

Ṛgveda Saṁhitā, Vaidika Saṁsodhana Maṇḍala, Poona.

Śatapatha Brāhmaṇa, Bibliotheca Indica, 1903.

Śabdakalpadruma, Calcutta, Saka, 1808.

Smṛtiśāstra-sāṁgraha, Jivananda Vidyasagar, Calcutta.

Smṛticandrikā, Anandasrama Press, Calcutta.

Śvetaśvatara Upaniṣad, *Īśādidasopaniṣadaḥ*, Motilal Banarsidass, Delhi.

Taittirīya Upaniṣad, *Īśādidasopaṇiṣadaḥ*, Motilal Banarsidass.

Taittirīya Āraṇyaka, ASP, 1897, Motilal Banarsidass, Delhi, 1985.

Taitirīya Brāhmaṇa ASP, Vol. 37, 1979, Anandashrama Samskrit Granthavali, Vol. 37.

Taittirīya Saṁhitā, ASP, 1902, Svādhyāya Maṇḍala, Pardi.

Tāṇḍya Mahābrāhmaṇa, Kashi Sanskrit Series, Chowkhamba Sanskrit Series Office, Banaras, 1936.

Vājasaneyi Saṁhitā, Motilal Banarsidass, Delhi.

Varāha Purāṇa, ASP, Poona.

Vāyu Purāṇa, ASP, Poona, 1965.

Vedānta Sūtra, Śānkarbhāṣya.

Viṣṇu Purāṇa, Venkatesvara Press, Bombay, 1904.

Yājñavalkya-smṛti, NSP, Bombay.

B. Reference Books

Abyankar, K.V., *A Dictionary of Sanskrit Grammer, GOS*, Baroda, No. 134, Oriental Institute, Baroda, 1977.

Agrawala, V.S., *Matsya Purāṇa : A Study*, All India Kashiraja Trust, Varanasi.

Aiyangar, K.V.R., *Śrāddha Kāṇḍa*, ed., Kṛtyakalpataru, GOS, Baroda, Vol. CX.

Bellingham, David, *An Introduction to Greek Mythology*, Apple Press, London.

Bergaigne, A. *La Religion Vedique*, tr. by V.G. Paranjape, Arya Samskriti Prakasana, Poona, 1973.

Bhawe, S.S., *Soma Hymns of the Ṛgveda, A Fresh Interpretation*, Oriental Institute, Baroda, Pt. I 1957; Pt. II 1960; Pt. III 1962.

Bhattacharji, Sukumari, *Indian Theogony*, Firma KLM Private Ltd., Calcutta, 1978.

Bloomfield, M., *The Hymns of Atharvaveda, SBE*, Vol. 42, Motilal Banarsidass, Delhi.

Bloomfield, M., *The Religion of the Veda*, The Knickerbocker Press, New York.

Burrow. T., *The Sanskrit Language*, Faber and Faber, First Edition, London.

Chatterjee, Sastri Asoke, *Upaniṣadyoga and Pātañjala Yoga, A Comparative Approach*, Ashutosh Granthmala, No. VII, University of Calcutta, 1989.

Caland, W. (tr.), *Pañcaviṁśa Brāhmaṇa*, Asiatic Society of Bengal, Calcutta, 1931.

Cavendish, Richard, *An Illustrated Encyclopaedia of Mythology*, Crescent Books, New York, 1984.

Chitrav, Siddheswar, *Prācīna Caritra Kośa*, Bharatiya Caritra Kosa Mandala, Poona, 1984.

Dandekar, R.N., *Vedic Mythological Tracts*, Ajanta Publications, Delhi, 1979.

Dange, S.A., *Vedic Myths in Social Prespective*, Vishveshvarananda Vishvabandhu, Institute of Sanskrit and Indological Studies, Punjab University Hoshiarpura, 1982.

Dange, S.S., *Mytho-Social Study of the Bhāgavata Purāṇa*, Ajanta Publication, Delhi, 1984.

Darmesteter, J. (tr.), *The Zend-Avesta*, Pt. I, *SBE*, Vol. IV, Oxford University Press, 1880.

Desai, Nileshvari, *Ancient Indian Society, Religion and Mythology as depicted in the Mārkaṇḍeya Purāṇa — A Critical Study*, M.S. University of Baroda, Baroda.

Devasthali, G.V., *Religion and Mythology of the Brāhmaṇas*, University of Poona, 1965.

Deussen, Paul, *The Philosophy of the Upaniṣads*, English, tr. by Rev. A.S. Geden, Dover Publications, New York.

Dixitar, V.R.R., *The Purāṇa Index*, University of Madras, Vol. I 1951; Vol. II 1952; Vol. III 1955.

Eggeling, J. (tr.), *Śatapatha Brāhmaṇa*, *SBE*, Vols. 12, 43, Motilal Banarsidass, Varanasi.

Fatah Singh, *Vedic Etymology*, National Publishing House, Delhi.

Geldener, K.F., *Der Ṛgveda*, *HDS*, Vol. 35.

Gonda, J., *A History of Indian Literature*, Fasc. 1 Otto

Harrassowitz, Wiesbaden.

Gonda, J., *Epithets in Rgveda*, The Hague, 1959.

Gonda, J., *Loka — World and Heaven in the Veda*, N.V. Noord-Hollandsche Uitgevers Maatschappij, Amsterdam, 1966.

Grassmann, H., *Worterbuch Zum Ṛgveda*, Otto Harrassowitz, Wiesbaden, 1955.

Griffith, R.T.H., *The Hymns of the Ṛgveda*, Chowkhamba Sanskrit Studies, Vol. XXXV, Varanasi.

Grinswold, H.D, *The Religion of the Rigveda*, Motilal Banarsidass, 1971.

Gyani, S.D., *Agni Purāṇa — A Study*, Chowkhamba Sanskrit Studies, Vol. XLII, Varanasi, 1964.

Hackin, J., *Asiatic Mythology*, George G. Harrap & Co. Ltd., London, 1963.

Hastings, James (ed.), *Encyclopaedia of Religion and Ethics*, Vol. III, New York, 1967.

Hazra, R.C., *Studies in the Purāṇic Records on Hindu rites and customs*, University of Dacca, Bulletin No. XX, Dacca, 1940.

Hopkins, E.W., *Epic Mythology*, Motilal Banarsidass, Delhi, 1974.

Hillebrandt, A., *Vedique Mythologie*, English Transl. *'Vedic Mythology'* by Rajeshvar Sarma, Motilal Banarsidass, Delhi, 1980.

James, E.O. *Myths and Rituals in the Ancient Near East*, Frederick A. Praeger, New Delhi, 1958.

Joshi, J.R., *Some Minor Divinities in Vedic Mythology and Rituals*, Deccan College Post-Graduate and Research Institute, Poona, 1977.

Kane, P.V., *History of Dharma-Sastra*, Government Oriental Series, BORI, Poona, Vol. I, 1930; Vol. II, pt. I 1941; Vol. II pt. II, 1941; Vol. III 1946; Vol. IV 1952; Vol. V, pt. I, 1958; Vol. V, pt. II, 1962.

Kantawala, S.G., *Cultural History of Matsya Purāṇa*, The M.S. University of Baroda, Baroda, 1964.

Kapadia, K.M., *Hindu Kinship*, Popular Book Depot, Bombay, 1947.

Keith, A.B., *The Religion and Philosophy of the Veda and Upaniṣads, HOS*, Vol. 31 & 32, Motilal Banarsidass, Delhi, 1976.

Kuiper, F.B.J., *Proto-Munda Words in Sanskrit*, N.V. Noord-Hollandsche Uitgevers Mattashappij, Amsterdom, 1948.

Lakshman Sarup, *The Nighanṭu and Nirukta* (Translated) Motilal Banarsidass, Delhi, 1984.

Macdonell, A.A., *A Vedic Reader for Students*, Geoffrey Cumberlege, Oxford University Press, 1954.

Macdonell, A.A., *Vedic Mythology*, Motilal Banarsidass, Delhi, 1981.

Macdonell, A.A., *A History of Sanskrit Literature*, Motilal Banarsidass, Delhi, 1962.

Majumdar R.C. and Pusalkar A.D., *The Vedic Age*, George Allen and Unwin Ltd., London, 1951.

Max-Müller, F., *A History of Ancient Sanskrit Literature*, Chowkhamba Sanskrit Studies, Vol. XV, Chowkhamba Prakashan, 1968.

Max-Müller, F., *Lectures on the Science of Language*.

Muir, J., *Original Sanskrit Texts*, Vol. V, Oriental Publishers and Distributors, New Delhi, 1976.

Murray, A., *Manual of Mythology*, Carol Publishers, New Delhi, 1986.

Oldenberg, H., *Vedic Hymns* (Transl.) *SBE*, Vol. 46, Motilal Banarsidass, Delhi, 1979.

Pandit Bindu (Mrs.), *The Origin and Development of the Doctrine of Transmigration in the Sanskrit Literature of Hindus*, unpublished Ph.D Thesis submitted to the University of Bombay, 1957.

Pargitar, F.E., *Mārkaṇḍeya Purāṇa*, English Transl., Indological Book House, 1969.

Parpola, Asko, "The Sky-Garment", *Studia-Orientalia*, Vol. 57, Helsinki, 1985.

Patil, D.R., *Cultural History From the Vāyu Purāṇa*, Deccan College, Post-Graduate and Research Institute, Poona, 1946.

Pandya, Shastri Tulajashankar, *Mārkaṇḍeya Purāṇa*, Gujarati Translation.

Pusalkar, A.D., Majumdar, R.C., *Vedic Age*, Bharatiya Vidya Bhavan, 1971.

Pusalkar, A.D., *Studies in the Epics and Purāṇas*, Bharatiya Vidya Bhavan, Bombay, 1955.

Radhakrishnan, S., *Indian Philosophy*, Vols. I & II, Blackie & Son Publishers Pvt. Ltd., 1983.

Rajwade, V.K. (ed.), *Nirukta of Yāska* (with Marathi translation), Ichakaranji Granthmala, Vol. 9, Poona, 1935.

Ranade, R.D., *A Contructive Survey of Upanisadic Philosophy*, Poona Oriental Series, No. 7, Oriental Book Agency, Poona, 1926.

Rao, Gopinath, *Elements of Hindu Iconography*, Vol. II, Pt. II, Delhi, 1971.

Raval, A.J., *Indian Society : Religion and Mythology, A Study of the Brahma-Vaivarta Purāṇa*, D.K. Publication, Delhi, 1982.

Roer, E., Mitra R.L. and Cowel E.B., *The Twelve Principal Upanisads*, Vols. I, II, and III, Nag Publishers, Delhi, 1978.

Satvalekar, S.D., *Atharvaveda Kā Svādhyāya, Kāṇḍa 1*, Svādhyāya Maṇḍala, Aundh, *Atharvaveda kā Subodh Bhāṣya*, Pt. IV, *Kāṇḍa* 11-18, Svādhyāya Maṇḍala, Pardi, 1958.

Shende, N.J., *The Religion and Philosophy of the Atharvaveda*,

BORI Series No. 8, BORI, Poona, 1952.

Sheth, Surabhi, *Religion and Society in the Brahma Purāṇa*, Sterling Publishers Pvt. Ltd., New Delhi, 1979.

Stürtevant, Edgar H., *An Introduction to Linguistic Science.*

Surya Kanta, *A Practical Vedic Dictionary*, Oxford University Press, Delhi, 1973.

Tripathi, Gayacharana, *Vaidika Devata*, Vols. I & II, Bharatiya Vidya Prakashan, 1983.

Upadhyaya, Baladeva, *Purāṇa-vimarśa*, Chowkhamba Sanskrit Series, Varanasi, 1965.

Upadhyaya, Gangaprasada, *Śatapatha Brāhmaṇa*, Vols. I-III, with Hindi commentary. The Research Institute of Ancient Scientific Studies, New Delhi.

Varma, Siddheshvar, *Etymologies of Yāska*, Vishveshvarananda Institute Publications, Hoshiarpur, 1953.

Velankar, H.D., *Ṛgvedic Maṇḍala* VII, Bharatiya Vidya Bhavan, Bombay, 1963.

Vettam Mani, *Purāṇic Encyclopaedia.*

West, E.W. (tr.) *Pahlavi Texts*, *SBE*, Vol. 24, Motilal Banarsidass.

Wilkins, J., *Hindu Mythology, Vedic and Purāṇic*, Indological Book House, 1972.

Williams, Monier, *The Sanskrit English Dictionary*, The Clarendon Press, Oxford, 1899.

Wilson, H.H., *Ṛgveda Saṁhitā*, 6 vols., Nag Publishers, Delhi.

Wilson, H.H., *Viṣṇu Purāṇa* (English tr.), Punthi Pustaka, Calcutta, 1961.

Winternitz, M., *A History of Indian Literature*, Vol. I, Translated into English by Mrs. S. Ketkar, University of Calcutta, 1927.

Winternitz, W.D. (tr.), *Atharvaveda*, Vols. I & II, Motilal Banarsidass, Delhi, 1962.

Zimmermann, S.J., *Peterson's second selection of Hymns of the Ṛgveda*, III Edition ed. by V.G. Paranjape, 1938, Bombay Sanskrit and Prakrit Series, vol. LVIII, published by BORI, Poona.

C. Articles in Journals

Bruce, Lincoln, "The Hell-hound", In *Journal of Indo-European Studies*, 7, (3-4), 1979, pp. 273-85.

Chapekar, N.G., "Yama and Pitar", In *Dr. S.K. Belvalkar Felicitation Volume*, pp. 36-42.

Dandekar, R.V., "Some Aspects of Vedic Mythology : Evolutionary Mythology", In *University of Ceylone Review*, 12 (!), pp. 1-23.

Dange, Sindu S., "Trikadrukebhiḥ Patati, the RV 10.14.16, An Interpretation", In *Proceeding and Transactions of AIOC*, No. 27, 1974, Kurukṣetra, pp. 221-23.

Dangc, Sindu S., "A lost (!) funeral custom from the Ṛgveda (10.135)", In *Proceedings and Transaction of AIOC*, No. 28, 1976, Dharwad, pp. 219-25.

Dhal, U.N., "Colour Concept of a Deity", *Visveshvarananda Indological Journal*, June/December, 1983.

Dixitar, R., "The Purāṇas : A Study", In *IHQ*, Vol. 8, 1932.

Hazra, R.C., "Rgvedic Rudra, as extremely unsocial and non-cooperating god", *JOIB* 25 (34), pp. 213-22.

Kantawala, S.G., "The Cult of Manes as Depicted in the Matsya-Purāṇa", In *JOI*, Baroda, June, 1956, Vols. V, No. 4, and Vol. VI, No. 1, September, 1956, pp. 403-10, 22-31.

Kantawala, S.G., "Some Remarks on the Naciketas-Legend", In *Ludwick Sternbuck Felicitation Volume*, pt. I, Lucknow, 1979, pp. 293-302.

Kantawala, S.G., "Two Legends from the Purāṇas : A Study in the Upabṛhamaṇa", In *Indological Taurinensia*, Vol. 8, 9.

Kantawala, S.G., "Purāṇic Etymology on the Vocable 'Purāṇa", Indological Studies, In *Journal of the Department of Sanskrit*, University of Delhi, Vol. II, Part I.

Lal, S.K., "Nirṛti", In *JOIB*, Vol. 24 (3-4), 1975, pp. 301-12.

Pathak, P.V., and J.P., Naik, "Tectonic Upheavals in the Indus Region and Some Rgvedic Hymns (Part III) : Nirṛti and the significance of oblations to Nṛṭi at Irina", In *ABORI*, LXVII, Pt. I-IV, 1986, pp. 265-69.

Pradhān, Śruti S., "The Yama and Yamī Sukta — New Prespectives", In *ABORI*, Vol. LXXI, pts. I-IV, 1991, pp. 109-38.

Shende, N.G., "Mythology of Yajurveda", In *Journal of Bombay University*, Vols. 26 (2) 34-71; 27 (2) 29-94.

Shende, N.J., "Mṛtyu", In *Journal of Bombay University*, Vol. 27.

Glossary

ādhibhautika : Caused by living beings (-pain etc.)

ādhidaivika : Caused by fate (-pain etc.)

adhvaryu : Director of sacrifice — one of the four priests at a sacrifice. Others are *hotṛ*, *udgātṛ* and *brahman*.

ādhyātmika : Spiritual, caused by mind.

ahimam : Not cold.

ajāmi : Non-akin.

amāvasyā : No-moon day.

anagnidagdha : Not burnt with fire.

aparā : The knowledge of the four *Vedas* along with the six *Vedāṅgas*.

arcimārga : The path brightened by rays.

arghya : Water meant for worship.

āśrama : The four stages of life, i.e., *Brahmacarya*, *Gṛhastha*, *Vānaprastha* and *Saṁnyāsa*.

aṣṭaka : Consisting of eight parts.

asura : demons, in perpetual hostility with the god.

atharvans : Hymns of the *AV*.

Ātman : The 'self' residing in all as immanent Godhead.

bhayānaka rasa : Sentiment of fear. One of the nine sentiments in poetry.

Brahman : The impersonal absolute existence or the supreme self; the *Vedas*.

brahman priest : The possessor of the sacred love; ***also see*** *adhvaryu.*

Brāhmaṇas : Works primarily dealing with the sacrificial aspect of the *Veda.* They form a part of the *Veda.*

Bṛhaspati : Lord of prayers or speech; name of a god; the principal priest at a sacrifice.

ḍamaru : A small hour-glass shaped drum, held by Śiva in one of his hands.

dānava : Demon; ***also see*** *asura.*

daṇḍa : Staff, rod.

devajāmi : Sister of the gods.

devayāna : Path of the gods.

dharma : Ordinance; law; religious duty, moral law.

dharmapati : Protector of *dharma.*

dhūmamārga : Path darkened by smoke.

duṣkṛt : Evil-doers.

dvipadā : *VS,* XXV. 46-47.

gāyatrī : Vedic metre having three lines of eight syllables each.

grāhī : illness.

Gṛhyasūtra : *Dharmaśāstra* texts dealing with the rituals and other duties of the house-holders.

Haoma : An Avestan god.

harmya : Palace.

havana : Offering oblations.

Havyavāhana : Conveyor of the oblations.

Hotṛ : The sacrificer, priest who recites the hymns to praise the gods, and invites them to a sacrifice.

iṣṭāpūrta : The merit acquired by sacrifices and the religious merit.

jāmi : Closely related-like a sister.

jīva: Individual self, it is the *Ātman* with its coverings of body, mind and senses.

kalpa : One of the six *Vedāṅgas* describing the rituals and giving rules for ceremonial and sacrificial acts.

kāṇva : Born in the family of Kaṇva.

kapota : Pigeon.

karmavipāka : The fruction of an individuals actions done in this and previous lives.

kravyavāhana : Bearer of the oblation to the manes.

kravyāda : The corpse-devouring fire.

kṣatriya : The warrior class.

Lokapāla : Guardian of the region.

Mahāpitṛyajña : Sacrifice to the manes.

mantra: Vedic hymn, sacred text, sacrificial formula, magical spell.

manuṣya : Human being.

manvantara : The period or the age of Manu. This period according to Manu S. 1.79 comprises of 4320000 years. They are 14 in all, presided over by their own Manu. The running *manvantara* is the seventh.

martya : Mortal.

māyā : Illusion.

mokṣa : The total liberation resulting in freedom from rebirths which is the ultimate goal of life.

muhūrta : Moment.

Nārāyaṇa : Name of Viṣṇu.

naimittika : Occasional, religious acts done on some special occasion.

Nirbhūti : Extermination, vanishing.

Nirṛti : Destruction.

nitya : Daily.

Oṁ : The sacred syllable, a symbol of *Brahman*.

pitṛ : Fathers, manes, dead relatives.

pitṛloka : Region of the Fathers.

pitṛmedha : Rites for the Fathers.

pitṛyāṇa : Path of the Fathers.

pragāthā : A combination of *Bṛhatī* and *Satobṛhatī*.

prāṇa : Breath of life.

preyas : Pleasant.

puruṣa : The cosmic Man, as the sole and original source of Universe.

padbīśa : Foot-fetter.

palāśa : Name of a tree.

pāpadevatā : Evil-goddess.

parā : The knowledge of *Brahman*.

parābhūti : Defeat, insult.

parame vyoman : In the highest heaven.

parvan : Junctions of the halves of a month.

pāśa : Noose.

rākṣasa : Demon, ***see under*** *asura*.

ṛk : Ṛgvedic hymn.

ṛṣis : Sages, the seers of the *Veda*.

salakṣmā : 'Of the same type', akin.

śamī : Name of a tree.

sāṁkhya : One of the six systems of the Indian.

saṁsāra : The ceaseless cycle of birth, Philosophy, death and rebirth to which the individual is subject to as long as the remains ignorant of his identity with *Brahman*.

saṁskāra : Purificatory rites, sacred rites on ceremonies.

śāntikarman : Post-cremation rites.

śikṣā : **See** *Vedāṅga.*

somyāsaḥ : Soma-loving.

śrāddha : Ceremony in honour and for the benefit of the dead relatives observed at various fixed periods.

śreyas : Better, more beautiful, glorious.

śṛṅgāra : Sentiment of love, one of the nine sentiments of poetry.

sukṛt : Pious deeds.

sūkta : Vedic hymn.

sūtra (style) : Aphorism.

svapna : Dream

tantu : Thread.

tīrtha : Holy places.

tulādhāna : mounting on the balance in the balance ordeal.

udgātṛ : Priest — chanter of the *Sāman.*

ulūka : Owl.

ūrjas : Vigour, vital power.

Vaivasvat : Son of Vivasvat.

Vālakhilya : The eleven additional hymns at the end of VIIIth *maṇḍala.*

vānaprastha : **See under** *āśrama.*

varṇa : The caste-system. The four main classes are brāhmaṇas or the priest class, kṣatriya or the warrior class, vaiśya or the merchant class and śūdra or the servant class.

varuṇānī : Consort of Varuṇa.

vedāṅga : Auxiliary sciences of the *Veda.* They are six in number — *Śikṣā* (phonetics), *Kalpa* (rituals),

Vyākaraṇa (grammar), *Nirukti* (etymology) *Chandas* (metre) and *Jyotiṣa* (astronomy).

vedānta : The *Upaniṣads*, religious philosophy which has evolved from the *Vedas*.

Viṣurūpā : Non-akin.

vivanhvant : An Avestan god. Counterpart of the Vedic god Vivasvat.

vrata : Observances.

vrātya : Non-Āryans who had been admitted to the brāhmaṇa caste.

yajña : Sacrificial rites.

Yajus : The *mantras* of the *YV*.

yamaloka : The region of Yama.

yava : Barley.

yojana : A measure of distance equal to 4 *krośas* or 8/9 miles.

Index

(The references to the *Vedas*, the *Mahābhārata* and the *Purāṇas* is very frequent and so not included in this index)

Pl. 1. Yama, eighth century, Śiva temple, *garbhagṛha*, south wall, Indore.

Pl. 2. Yama, twelfth century, Darasuram, Thanjavur.

Pl. 3. Yama, tenth century, Kalleśvara temple, *Mukhamaṇḍapa*, ceiling, Betur.

Pl. 4. Yama, early eighth century, Viṣṇu Brahmā temple, *Gūḍhamaṇḍapa*, south wall, Alampur.

Pl. 5. Yama, last quarter of seventh century, Sangameśvara temple, *Gūḍhamaṇḍapa*, south wall, Kudaveli.

Pl. 6. Yama, tenth century, mailarliṅga temple, *Mukhamaṇḍapa*, ceiling, Patasivaram.

Pl. 7. Yama, eighth century, Government Museum, Alwar.

Pl. 8. Yama, god of death, Pratihar, tenth century AD, Jhalawar, Rajasthan, stone.

Pl. 9. Yama, Thirteenth century AD, Orissa, stone.

Pl. 10. Showing Varuṇa, unidentified dikpāla and Yama, *c.* ninth century, Kallesvara temple, *Mukhamaṇḍapa*, ceiling, Aralaguppe.

Pl. 11. Nirṛti and Yama, standing *c.* tenth century, Hinglajgarh (Mandasore, MP) Indore.

Pl. 12. Yama, dikpāla, standing, *c.* tenth century, Hinglajgarh.

Pl. 13. Yama and Nirṛti, *c.* tenth century, Hinglajgarh.

Pl. 14. Yama, dikpāla, standing, *c*. tenth century, Hinglajgarh.

Pl. 15. Yama, dikpāla and a *surasundarī*, standing,
c. tenth century, Hinglajgarh.